Shifting Boundaries

SHIFTING BOUNDARIES

Contextual Approaches to the Structure of Theological Education

Barbara G. Wheeler
and
Edward Farley,
Editors

Westminster/John Knox Press
Louisville, Kentucky

Book design by Gene Harris

First edition

Published by Westminster/John Knox Press
Louisville, Kentucky

PRINTED IN THE UNITED STATES OF AMERICA

9 8 7 6 5 4 3 2 1

Library of Congress Cataloging-in-Publication Data

Shifting boundaries : contextual approaches to the structure of theological education / Barbara G. Wheeler and Edward Farley, editors. — 1st ed.
p. cm.
Includes bibliographical references.
Contents: Reconceiving practice / Craig Dykstra — Situating the structure / Rebecca S. Chopp — The historical consciousness and the study of theology / Walter E. Wyman, Jr. — Theological and religious studies / Francis Schüssler Fiorenza — Beyond a mono-religious theological education / Paul F. Knitter — Overcoming alienation in theological education / Peter J. Paris — Christian social ethics as a theological discipline / Thomas W. Ogletree — Theology against the disciplines / John B. Cobb, Jr. — Celebrating difference, resisting domination / Mark Kline Taylor — Toward a fundamental and strategic practical theology / Don S. Browning.
ISBN 0-664-25172-2

1. Theology—Study and teaching. 2. Religious education—Study and teaching. 3. Theological seminaries. I. Wheeler, Barbara G. II. Farley, Edward, 1929–
BV4022.S45 1991
207′.1′1—dc20 91-17578

Contents

Contributors

Don S. Browning, Alexander Campbell Professor of Religion and Psychological Studies, Divinity School, University of Chicago

Rebecca S. Chopp, Associate Professor, Candler School of Theology, Emory University

John B. Cobb, Jr., Emeritus Professor, School of Theology at Claremont

Craig Dykstra, Vice-president, Religion, Lilly Endowment Inc.

Francis Schüssler Fiorenza, Charles Chauncey Stillman Professor of Roman Catholic Theological Studies, Harvard Divinity School

Paul F. Knitter, Professor of Theology, Xavier University, Cincinnati

Thomas W. Ogletree, Dean and Professor of Theological Ethics, Yale Divinity School

Peter J. Paris, Elmer G. Homrighausen Professor of Christian Social Ethics, Princeton Theological Seminary

Mark K. Taylor, Associate Professor of Theology and Culture, Princeton Theological Seminary

Barbara G. Wheeler, President, Auburn Theological Seminary

Walter E. Wyman, Jr., Associate Professor of Religion, Whitman College

Introduction

In recent years, theological education has undergone the beginning of a reexamination. A growing literature of books and articles,[1] ongoing studies such as those pursued under the rubric of Issues Research by the Association of Theological Schools, and discussions of the subject by the faculties of particular schools[2] all attest to a new critical self-consciousness about both the *theology* and the *education* of theological education.*

I

The debates and deliberations of the recent period represent a marked departure, in both form and sub-

*In this volume, the term *theological education* usually refers to the activities of seminaries and divinity schools, and sometimes is further specified as those activities that prepare clergy for their role and tasks. Several recent writers and most of the authors in this volume question the clerical orientation of contemporary theological education, and some (see especially Farley, "Should Church Education Be Theological Education?" in *The Fragility of Knowledge*, 85–102) argue that "theological education" should be conceived broadly as all education, whatever the institutional locus, that has a theological character.

stance, from earlier approaches to the criticism and reform of theological education. The form of recent activities has been distinctive in several ways. First, the chief participants have been faculty members in theological schools. This is a new development. Although faculty members have made important contributions to the controversial and constructive literature on theological education[3], a great deal of the writing on the subject and almost all public discussion have been conducted—in this sector of higher education as in others—by presidents and deans. Second, perhaps as a consequence of the major role that faculty have played in recent activities, the books, articles, conferences, and seminars of the last decade have been distinctively scholarly in approach. This too is a major departure from past practice. With a very few exceptions, it has not been our habit in North America to treat the topic of theological education as deserving of painstaking scholarship. In the 1960s and 1970s, for instance, there was an extended debate about whether theological education should be reshaped as a more explicitly professional education, but at no point was any analytical groundwork laid that sorted out all the different conceptual and historical strands that have become tangled in the term *professional.* As a result, the discourse on professional education, like many others in the history of American theological education, was largely a polemical one. Only since the early 1980s have theological educators begun to establish a scholarly tradition that focuses on their own practice.

The third distinctive formal feature of the recent round of writing and discussion is its theological character. Yet again, this feature makes the work of the last ten years very different from what went before. North Americans rarely participated in the long European tradition of arguing on theological grounds about how theological schools should define their mission, what should be included in the course of theological studies, and how those studies should be organized. North Americans have, of course, had public theological wrangles about theological education, in fact some violent ones, but these battles have focused not on the theological rationale for a particular program of studies but rather on the theological orthodoxy of those who will be permitted to teach. More frequently, however, theological education in the United States has been conceived not as a theological problem, but as a matter of practical application and technique. Our attention has been focused not on the theological grounds and reasons for doing what we do, but on questions of how to do it effectively.

But the authors and discussants who have contributed to discussions of the issues during the last decade do not generally view theological education as that kind of technical problem. Most have treated theological education as a form of Christian practice and thus the question of what should be its nature and purposes as a theological question. The result has been a nascent practical theology of theological education, a literature that has shifted from the long-standing focus on narrowly technical questions about how to be effective to theological ones about what goals should orient the practice of theological education and what shape the practice itself should take.

Just as notable as some of these formal changes—the involvement of faculty, the rapid appearance of scholarly resources for thinking about theological education, and the new theological cast to the conversation—have been the substantive directions of the writing and discussion. Several important challenges to the conventional wisdom about theological education have emerged. A primary target of criticism has been the assumption, so widely held that it is often taken to be self-evident, that theological education is best conceived as the preparation of clergy for their tasks. Against this prevailing view, several writers argue that theological education will not serve adequately as preparation for ministry or any other end until it ceases to be oriented to ministerial functions and regains a theological focus that it has lost. These writers, a diverse group that includes Edward Farley, Charles M. Wood, Francis Schüssler Fiorenza, and a group of feminists called the Mud Flower Collective (Katie G. Cannon,

Beverly W. Harrison, Carter Heyward, Ada María Isasi-Díaz, Bess B. Johnson, Mary D. Pellauer, Nancy D. Richardson, and Delores S. Williams), do not advocate a new priority for the contemporary academic discipline of theology or for the so-called classical disciplines that are sometimes grouped as "theological" studies to distinguish them from "practical" ones. Indeed, they argue that current schemes of disciplinary organization and the very concept of disciplines have undermined the theological character of theological education. The proposal that theological education become more theological is intended not to privilege any current field or area of study but, by making theological understanding its primary goal, to call into question the criteria and boundaries that define all of them.

Recent writers have also taken aim at the widely accepted convention that the process of theological education is best understood as the application of theory to practice. Edward Farley and other writers have traced the history of this conception of the theory/practice relationship in theological education. In their account, it replaces an earlier one-way movement from authoritatively written Word, systematically and confessionally explicated, to ecclesiastical and ministerial "means of grace." When theological education incorporated historical and other critical methods, the studies of an authoritative text as the basis of practice were supplanted by a cluster of historical and critical disciplines. At the same time, professionalism was creating a growing number of practical disciplines. The structure and direction of the relationship, however, remained unchanged. As the Bible had served as the ground for applicatory acts, theory now grounded practice. Recent writers have two objections to this theory-to-practice model. Edward Farley and Charles Wood are critical of the way it reduces all nonpractical theological studies to the status of theory for clerical practice.[4] Joseph Hough and John Cobb fault it for not providing an adequate description of the complex ways that thinking and action are related to each other.

II

Despite the force of these and other challenges to conventional thinking about theological education, such as the charges leveled by the Mud Flower Collective and others against the white and male hegemonies of its pedagogical ethos, it has not been easy to imagine how the actual programs of schools might be changed to meet the challengers' objections and to promote the new goals and values they propose. What intervenes between new visions for theological study and revised curricula is a structure, a pattern of studies that dictates what theological education shall include and how it shall proceed.

This pattern, which divides theological study into four areas (Bible, theology, history of the church, practics) was created by what were once strong and self-conscious convictions about the structure of theological knowledge and the sources of theological authority—the conviction, for instance, that the Bible, explicated but critically unquestioned, is the sole and comprehensive source of norms for all other theological knowledge and for religious action. As historical consciousness and other movements have undermined such basic convictions in many quarters, parts of the structure have been developed or replaced. But the structure itself has not been revised. The divisions into study areas (which have assumed the status of disciplines) and the relationships among the areas remain as they were, and these divisions and relationships carry with them and hold in place deep presuppositions from an earlier time. The incongruous nature of this arrangement—the structure we have inherited was never meant to arrange its current contents—creates two serious problems for the reconception and reform of theological education.

First, the structure of studies brings outmoded assumptions and norms to bear on our current educational practice. It forces us into certain patterns of thinking and acting. The theory-to-practice procedure, for instance, so common in most discourse about theological education and in so many educational programs, is codified and continuously re-presented to us by a structure that consists of three "theoretical" disciplines that are defined as in some way grounding a cluster of practical ones. Even if we judge such a procedure to be unsatisfactory, we have a hard time escaping it. Theory-to-practice notions are a case in point. Criticisms of that way of relating theory and practice have been advanced in various arenas for more than half a century. Various attempts to reform practical studies along the lines of more complex and reciprocal ideas about the theory-practice relationship have, however, always failed, because they have left in place an overall structure of studies that does not admit such ideas and that maintains in the very way it is put together the pattern and movement of theory-to-practice.

Second, the current structure of studies creates a problem for any proposed revision of theological education, because it has no currently convincing rationale or internal logic. At one time it reflected with some precision how the literatures and dimensions of theology fit together. The various elements that the structure now orders, however, bear little relationship to that earlier picture of theology as a unity. Nor, when they were added, were they conceived as parts of any one new conception of theological knowledge. As a result, the structure now portrays not the order and unity of theology, but—to use Edward Farley's term—its fragmentation by diverse movements and developments of the last several centuries. This is why attempts to "integrate" the pieces of the theological curriculum are invariably frustrated. These pieces of both structure and content have diverse origins and refer to vastly different assumptions and worldviews. Thus they cannot be melded into any coherent, integrated whole.

A structure that creates such formidable problems, that imports discarded assumptions and norms into current educational practice and functions as an obstacle to educational coherence, seems an obvious candidate for fundamental review and reform. Yet the overall structure of studies and the priorities and values it presupposes are rarely scrutinized in discussions of theological education. Even those whose agenda is radical reform usually assume that the changes they advocate must be fitted into the prevailing pattern of studies. Why is so little attention paid to so important a matter? The principal reason is that the structure of studies is simply taken for granted, and its power to shape perceptions and behavior goes unnoticed. Not only does the structure of studies bring certain presuppositions to bear on practice, but the structure itself has become part of the presuppositional package that theological educators bring to the reexamination of their practice. The four fields, the theory-to-practice relationship that arranges them, the subdivision of the practical area into functional ministry specialties, and the centrality of historical-critical methods are taken simply as given and thus function as norms against which the adequacy of new ideas and proposals is evaluated. Proposals to revise the curricula that incorporate these essential features of the current structure are generally acceptable. Those that omit any of them are usually found deficient. Whether these structural features should continue to stand does not often become an issue.

One of the major contributions of the recent literature on theological education has been to raise that issue, to demonstrate that the structure of studies and its prominent features are historically rooted patterns that can be questioned and that are in some ways so antiquated and inappropriate that they demand critical assessment and change to meet new historical conditions. Even when the inadequacies of the structure and its historically contingent character are made clear, however, conversations about the pattern of studies are difficult to initiate and sustain because they threaten the self-definition of the participants. Theological schools are organized into departments staffed by academic specialists whose reasons for being are intimately connected to the justifications for those departments held in place by the structure of studies and its presuppositions. It is not easy for the explorer of theological education to strike a pose of indifference on the matter of whether or not the explorer's own scholarly endeavor should continue to exist! The resistance to inspecting underlying structures and their values and assumptions is not only an individual matter. The existing pattern is more than a pedagogical arrangement; it is also a socioeconomic reality of departments whose fragile existence depends on an unstated comity agreement of mutual approval and support within the existing structure. Thus groups of faculty members, formed into departmental teams, adapt to criticism by adding courses, by making faculty appointments to departments, and by interdepartmental teaching, but they resist changes in the structure itself or even discussions that pose the possibility of such changes.

Such discussions are, however, critically important. Virtually every well-known problem of theological education—the lack of integration of the disciplines, the failure of the "scholarly" aspect of theological education to have much effect in ministry, the theological aridity of most practical studies, the hegemony of white, male, and Western history and experience—is anchored in the overall pattern of studies. A school organized according to that pattern, as (with small variations) are all North American seminaries and divinity schools, can undergo minor, cosmetic curriculum changes but not true reform. Real and lasting reform waits on a thorough examination of the structure of studies, the exposure of the presuppositions and goals it supports, the critical evaluation of its subdivisions and their diverse contents, and the fundamental restructuring of the pattern of studies along the lines of the purposes and values we most seriously seek to advance.

III

The purpose of this volume is to provide resources for those inevitably difficult but crucially important discussions of structure and of associated issues—discussions that are required to discern the shape and direction for actual structural change. The authors whose work is collected here approach the question of the pattern of studies by different avenues, but they also share a common context. All build upon or respond to the several recent works already mentioned, especially those that criticize the present structure of studies and propose new structures or patterns.

These recent structural proposals are of two types. Charles Wood and Edward Farley argue that the pattern of theological education should be determined and unified by the structure and movement of theology itself, not, as is now the case, by the "paradigm" of functional specialties that clergy are expected to perform. Theological education focused on the goal of theological understanding, both argue, is more adequate preparation for religious leadership than training focused specifically on professional functions.

Both Wood and Farley define theology broadly, not as a discipline identified by a single method or subject matter, but as a series or collection of studies unified by its goal. For Wood, Christian theology is "a critical inquiry into the validity of Christian witness."[5] Though he recognizes that any set of disciplines into which this inquiry is divided may become reductionistic, as the present disciplines have, he nonetheless proposes three "potential" new ones, lest theological inquiry, for lack of disciplinary housing, become unstable and vulnerable to corruption by ancillary disciplines on which it relies.[6] Wood's potential disciplines are, like theology as a whole, oriented to questions: Is the Christian witness authentic? (historical theology); Is it true? (philosophical theology); Is it enacted in a manner appropriate to its context? (practical theology). Wood further suggests that each of these interrogatively constituted dimensions of theology is structured internally by a relationship between two moments: "vision," a moment of broad understanding; and "discernment," the grasp of differences. Wood recognizes that vision and discernment correspond in some ways to the more familiar categories of theology and practice. But he rejects the current convention that identifies some disciplines with broad theoretical apprehension and others with application in specific circumstances. Rather, he insists, each of his potential disciplines is structured by the dialectical movement between vision and discernment.[7]

Farley defines theology as reflective activity that has as its goal "wisdom" about "the believer's existence and action in the world." Such reflection, according to Farley, entails certain "fundamental modes of interpretation" whose "disciplining" should provide the structure of theological study. On Farley's reading, these modes are five. Three are "primary": the interpretation of tradition, the interpretation of truth, and the interpretation of action. Two are "synthetic": the interpretation of situations and the interpretation of vocation. These five modes, plus a course of "foundational" studies that are prerequisite to setting out on this five-sided project of interpretation, constitute a pattern for theological education more likely than the present one, in Farley's view, to lead to the wisdom that theology intends.[8] Several essays in this book offer appreciations or critiques of Farley's proposal and locate their own proposals and recommendations in relation to it.

A different starting point for reorienting the structure of studies is proposed by Joseph C. Hough, Jr., and John B. Cobb, Jr., in *Christian Identity and Theological Education*. Hough and Cobb propose to retain the preparation of church leadership as the explicit and orienting goal of theological studies, but to change the image and definition of professional leadership from a functionalist one to a far more complex model that they call "the Christian practical thinker." The Christian identity of this practical thinker would be formed, in the pattern of studies they set forth, by a basic course in the internal history of the Christian tradition, taught in a critical, inclusive, and global perspective. To this basic course would be added a variety of exercises in "reflective practice," a process of reflective research-in-action that they present as an alternative to the theory-to-practice procedure. Although the Hough/Cobb proposal is directly focused on the preparation of church leaders in a way that Farley's and Wood's are not, Hough and Cobb explicitly eject training in the functions of ministry from the theological curriculum. Such training, they argue, should be carried out under ecclesiastical supervision in the actual settings of practice.[9] A book of essays on the Hough/Cobb proposal has recently appeared.[10] Though there are few specific references to Hough's and Cobb's work in the papers in the present volume, several of the authors take a similar approach, arguing that a revised understanding of practice is the starting point for significant reform of the pattern of theological education.

IV

The first three essays in this volume identify concepts or orientations that pervade contemporary education and that must, the authors argue, be fundamentally changed (Dykstra and Chopp) or revised and intensified (Wyman).

For Craig Dykstra, practice is the pivotal theme. Dykstra takes aim at a concept of practice that is, in his view, harmfully individualistic (practice is understood as some*one* doing something), technological (theory is applied in practice as science is applied in technology), ahistorical (the history of practices is deemed irrelevant to their single goal, effectiveness) and abstract (cut off from their history, practices are also cut off from the communities that carry them out). Following Alasdair MacIntyre, he proposes a different understanding: practices are cooperative human activities that are socially established over time. This picture of practice, which has moral, historical, epistemological, and theological dimensions, becomes the basis for his structural sketch. No longer should theological study move from theory to practice. Instead, all of its parts and divisions should attend to the ways that practices have created and permeate all aspects of theology and church life. Some fields should study the history of practices, others their inner rationality and truth; and still others should teach practices by disciplining students' participation in them at increasing levels of complexity. Dykstra does not propose a new lineup of fields or disciplines, but he does suggest that if practices were to become the focus of all theological study, the agenda for what is currently the "practical" field would be greatly reduced.

Rebecca S. Chopp reviews the accomplishments of a reform movement already underway, the feminist attempt to reorder theological education by criticizing the partiality of the version of church history and tradition that is generally taught; defining new research areas; providing new models of God, church, and community; and insisting on inclusive forms of language and equal roles for women and men in the theological community. Behind these efforts she identifies two forms of feminism, one that argues for the equality of women and another that stresses the uniqueness of their perceptions and contributions. Yet despite the success of feminists in advancing both perspectives (at least in some settings), the deep inadequacies of the pattern of theological studies have not—Chopp maintains—been addressed, either by feminists or in new structural proposals such as Farley's that are sympathetic to feminist goals. A third form of feminism, labeled by Chopp "poststructuralist," which focuses on gender identity as a social construct and the way that other social constructs are gender identified, reveals the deeper problem: The pattern of theological studies is thoroughly warped by the identification of knowledge with the autonomous subject position and public realm of the masculine and of religion with the dependent subject position and private realm of the feminine. Chopp does not propose a structural adjustment to correct this. Rather, she implies, it is too soon for new structures. First, the gender-bound presuppositions of the present structure must be completely unmasked and alternative conceptions of gender displayed and developed.

Walter E. Wyman, Jr., writes about a reform movement in theological education, the historical reorientation of theological studies, that is not only in full swing but that has, in the view of many, triumphed and become dominant. Wyman poses the question: Should historical studies continue to hold a place of prominence in a pattern of organization that has recently been subjected to such devastating critique? His response is emphatically positive. Historical consciousness is a core ingredient of knowledge and belief in our time. Therefore the elements of historical consciousness, historical-critical methods and a "historicizing" worldview, must be *more* central to the pattern of studies than they currently are. The presence of historians and the study of history in theological education are not sufficient to ensure this. Wyman does not lay out a structure that guarantees the right kind of attention to goals he promotes. Like Chopp, however, he sets conditions for the pattern of studies: historical-critical method and historicism must become specific themes of theological reflection; historical studies must be understood as the "body" of theological study, as Schleiermacher long ago proposed; historical studies must along with other studies take on the theological task of critical reflection on meaning and truth; and historical consciousness must inform all theological specialty areas, whatever they may eventually be determined to be.

The three papers that follow (Fiorenza, Knitter, and Paris) also draw attention to pervasive themes or features of the present structure of studies and suggest how reconception of a particular theme or dimension can help to reorient the whole. Unlike the previous writers, however, who portrayed the reorientation of theological education as chiefly an internal matter, these authors believe that important resources for the reconstruction of theological education can be found in the university, an institution with which theological education has had an uneasy and ambiguous relationship. Despite the problems of the past, argue the authors of these papers, new intellectual and institutional alliances with the university and the studies it houses are required for theological education's restructure and reform.

Francis Schüssler Fiorenza begins by classifying existing schemes that relate theological and religious studies. He creates two categories: one for schemes that contrast theological studies and religious studies as subjective faith versus objective knowledge, as epistemic privilege versus scientific neutrality, and as advocacy versus disinterest; and a second for those that absorb one body of studies into the other, making one a subcategory or case of the other. Fiorenza rejects both these modes of relationship and also the possibility of distinguishing theological studies from religious studies as explanation is distinguished from understanding or as life-praxis is from meaning. Indeed, the dialectic between the terms of each of these pairs describes what should be (in preference to theory applied in practice) the movement *internal* to both theological and religious studies. In other words, each should be structured by the disclosive and active aspects of praxis, which Fiorenza identifies as the "hermeneutical link" between the theological and religious studies. Is there then any difference between them? Fiorenza suggests that theological studies are distinguished by their goal of reconstructing the identity of a particular tradition in relation to practice, religious studies by their character as human sciences with practical intent. Religious studies remind theological studies that they must be critical; theological studies challenge religious studies to be practical. Whatever the internal structure of theological studies (this Fiorenza does not specify in this essay, though he has made provocative suggestions elsewhere[11]), patterns of theological education must be institutionally and educationally "crisscrossed" with religious studies for theological education to maintain its critical integrity.

Paul F. Knitter taxes theological education for its "mono-religiosity." He sets as the goal of theological education an adequate response to the "trilemma" of modernity: how at the same time to maintain a sense of tradition, take account of pluralism, and confront domination and oppression. Bipartite "revisionist" structures that attempt to correlate tradition and experience will not, he argues, accomplish this, because Christian tradition and experience by themselves are inaccessible to the kind of theology that addresses the trilemma. Thus Christian theology, for its own reconstruction as well as for its understanding of other religious perspectives, must be "married" to religious studies, especially studies of other religions. Knitter makes no specific structural suggestions for the pattern of theological studies, but he does lay down firm rules of engagement for the analogical and practical encounter, in all fields and disciplines, with other religious traditions.

Peter J. Paris traces the history of the presence of African Americans in theological education. The movement has, he says, had two stages. When African Americans first gained access to predominantly white seminaries, special programs and positions for African Americans were created at the institutional margins. Then the Black Theology Movement challenged white theological education in far more fundamental ways, creating a "crisis of confidence" for many African American students in the core of theological studies. This alienation is unnecessary, Paris maintains, because African American theological studies address fundamental moral and religious problems of sustenance and empowerment that are common to all groups. Paris's proposal would bring the "basic requirements" of liberation and survival to the center of a curriculum constructed in "dialogical" relation to the study of the arts and the human sciences in the university, creating a new "ethos" of concern for justice, peace, and the integrity of creation that would accommodate students' and faculty members' diverse goals and backgrounds.

Like the authors of the essays that precede his, Paris implies that many things in and about theological education must change for it to be adequate to its purposes (for Paris, both new ways of focusing studies and new partnerships are required), but he does not specify a comprehensive new pattern of studies that this change would entail.

The last four papers in the volume (Ogletree, Cobb, Taylor, and Browning) resemble the others in their concern for a theme or feature of the present pattern of studies, but these essays also take on questions of structure directly, each in a very different way.

Two of the authors oppose the notion of a structure of studies of the sort that Farley and others have proposed. That is, they resist the suggestion that theological education should be reordered by creating a new pattern and order of fields of disciplines. Thomas W. Ogletree, citing Farley's work in *The Fragility of Knowledge*, argues that theology can no longer be structured as a map of specialized "sciences." He accepts Farley's hermeneutical modes as a way to define theology, but he does not think that they delineate or imply a "fixed number of sub-specialties that might complete the spectrum of theological studies." Rather, there should be as many subspecialties as "prove practically illuminating in the quest for theological understanding," each a "vantage point" or perspective that enriches the theological whole. These vantage points must, however, be *theological;* they must be structured internally by modes proper to theology, such as those Farley has proposed. Ogletree then proceeds to show how one specialty area, Christian social ethics, can be a theological discipline if it permits its critical investigations to be guided by a hermeneutics of action, a hermeneutics of situations, and at points, other interpretative modes as well—all oriented to Christian social ethics' special theological responsibility, critical reflection on the consequences of human action in the creaturely realm.

John B. Cobb, Jr., writes against disciplines and specialty areas. The task of theological education in a time of crisis like the present, he insists, is to delineate alternatives. The university, splintered into specialty fields, has failed to provide such alternatives; therefore, disciplines, which have so far proved themselves incapable of taking responsibility for human beings, must not play a prominent role in the pattern of theological studies. Cobb makes clear that for him disciplined thinking is important and that specialized inquiries are often appropriate. He argues, however, that if theology either aims to be a discipline or agrees to house a pattern of permanently "canalized" studies, it will lose its proper focus on the well-being of the church and the world. He concludes with a sketch of theology and theological education as they would look if they were focused on the "urgent questions" of belief, value, and practice that Cobb is convinced should serve to orient all teaching and research.

Mark K. Taylor takes a position on the question of structure by sketching one. He agrees with Edward Farley that modes or strategies for interpreting what the Christian's situation requires provide the template for the movement and structure of theological education. In contrast to Wyman, who argues that the pattern and movement of theological studies must give priority to an awareness that "we are children of time," Taylor asserts that diachronic strategies that "move between the horizons of past and present" are insufficient, even in their most sophisticated forms, to situate the subject in the complexity of the present. This task requires synchronic strategies, which move between different horizons or boundaries in the present. Such strategies are, however, neglected in theological education. They are marginalized in the pattern of studies, Taylor charges, by the hegemony of the diachronic. What is lost when they are crowded out is very important—the opportunity to judge beliefs and practices not only by their correlation with past understandings, which is the contribution of diachronic procedures, but also by their consonance with other, different systems of understanding in the present. To redress the present imbalance, Taylor proposes a two-part diachronic strategy: an "intercultural hermeneutic" that requires ethnographic descriptions, including self-descriptions, and the theological critique of what is described; and a "social-political hermeneutic" that explores situations of injustice and domination in a specially disciplined conversation, one that requires the inclusion of those who are most widely distant from the centers of power, equal roles for the conversation partners, an openness to the particularity of the other, and a willingness to engage in conflict. Taylor makes clear that synchronic interpretation, essential as it is, is not adequate by itself to the complexity of the situations that Christians must interpret. Thus he presents his strategies as complement and partner to diachronic strategies, creating, by implication, a twofold pattern of studies structured by interpretative modes.

The final essay, by Don S. Browning, tackles the question of structure by proposing a complete pattern of studies. Browning begins with an account of the recent vigorous conversation about practical theology. In the course of these conversations, the field's narrow focus on the assignment of the minister has, he points out, shifted to a broader concern for the witness of the church in the world. The conversations have also been deeply influenced by expansive definitions of praxis in the writings of contemporary philosophers and theologians. But the profound implications of these shifts, Browning suggests, have yet to be understood. The view of praxis increasingly adopted by practical and other theologians renders "all humanistic studies, including theological studies, . . . practical and historical through and through." In this light, Browning reorganizes theological studies under the rubric of "fundamental practical theology" and provides a preliminary sketch of its constituent parts or movements: descriptive theology (in which "situated and theory-laden religious and cultural practices" are "thickly" described); historical theology (in which questions from theory-laden practice are put to historic texts and traditions); systematic theology (in which "new horizons of meaning" are fused between contemporary practices and historic Christian witness, and the validity of such new meanings is questioned); and strategic practical theology (in which new strategies for action are devised). Browning then suggests how these movements might be translated into actual curricular plans, either as stages of a whole program of studies or as segments of individual courses that lead students through all the hermeneutical steps of fundamental practical theology. He illustrates how such a course might be constructed by describing one that he actually taught.

As the foregoing descriptions suggest, the writers whose works comprise this collection approach the question of the structure of studies by quite different avenues. The majority criticize dimensions or presuppositions of the present structure and propose fundamental changes in those dimensions or assumptions. But, as earlier noted, they do not propose wholly new structures. Some (Dykstra, Wyman, and Knitter, for instance) seem to assume that the current pattern of studies will remain much the same. For these writers, one can infer, profound change is accomplished by infusing the present structure with some new idea or mind-set. Others (notably Taylor) portray the present structure as itself an obstacle to adequate theological education and therefore sketch a major structural revision. These two positions become explicit in the papers of Ogletree, Cobb, and Browning. These three are in close agreement about the goal of theological study: it should provide critically reflective guidance for faithful persons and communities in the world. They disagree deeply, however, about the role of structural revision in promoting that goal. Ogletree thinks that it is not possible, that no particular table of organization can be inferred from the goal of theological formation. Cobb thinks that structural revision, if it serves to create new field areas and disciplines, is undesirable; and Browning, joining Farley, thinks that it is necessary in order to break the hold of old ideas and worldviews. This last disagreement stems from the problem framed earlier by Charles Wood. Disciplines and field areas stand in constant danger of reductionism and irresponsible self-service. Yet theology without structures and divisions, even if oriented to compelling new purposes, may find it difficult to set a steady course and to resist the corrupting influence of powerful disciplinary structures elsewhere. Which set of dangers is greater? These writers do not agree.

The differences just described are essentially strategic. One group focuses on the presuppositions and hidden assumptions of the present pattern of studies, convinced that they are the key to comprehensive change. The other seeks to redefine and rearrange the structural elements of the pattern, certain that a new order is required to undergird new practices. This difference, however, significant as it is, should not be permitted to mask the important feature the papers have in common: All are responses to what their authors perceive to be massive changes in the context of theological education, changes so great that they demand the reformulation of theology and hence theological education.

The shift that the papers record and respond to has numerous aspects. They include the erosion of earlier assumptions about authority and universality, a heightened awareness of pluralism and the historically determinate character of experience, and a new sensitivity to the oppression and domination of some groups by others. In theology and church life, the shift has produced many changes—the historicizing and pluralizing of theological knowledge, the growth of disciplines and subspecialties, a preference for democratic forms of church governance—and created a sense of the urgency of many further changes, especially those that undercut the hegemony of white, male experience and that challenge technocratic assumptions about theory and practice.

The shift and the climate of change it has created affect the authors in several ways. First, aspects of the shift provide the themes of their essays. Each of these authors can be read as describing and framing a theological educator's response to a major feature or dimension of the contemporary context. Second, the pervasiveness of the shift and its attendant changes highlights the importance and inescapability of context. Aware of how changed conditions have made the present structure of studies and its presuppositions inadequate and in some cases harmful, these authors are acutely conscious of the contextuality of all practices and proposals—none completely transcends the time and place of its origin—and of the necessity that their own recommendations be carefully fitted to the settings for which they are made. Third, the massiveness of the changes to which these authors are responding intensifies the difficulty of their task. It is no simple matter to propose a new structure for all of theological study when so much is new, so much is still changing, and so much from the past must be dismantled and reshaped. Not surprisingly, then, most of these uthors focus on a *part* of the task of redesign and reconstruction rather than produce larger sketches of the shape and internal organization of the whole. Their heightened sense of context has taught them that, if future structures are to hold up for very long, both the criticism of existing foundations and the construction of new elements must proceed with great thoroughness and care.

V

Even complete and specific proposals such as the one Browning has set forth in this volume and those other authors have offered elsewhere are not recipes or prescriptions for new programs at particular schools. The theological and ethnic traditions of an institution, its ethos, the makeup of its faculty, the immediate needs of its students, and the expectations of other institutions and of its constituency are all powerful forces in molding the actual educational practices of a school, and such forces play major roles in determining the shape and direction of any changes a school may seek to make. Of what practical use, then, are the papers collected in this volume and the larger body of writing of which they form a part? How can blueprints for new structures and critical studies of deep presuppositions, which David Kelsey has accurately characterized as forming a "Utopian" literature on theological education,[12] make a real difference as the faculty and constituency of a school try to improve the programs that an institution offers?

Studies of structure and presuppositions have three concrete uses in such situations.

First, they serve as examples of a *level* of discussion that is an essential step toward significant and lasting educational change, but that is, nonetheless, often short-circuited. In recent years, as strategic planning has become the vogue in theological schools, faculties and boards of trust have become adept at an abstract and general sort of discussion about theological education, often leading to the drafting of an institutional mission statement that is itself general and abstract. Faculties are also practiced in the specific negotiations required to revise curricula. Connecting these two kinds of discussion, however, usually proves very difficult. Mission statements are so broad that they neither require nor rule out very much by way of specific curriculum elements.

A thorough discussion of the overall pattern of studies and the presuppositional baggage it carries supplies the missing link between general considerations of purpose and specific elements of a curriculum. If this link is not forged, any curriculum adjustments are likely to be superficial and short-lived. As noted earlier, the deep structure of studies—its division into field areas and the movement that is judged to occur among them—shapes attitudes, expectations, and educational behavior in powerful ways. Unless the existing pattern and its presuppositions are aired and critically evaluated, and unless any proposed innovation is treated to similarly searching analysis, real and lasting reform is not possible.

These essays or similar writings should, therefore, be used to stimulate the kind of discourse they exemplify. Adequate discussions of structure, as these essays illustrate, will require those who participate to engage in rigorous thinking (and probably writing) and extended deliberations. A faculty or other group that takes the essential step of understanding structure and presuppositions must, in other words, involve itself in the scholarly study of theological education.

Second, these essays provide an *agenda* for discussion. Though the list of topics treated in this volume is by no means exhaustive, most of the topics it presents—the relation of theory and practice, feminist and other liberation challenges to current conceptions of knowledge and religion, the role of historical consciousness, the relation of theological studies to the study of other cultures and religions, and the role and status of disciplines—refer to realities that are common to the situations of most theological schools. However diverse their traditions and heritages, Christian seminaries and divinity schools in the United States share a social and religious context that makes such topics important.

This holds true even for institutions allied with traditions that have resisted certain cultural trends and developments, such as the professionalization of the ministry or the ordination of women. Broad cultural and intellectual developments such as the ones identified in these essays are as subtly and pervasively formative for those who ignore or oppose them as for those who readily adopt them. For example, many small institutions do not have departments or other formal organizational divisions of the faculty. These schools may be tempted to think that they are therefore exempt from the problems and confusions created by the fourfold structure of studies and the theory-to-practice movement it enforces. A close study of the curriculum of these schools, however, and an honest inventory of the criteria that are used in determining whom to hire and what to teach will almost certainly reveal that the classic pattern of studies is both present and powerful in the making of crucial academic decisions.

Thus institutions that seek to weld a program of studies fitted to contemporary circumstances as well as to their historical identity should use these essays and other recent work as a partial checklist of topics that, one way or another, must be grappled with in any quest for a more coherent pattern of theological study. Once a school has begun to study and discuss this list of topics, other important issues that these writers have overlooked in the general situation or that have special import for the school in its particular context will no doubt emerge.

Third, these essays serve as a reminder of the *genre* in which any reexamination of theological education should seek to locate itself. Diverse as they are, all the papers in this book are *theological* studies of theological education. What makes them so is the seriousness with which they take the situation of theological education and the resources of the Christian gospel that theological education can claim in order to address its situation. These writers have not focused on the reform of theological education out of a concern for academic tidiness, a need to rearrange the traditional areas of study in patterns that are more orderly and symmetrical; nor is their motive public relations, a need to respond to the loudest complaints about theological education by showing that it can be modified to prepare ministers to function more effectively in ministry. Rather, these authors take theological education seriously because the world situation is serious. All would concur with John Cobb's "trite but true" judgment that the situation is characterized by crises—global ecological imbalance, recalcitrant racism and patriarchalism, unstable and unjust political arrangements, the possibility of nuclear destruction. Neither the hyperspecialized disciplines of theological and religious scholarship, as Cobb and Farley have pointed out, nor the technical and functionalist professionalism at which Dykstra, Hough and Cobb, and others take aim provides the resources for constructive responses to these crises. Therefore, a pattern of studies that is riddled with specialization and functionalism must be reformed, indeed replaced, by new patterns that take shape as Christians in community reach for a theological understanding of the world situation and of the requirements of their witness in it.

This is a large challenge. The present pattern of studies is entrenched and held firmly in place by habits and forces already described. The challenge is made even larger by recognition that every concrete situation of praxis is in some measure unique. If theological education is indeed a form of Christian praxis, as the writers in this volume maintain, this means different theological schools will interpret both the world situation and the problems of the present pattern of theological studies somewhat differently, leading to different proposals for reconstruction and renewal. Hence each school, or at least each type of school, must do much of the work of criticism and reconstruction for itself. Each must, in other words, devise its own practical theology of theological education. As schools proceed on this course, which is likely to be long, slow, and difficult, the work of recent writers, including those who have contributed to this book, will serve not as specific answers or solutions to the questions that arise, but as guidance, encouragement, and reminder that the task of reforming theological education is both theological and urgent.

Barbara G. Wheeler

NOTES

1. Prominent in this literature have been several monographs: Edward Farley, *Theologia: The Fragmentation and Unity of Theological Education* (Philadelphia: Fortress Press, 1983), and *The Fragility of Knowledge: Theological Education* in the Church and the University (Philadelphia: Fortress Press, 1988); Joseph C. Hough, Jr., and John B. Cobb, Jr., *Christian Identity and Theological Education* (Chico, Calif.: Scholars Press, 1985); The Mud Flower Collective, *God's Fierce Whimsy: Christian Feminism and Theological Education* (New York: Pilgrim Press, 1985); Charles M. Wood, *Vision and Discernment: An Orientation in Theological Study* (Atlanta: Scholars Press, 1985); and Max L. Stackhouse, ed., *Apologia: Contextualization, Globalization and Mission in Theological Education* (Grand Rapids: Eerdmans, 1988). Several collections have also appeared, including Don S. Browning, ed., *Practical Theology: The Emerging Field in Theology, Church and World* (San Francisco: Harper & Row, 1983); Lewis S. Mudge and James N. Poling, eds., *Formation and Reflection: The Promise of Practical Theology* (Philadelphia: Fortress Press, 1987); Joseph C. Hough, Jr., and Barbara G. Wheeler, eds., *Beyond Clericalism: The Congregation as a Focus for Theological Education* (Atlanta: Scholars Press, 1988); and Don S. Browning, ed., *The Education of the Practical Theologian: Responses to Joseph Hough and John Cobb's Christian Iden-*

tity and Theological Education (Atlanta: Scholars Press, 1989). For a bibliography of works on theological education since 1983, see W. Clark Gilpin, "Basic Issues in Theological Education: A Selected Bibliography, 1980–1988," *Theological Education* 25 (Spring 1989): 115–21.

2. Although many faculties have gathered to discuss theological education at deeper than merely cosmetic levels, two examples especially come to mind. In the 1970s, the Protestant theological faculty at the University of Heidelberg gathered and responded to essays submitted by faculty members. This event and its published text are unusual on two counts. First, the essays were not the usual "state of the discipline" statements issued along the lines of the department and guild representatives. They were on such topics as "European Theology and the Church on the Horizon of the *Ecumene,*" "The Old Testament and Theology," and so forth. Second, each essay was responded to extensively by one of the faculty members, Georg Picht. See Georg Picht and Enno Rudolph, eds., *Theologie—was is das?* (Berlin: Kreuz-Verlag, 1977). In the 1980s, the faculty of Andover-Newton Theological School gathered for extensive discussions of issues of theological education, determined to be sensitive to the complexity and dimensionality of the present situation. The outcome was a book that combined such themes as the nature of theology, globalization, contextuality, and doxology.

3. The most notable contributions of faculty members to the earlier literature on theological education were several comprehensive studies. The most recent of these was the work of H. Richard Niebuhr, Daniel Day Williams, and James M. Gustafson, published as *The Advancement of Theological Education* (New York: Harper & Brothers, 1957), and *The Purpose of the Church and Its Ministry: Reflections on the Aims of Theological Education* (New York: Harper & Brothers, 1956).

4. See especially Farley in *Practical Theology,* ed. Browning.

5. Wood, *Vision and Discernment,* 21.

6. Ibid., 57–58.

7. Ibid., 66ff.

8. Farley, *The Fragility of Knowledge,* 113–70.

9. Hough's and Cobb's structural proposal and a sample curriculum based on it is presented in *Christian Identity and Theological Education,* 95–131. The discussion of practical Christian thinking and reflective practice precedes it, pp. 77–94.

10. Browning et al., *The Education of the Practical Theologian.*

11. See Francis Schüssler Fiorenza, "Foundational Theology and Theological Education," *Theological Education* 20 (Spring 1984): 107–24.

12. Kelsey uses the phrase in a forthcoming book from Westminster/John Knox Press.

1

Reconceiving Practice

Craig Dykstra

Theology and theological education are burdened by a picture of practice that is harmfully individualistic, technological, ahistorical, and abstract. This current picture, implicit in our imaginations and explicit in our actual ways of doing things, is implicated in many of the problems that communities of faith, theology as a body and activity of thought, and theological education in all its contexts are now struggling to overcome.[1] Unless a revised understanding of practice takes root in our endeavors, these problems will remain unresolved. But there is an alternative to the current picture available to us, one that has potential to reorient our ways of thinking theologically about practice. Then certain dimensions of our understandings and practice of theological education, not only in seminaries and divinity schools but also in congregations, might be improved.

I

What is the current picture? When we imagine practice, we see someone doing something. And when we think of practice in relation to theology and theological education, we see, I would suspect, someone doing something like preaching to a congregation, teaching a class, moderating a meeting, or visiting someone in the hospital. Usually, the person we see doing one of these things in our mind's eye is a clergyperson. This picture, I suggest, is the one that comes first, most naturally, almost automatically into view. This is the picture of practice that much of the church and almost all of theological education takes for granted.

One of the problems with this picture that is quickly picked out and has been much discussed lies in the assumption that the practice is the practice of a clergyperson. The fact that we focus on clergy so readily is evidence of the pervasiveness of what Edward Farley calls "the clerical paradigm," which he says governs theological education in general and practical theology in particular.[2] This is surely a problem, for the many good reasons Farley discusses. But it is not a problem intrinsic to our understanding of practice. Were we to substitute a layperson in our minds (or in the actual situation), the basic problem with our view of practice would not be solved.[3] This is because the emphasis on clergy is only a symptom and manifestation of deeper issues.

Closer to the heart of the problem is the fact that we almost automatically see some*one* doing something. It is true, of course, that the one doing something (let us call him or her "the practitioner") is often doing it in the presence of others.[4] Indeed, the practitioner is doing it *to* the others, often *for the sake of* the others who are there. But notice the assumptions here. The person doing something to and for others is the one engaged in the practice. The preacher, the teacher, the counselor is the one who is doing the thing we are interested in. The others are objects or recipients of the practice. If we pay any attention at all to what the others are doing, it is in terms of the effects generated in them by the practice of the practitioner. The others are not themselves engaged in the practice. Our assumptive vision of practice is that it is something *individuals* do. This points to what I mean when I say that our current picture of practice is individualistic.

Why does the fact that our picture assumes that practice involves individuals doing something make the picture individualistic? After all, there is no getting away from the fact that practice does involve individuals doing things. True. The problem is not what is included in the picture. The problem lies in where we focus and in what is left out. Our point of focus is the individual actor. What is left out is the larger social and historical context in which individual actions take place.[5] From the point of view of an alternative understanding of practice that I will be developing, practice is not the activity of a single person. One person's action becomes practice only insofar as it is participation in the larger practice of a community and a tradition.

The individualism of the current picture is related to another of its features. When we think of practice, we picture the practitioner as someone who knows what he or she is doing, and we expect that person to carry out his or her practice effectively. "Good practice" does not mean just the exercise of routine, mechanical technique. It means knowledgeable, thoughtful action. This is why we invest so heavily in the professional education of practitioners. We want them to know what to do and how to do it, and we insist that they know why as well. We want them to recognize the point of what they are doing and to be aware of the reasons for doing something one way rather than another. They should be able to give explanations of their action in the light of the situations in which they do what they do. We want them, in short, to be guided in their practice by theory.

This is all good, of course. We would not want practitioners *not* knowing what they are doing. It is not desirable that people be stupid and ineffectual in their practice. Rather, the problem lies in what this picture naturally suggests most aids and forms intelligent practice.

In the case of the professional education of ministers, the social sciences have had a fairly considerable role to play—particularly in that part of theological education we call "practical theology." The reason is that these sciences seem to be quite useful in providing the kind of theory (the kinds of reasons and explanations and predictions) that helpfully guide action. The value of other theoretical disciplines, such as biblical studies, history, and systematic theology, in guiding action is more difficult to discern. Usually, in fact, we cannot find ways to think of them in these terms at all. Therefore, these areas of study are relegated to providing the "content" for practice; that is, what is preached and taught.[6] Or we take the tack that these "academic" disciplines shape the practitioners' character; teach them to be better, clearer thinkers; or help them become more discerning in their perceptions and interpretations of the people and situations in which they work—all examples of influencing practice in some indirect way.[7] Even so, making connections between the so-called academic and practical fields seems difficult, not only to students but to teachers and scholars as well.[8]

The problem, again, is with the assumptions behind the current picture. The picture is a technological one. We assume the theory-practice relation to be a form of the science-technology relation. "Practice" means for us "making something happen." Practitioners are not supposed just to be doing something. They are supposed to be doing something to something or someone *in order to gain some desired outcome or result*. The reasons we consider for doing any particular thing are the *effects* it generates. The criterion by which practice is evaluated is whether it produces the effects we expect. That is, the criterion is effectiveness.

When theory and practice are related in this way, the kind of theory that is particularly relevant to practice is theory that helps us understand and trace causal relationships. Under the power of this picture, what we need to know from theory is how things work. When we know that, we can see how best to intervene in their workings and influence the course of events. Theory that can help us do that is highly valued. Theory that cannot do that (or can do so only marginally) is not valuable to practice.

This way of understanding practice not only focuses our attention on issues of cause and effect; it prescinds moral questions. Moral issues are not so much excluded as they are kept hidden or extraneous. This is because moral questions are made extrinsic to cause-and-effect relations, and thus to both theory and practice understood this way. When practice is procedure, its value depends upon its utility. Morality, then, has to do with the value of the results or effects of practice rather than with anything intrinsic to practice itself. Morality and practice have become separate issues in this.

Again, the problem has to do with focus and exclusion. We do not want people to be *in*effective. Nor should we deny that there are often causal relations among events that, if we understand them, are important to know about and do something with. The problem is that we easily assume that *all* relations are causal; that practice is fundamentally intervention into a causal network and thus always the purposeful creation of change (especially in other people or in groups and institutions); that the creation of such change is both within our power and the point or purpose of any and every practice; and that the criterion of all practice must be an extrinsic one such as effectiveness. And with these assumptions we are forced to conclude that if we do not know how or do not have the power to intervene in certain causal relations in order to make change, there is nothing to do. Lacking such understanding and ability, we are left with no practice, or, what practice there is, is mere habit or technique with no point. This is what I mean by a technological understanding of practice.

If we conceive of practice technologically, it is likely that our conception will also be ahistorical and abstract in character. When "practice" refers to what someone does to and for someone or something else in order to create change, and if we come to know how to do that by understanding the causal relations involved, our tendency is to focus primarily on *present* circumstances and the possibilities inherent in them. We do, of course, often try to trace what has led up to the present circumstances in order to discern better what the causal relations involved are, but our interest in the past is exhausted by what it can tell us about this. Furthermore, our historical interest is in the history of the current situation, not in the history of practice. Practice is *applied* to a situation—perhaps historically (or better, genetically) understood—but the practice itself is not regarded as part of the situation to be understood historically. Indeed, practice, technologically understood, can have no real history. Practices may be repeated (that is, one may do the same kind of thing in sufficiently similar situations), but each practice is essentially a singular event, beginning and ending upon its intervention into each situation. Practice has no internal history of its own.

In theological schools, the assumed ahistoricism of practice is evident in how little work is done in the various subfields of practical theology on the history of Christian education, homiletics, pastoral care, church administration, and so forth.[9] We see little reason to analyze carefully the continuities and discontinuities of practice in various historical periods, traditions, and cultures. The research of this kind that does exist is marginal to the curriculum largely because its relevance to contemporary practice is so difficult to discern. When it is perceived to be relevant, it is usually as data out of which certain methods and techniques or, more generally, principles and guidelines may be recovered from earlier periods for use today.

The assumption that the value of history is the current usability of technical resources found there is an indication of what I mean by the abstractness of the current picture of practice. What we are after are theoretical principles and guidelines, together with tested methods, approaches, and techniques, which we regard as historically and culturally neutral.[10] We get these principles and methods mainly from contemporary theory-building and experimentation. If we turn to historical documents for help at all, we do so assuming that our task is to abstract the principles and methods from any historical narrative or tradition of which they may be a part. The tradition or context is, intentionally or unintentionally, distilled out. When we have these principles and methods, we may then employ them in our contemporary action. We understand, of course, that situations vary considerably and that our principles, guidelines, methods, and techniques must be applied differently in different situations, but we rely on theory together with direct observation rather than history or tradition to help us do this.

II

This, I suggest, is the picture that currently governs our understanding of practice in theology, in theological education, and to a large extent in the life of the church—particularly in the First World. The point is not that this is the only picture at all operative on the contemporary scene, or that all of its dimensions as articulated here prevail equally in every situation. Correctives to the tendencies we have lifted up do exist in many actual situations as well as in the minds of many thinkers. Various aspects of the current picture and many of its implications and effects have numerous critics. Nevertheless, this remains the dominant picture. It is the one around which most ministers and members of congregations orient church life. It is the one that most faculty in theological seminaries take for granted. It defines for many in the "academic" fields what the "practical" department is concerned with, and few in practical departments really question that definition, even when they chafe under its effects. This picture is the one that so naturally comes to mind for so many that conscious resistance to and articulated criticism of this one is required in order to function on the basis of any other.

Criticism of this picture may take place on two levels. One may criticize its implications and effects, or one may criticize the assumptions implicit in it. Both kinds of criticism are available across a broad literature.[11] But criticism, even if it is thoroughgoing, can take us only so far. What we really need is an alternative. Fortunately, an alternative is being put forward by some of those who have been most involved in the kind of criticism just mentioned. The picture of practice being suggested is quite different from the current picture in each of the aspects we have discussed. Its clearest formulation is provided by Alasdair MacIntyre, who defines a practice as

> any coherent and complex form of socially established cooperative human activity through which goods internal to that form of activity are realized in the course of trying to achieve those standards of excellence which are appropriate to, and partially definitive of, that form of activity, with the result that human powers to achieve excellence, and human conceptions of the ends and goods involved, are systematically extended.[12]

In the picture of practice carried by this definition, we do not first see an individual doing something. Rather, practice is inherently *cooperative,* so the lens broadens to include numbers of people. And these people are not doing things *to* one another so much as they are doing things *with* one another. Though each may be engaged in different specific actions, they are not doing different things. Individual actions interrelate in such a way that they constitute engagement in a common practice.

Jeffrey Stout's favorite example of a practice is baseball.[13] Baseball simply cannot be played alone. It is fundamentally cooperative. If you can't get a team together, you can't play the game. The players are gathered together, however, not in order to do different things *to* each other but to do one thing together – play baseball. Each player does, of course, do many things individually. We might see, for instance, Nolan Ryan pitching and Jose Canseco batting, while others are fielding, stealing bases, or watching from the dugout. Each of them, at a particular time, is doing something distinctive and individual. But at the level of practice, they are all doing the same thing – playing baseball.

Even this formulation may be too limiting, however; for the practice we have just been describing is "playing baseball" rather than "baseball itself." In the practice of baseball itself, Tommy LaSorda managing, Vin Scully and Joe Garagiola doing the play-by-play, and even my sons and I watching games on television and Roger Angell writing about it in *The New Yorker* are all included as well. A practice involves people doing things with one another, and normally at least some part of the time people will be doing what they do in physical proximity to one another. But not everyone engaged in a practice need be physically with others in order to participate.

Practice does not reduce to group activity. On the one hand, you do not have to be in a group to be participating in a practice. Prayer is a practice of the church. People praying by themselves are involved in this practice. Even though they are not at the moment involved in a group activity, they are involved in a "coherent and complex form of socially established cooperative human activity." It is cooperative because we pray, even when praying alone, as participants in the praying of the church. The principle is illustrated by an example MacIntyre uses—portrait painting.[14] Painting is something an individual does, so it is hard to see how this is a cooperative human activity. But the cooperation comes not primarily through persons interacting physically so much as it does through persons engaging in activities that gain their meaning from the *form* that emerges through a complex tradition of interactions among many people sustained over a long period of time. Portrait painting and private prayer are in this way social established forms of human activity, just as baseball is.

Conversely, the mere fact of a group of people doing something together does not mean we necessarily have a practice. Practice is participation in a cooperatively formed pattern of activity that emerges out of a complex tradition of interactions among many people sustained over a long period of time. This is what MacIntyre means when he says that a practice is "socially established." What is socially established is a "form" of human activity. Some cooperative human activities build up, over time, patterns of reciprocal expections among participants, ways of doing things together by which the cooperative activity is given not only direction but also meaning and significance. The form itself comes to embody the reasons for the practice and the values intrinsic to it. This is why, in order to participate in a practice intelligently, one must become aware of the *history* of the practice.

A practice cannot be abstracted from its past, because the past is embedded in the practice itself. To abstract the practice from its tradition is to reduce the practice to a group activity. An implication of this feature of practices is that a practice cannot be made up, created on the spot by an individual or even a group. Because practices come into existence through a process of interaction among many people over a sustained period of time, individuals can only participate in them; they cannot create them. This does not mean, of course, that new practices never emerge or that established practices do not change. As people participate in practices, they are involved in their ongoing history and may in the process significantly reshape them. Practices may be deepened, enriched, extended, and to various extents be reformed and transformed. Individuals, usually persons profoundly competent in a practice, may have considerable historical effect on its shape and direction.

The "form" of a practice is related to its value. In order for a socially established activity to be a practice, its form must be "coherent" and "complex" enough to generate "goods internal to that form" that may be realized through participation in the practice. Taking long showers, says Stout, is not a practice.[15] As an activity, it lacks the coherence and complexity necessary for generating value internal to the activity itself. It can certainly generate "external goods" (smelling better, feeling more relaxed), but the activity itself cannot simply through our participation in it make us better people or involve us in a kind of life that is itself good. A practice may do this.

MacIntyre uses his example of the practice of portrait painting to make this point. There are two different kinds of goods internal to painting, he says. The first kind is "the excellence of the products, both the excellence in performance by the painters and that of each portrait itself." The second kind is "what the artist discovers within the pursuit of excellence in portrait painting," namely, "the good of a certain kind of life."[16] That is, things of value arise through engagement in the practice itself. Some of these things are products emerging from the practice; others are the effects of the practice on the practicing persons and their communities—including the effects on their minds, imaginations, and spirits.[17]

The goods internal to a practice can be realized, according to MacIntyre, only by participating well in it. These goods "can only be identified and recognized by the experience of participating in the practice in question."[18] Baseball often seems an utter waste of time to those who do not participate in the practice. Only by getting inside the world of baseball, through playing the game, attending to its nuances, do its intrinsic values become evident. And, according to MacIntyre, we come to identify and recognize these goods more clearly and powerfully as we more fully satisfy the standards of excellence "appropriate to and, partially definitive of, that form of activity." Baseball may be played well or badly. It is baseball "at its best" that most clearly reveals the values embedded in it.

Furthermore, the criteria revealed and by which a practice is ultimately to be judged are not entirely external criteria. Some of the criteria—indeed, often the most significant criteria—are intrinsic to the practice, criteria that constitute the practice as the practice it is. Moral standards and values are built into practices. Practices themselves bear moral weight.

We must go beyond MacIntyre, however, to make another claim about practices. Practices bear more than moral weight; they also bear epistemological weight. The point here is that in the context of participation in certain practices we come to see more than just the value, the "good" of certain human activities. Beyond that, we may come to awareness of certain *realities* that outside of these practices are beyond our ken. Engagement in certain practices may give rise to new knowledge.

Some of this knowledge may be almost entirely somatic in nature. A fine batter comes to "know" what a ball will do, and his body will "know" what to do to hit it. It is possible that without such somatic knowledge, other forms of cognition for which this is a prerequisite become impossible. Edward Farley reminds us also how "social relationships mediate realities [through] their capacity to effect new powers of perceptiveness" and suggests that "what is true for physical perception carries over, it seems, into the more subtle realms of insight or perceptiveness into various regions of reality; the nuances of poetry, the complex interrelations of a bureaucracy, the shadings of human vocabulary."[19]

But Farley points this out while making a larger, theological point that runs much deeper. He argues that under certain conditions changes in perceptivity may take place that bring more than simply new perspectives on things. Sometimes, new *realities* appear on the horizon to be apprehended, thus generating new knowledge. More specifically, within what Farley calls "the situation of faith" there come into being "states of affairs which at one time had no existence and which now have emerged in the course of history and individual existence."[20] In the situation of faith, these new realities include a new way of life, a new form of existence, which in turn presupposes a transcendent source and ground.

It is important to ask whether participation in certain practices provides physical, social, and even intellectual conditions necessary to knowledge intrinsic to the life of faith.[21] Marianne Sawicki has argued that the New Testament itself makes clear that certain practices are in fact conditions to the possibility of "recognizing the risen Lord." She contends that both Luke-Acts and Matthew posit the insufficiency of their own words and stipulate that "action on behalf of the needy is not an implication of resurrection faith, but a precondition for it. Talk about resurrection is literally meaningless in the absence of such action."[22] The claim is that engagement in the practice of service is a *condition* for the knowledge of a reality absolutely central to faith—the reality of resurrection presence.

III

We have put forward an understanding of practice that is quite different from the standard current picture. Alasdair MacIntyre's discussion of the nature of "practices" as fundamental features of the moral life has provided us a way to move forward. But in order to discern the significance of practice for Christian life, we have needed to move beyond MacIntyre's historical-moral claim to make epistemological-theological suggestions. Once we have reached this level of discussion, it begins to become clear how intrinsic practices are to the life of faith.

In the prevailing picture, practice cannot be intrinsic to or constitutive of a way of life. Practice understood technologically, individualistically, and ahistorically is practice reduced to the merely functional. But things are different with the alternative picture. Our identities as persons are constituted by practices and the knowledge and relationships they mediate. Some of these are so central to who we are that we cannot give them up without our very existence undergoing transformation. Correlatively, communal life is constituted by practices. Communities do not just engage in practices; in a sense, they *are* practices.[23]

Our suggestions obviously raise a host of questions on all fronts. What status do practices so defined really have? Under what conditions do certain practices in fact have power to create new perceptivities and even make accessible to us such realities as are central to the life of faith? What have been the practices by which Christian life in the world has been sustained across the centuries? What have people done, and what has their doing meant? How have their practices taken on different shape and meaning in various historical and cultural contexts? What have people come to see and know and be through participation in these practices? How has that happened? What agencies are involved – both immanent and transcendent – and how? Where are these practices still alive in some form in the contemporary world? What does participation in them involve? What are their consequences and effects? What are the grounds of their possibility?

These questions admit of no easy answers, but there are good reasons to raise them here. First, the prevailing conception of practice fails even to generate such questions. That is a sign of its poverty. Second, to answer such questions we must cross the lines that now divide biblical studies, European church history, Reformed systematic theology, and religious education, to cite a few specific curriculum areas in contemporary theological study, from one another. And clearly, a list of pastoral activities will do us no good.

The identification, study, and pursuit of practices that are central to and constitutive of Christian faith and life are, in my view, among the signal tasks of Christian theological study. This is especially true today, when this task has been singularly neglected. Answers to questions about practices are relatively simple when we are talking about baseball or even portrait painting. But matters become quite complicated when we attend to practices that have histories often going as far back as biblical times and further, practices that have been embodied in various ways in societies and situations around the globe. Moreover, in the context of theological study, we attend to practices of a form of life that claims to bear intimacy with God as well as world-transforming power.

That there would ever be unanimity on what the constitutive practices of Christian life are or at what levels of discourse they ought to be identified is unlikely. But it is best not to strive for common agreement in any case, because some ways of construing practices may serve some specific purposes and occasions better than others. I articulated a series of practices in a previously published essay. The list included such practices as interpreting scripture, worship and prayer, confession and reconciliation, service, witness, social criticism, and the mutual bearing of suffering.[24] Margaret Miles's recent book *Practicing Christianity: Critical Perspectives for an*

Embodied Spirituality includes a section on "practices of Christian life." What she means by "practice" is consistent with the meaning we have been discussing here, and our lists overlap. She mentions a number of practices in her introduction and devotes a chapter each to ascetic practices, worship and sacraments, service, and prayer.[25] In these chapters, she poses some of the important questions we have suggested need pursuing.

An essay by Michael Welker provides an excellent example of a kind of analysis the historical and theological intricacy of practice in Christian life demands.[26] He asks what law is and how it relates to gospel. But rather than providing an intellectual history of the concepts, he engages in an acute multidisciplinary investigation of the basic human practice of securing expectations. The question Welker pursues is this: How do people commit themselves and others to obligations to one another in such a way that public security and a social future can be corporately secured? All human communities must find some way to do this. Welker shows how a distinctive practice of securing expectations lies at the heart of Christian life and traces how this practice emerges from cultic and legal practices reflected in Deuteronomy, everyday social issues refracted through the narratives recounted in Exodus, as well as the theological struggles engaged by Paul in the face of Christ's death.

The point here is neither to recommend a specific list of practices nor a particular way of identifying and studying them. The point is to call for their recognition and to suggest their centrality in Christian life and, hence, in theological study and theological education. Suppose that practices central to Christian life are conditions under which various kinds and forms of knowledge emerge—knowledge of God, of ourselves, and of the world; knowledge that is not only personal but also public. Suppose that through such practices, the virtues and character and wisdom of the communities and individuals who participate in them are formed. Suppose that through participation in practices of Christian life, the community of faith comes continually to awareness of and participation in the creative and redemptive activity of God in the world. If these suppositions are sustainable, practices deserve a pivotal place in Christian formation, theological study, and theological education.

IV

Edward Farley has suggested that we recover an understanding of theology as habitus.[27] I suggest that what such habitus involves is profound, life-orienting, identity-shaping participation in the constitutive practices of Christian life. If theology is habitus, then it follows that we learn theology (are formed in this habitus) by participation in these practices.

Participation in these practices, certainly participation at any significant level of depth and understanding, must be learned. We need more than just to be included in the practices. We need to come to understand them from the inside and to study and interpret carefully the realities we encounter through engagement in them.

In order to learn them and learn in the context of them, we need others who are competent in these practices to help us: to be our models, mentors, teachers, and partners in practice. We need people who will include us in these practices as they themselves are engaged in them and who will show us how to do what the practices require. We also need them to explain to us what these practices mean, what the reasons, understandings, insights, and values embedded in them are. And we need them to lure us and press us beyond our current understandings of and competence in these practices, to the point where we together may extend and deepen the practices themselves.

People best learn practices such as these when conditions like the following pertain:

1. When we are active in them, actually *doing* what these practices involve, engaging in them personally in particular physical and material settings and in face-to-face interaction with other people;

2. When we participate in them *jointly* with others, especially with others who are skilled in them and are able to teach them to us;
3. When the people involved in them with us are, or are becoming, personally significant to us—and we to them;
4. When we are involved in increasingly broader, more varied, and more complex dimensions of them, and when the activities we engage in in these practices become increasingly more wide-ranging in their context and impact;
5. When we come more and more to connect articulations of the significance and meaning of these practices and the ways the various practices are connected and related to one another with our own activities in them and with the reasons we ourselves have for engaging in them; and
6. When we come to take increasing personal responsibility for initiating, pursuing, and sustaining these practices, and for including and guiding others in them.

Participation in some of the practices of Christian life can and should occur naturally in the context of everyday life in a community constituted by them. But communities, especially in such culturally and socially fragmented situations as our own, cannot depend entirely upon this for initiating people into these practices and guiding them in them. The situation requires planned and systematic education in these practices. But such education must never be detached from participation in the practices; it cannot be satisfactory simply to describe and analyze them from afar.[28] Nonetheless, education must order this participation in such a way that all the practices are engaged in meaningfully and with understanding at increasingly broader and more complex levels. And that presupposes sytematic and comprehensive education in the history and wider reaches of the practices as well as in the interpretation and criticism of the reasons and values embedded in the practices. This is true in the theological education of children and youth as well as in the education of adults.

The range of such education is still more extensive than this, however. None of us live only in communities constituted by such practices as we have articulated, and such practices never exist in a vacuum. We both live and learn in multiple social contexts and institutions, each of which is constituted by a much broader plurality of practices than those on which we have focused. Our wider intellectual, political, social, and occupational lives involve us all in a great variety of practices. And because such contexts naturally infiltrate faith communities, this broad spectrum of practices is internal to congregations, to theological seminaries, and even to convents. We all live our lives in an intersection of many practices.

Theological education must concern itself with the mutual influences that various practices have on each other, as well as whatever complementarity and/or conflict there may be between the goods internal to ecclesial practices and others. Because we are all citizens, for example, we must inquire into the nature, effects, and implications of our simultaneous engagement in practices constitutive of Christian life and those central to public politics. We need to inquire into the continuities and discontinuities between medical practice in our society and practices of care for the ill and the dying that now are and have in the past been characteristic of the church. Various intellectual disciplines (such as physics, literary studies, and psychology) are also practices in the sense we mean. Inquiries into the relations between disciplines (including those that are theological and those that are secular) engage us in similar issues and are thus central to theological study and theological education.[29]

V

The understanding of practice we have been developing has manifold implications for theological inquiry and theological education. The constriction of the range of appropriate participants in theological education will need to be broken. The organization of theological study might well need to change significantly. And in response to both of these alterations, the kind of institutions responsible for theological education might well need to be significantly expanded and the educational processes structured by them considerably enriched.

Farley has ably critiqued the clerical paradigm in theological studies and the reduction of theological education to schools for clergy.[30] Theological study and theological education are appropriate to and necessary for all Christians. Once we recognize that a more significant and fruitful conception of practice refers to the ongoing and central practices that constitute the community's very life and that all its members are called to be participants in that practice, we are led to a broad vision of theological inquiry and education. The idea that theological inquiry and education is only for scholarly researchers and clergy begins to evaporate. But clergy, like others, do require theological education, and the patterns of study that now obtain in those schools powerfully influence most other institutions of theological education presently existing or likely to emerge. So I will conclude by developing some of the implications of our work on practice for these schools.

Clergy, like all Christians, need to be formed and schooled in the practices of the life of Christian faith. This should not be just beginning when candidates enter a theological seminary or divinity school. Prerequisite to seminary education are not just certain studies in the liberal arts and sciences, but education in ecclesial practices. The theological education of clergy is dependent upon and should be continuous with the theological education these same people receive as lay people.

To presuppose much of an education along these lines may be, under present circumstances, to traffic in an ideal. Seminary or divinity school education is not the first exposure or context of participation people have to any practices of the life of Christian faith; otherwise, they would not be enrolled. But it may well be their first exposure to some of them. And it is likely to be their first opportunity to explore ways in which all of the practices are carried out in contexts beyond those they have personally experienced. Because these practices, understood as practices that take place worldwide and over a long history, are so central to Christian life and community, a key task in clergy education is to insure that all students are exposed to and participate in all of these practices in some context and at some level and become aware of the breadth and depth to which these practices may extend.

The continuity of the theological education of clergy with their previous theological education is premised on the fact that clergy are involved in the same fundamental practices as are all other Christians. But clergy have some responsibilities and roles that not all of us do. They are responsible not only for their own participation in the practices of Christian life. They are uniquely responsible for the participation of whole communities in them. This requires that they organize these practices corporately in a particular situation and insure that the people of that community, young and old, are initiated into them, guided in them, and led in them. It requires them to work to insure that all the practices are learned by everyone in breadth and in depth, in their increasing complexity, and with ever more profound understanding. It requires them to work to insure that the practices happen and that the dangerous proclivities of the institutionalization necessary to sustaining a community in these practices do not subvert them.

Because clergy must be teachers of these practices in their own communities, it is essential that they know and understand the histories of these practices and the reasons, insights, values, and forms of judgment borne both by the traditions of which they are a part and by competent and wise contemporary engagement in them. But not only this. These insights, values, and forms of judgment are borne in Christian practices only because new perceptivities and the apprehension of distinctive, life-transforming realities gave rise to them. If the ever-fresh promise in the context of these practices is that new perceptivities are shaped and life-transforming realities are made available for apprehension in each new day, then this must be the heart of what is taught. Christian teachers are not ultimately teachers of practices; they are teachers of the gospel. The education that clergy are responsible for is education in truth and reality in and through those practices by which truth and reality may be made manifest.

This is what clergy are called to articulate and explain (or, better, expose and reveal) to others. Teachers, as they guide others in their participation in the practices of Christian life, must be able to make the inner workings and qualities of each practice available to those they teach in such a way that those workings and qualities open up to the reality and truth on which they are founded. Clergy ought to be teachers who can do this, and the theological education clergy receive ought to help them.

The present system of curricular fields and departments of seminaries and divinity schools leaves much of this unattended. Under the dominance of the current picture of practice, practical theology attends either to other issues or to a stripped-down form of practice that reduces it to know-how. The other fields disregard practice almost entirely. But we do not have to reform the structure of departments and fields in order to ameliorate this situation considerably. Every field of seminary education currently existing has contributions to make to the understanding and interpretation of every one of these practices—if they become aware that these practices actually permeate their own subject matters and are, to various extents, actually or potentially implicated in the practice of their own disciplines.

In the Bible, for example, we can see all of these practices being carried out—and in a great variety of situations and circumstances. Moreover, the coming of the Bible into its present form is itself the engagement of a people in many of these practices, as the various forms of criticism clearly show. The case is similar with respect to the historical study of any era, dimension, text, or community of the Christian tradition. But historical studies are not the only relevant ones. The practices carry a broad and complex range of theological, ethical, and philosophical assumptions, convictions, insights, and reasonings, all of which are in need of exposure, display, and continuing scrutiny. Here the systematic disciplines come heavily into play. They are essential for helping communities and persons know what they are doing and why as they engage in these practices. They are also essential for the continuing criticism and reform of these practices, the goods internal to them, and the knowledge that they make possible.

This is not to assert that the curriculum of seminary education can or should be exhausted by attention to these practices or that the historical, theological, and philosophical investigation of these practices should define and circumscribe every field. It is more than enough to say that all of these fields and disciplines are relevant and necessary to the kind of systematic investigation and understanding of these practices that clergy require. And all of these fields could be enhanced by recognizing and making explicit this relevance and necessity.

At this point, one might ask, If education in the history and inner workings and meanings of these practices were actually taking place in the Bible, history, and theology departments of a school, and especially if this were done in relation to actual engagement in these practices, would there be anything left for a practical theology department to do? My own response to this question is ambivalent. Ideally, I am inclined to think probably not.

Realistically speaking, however, and short of an entire reformulation of the departmental structure of theological education, attending to the history, inner rationality, and truth of the practices may be enough to ask of the "academic" fields. For the time being at least, disciplined reflection on and engagement in the practices as such may have to fall to those who teach in the departments and curriculum area we now gather under such rubrics as social ethics, church and society, and practical theology.[31] This would provide a context in which the practices and their engagement in the various concrete, contemporary situations and environments in which they are carried out would be *the* focusing subject matter.[32] It would be the responsibility of such fields to articulate these practices, describe them, analyze them, interpret them, evaluate them, and aid in their reformation. It would also be their focal responsibility to help students participate actively in them in actual situations of the kind they do and will face in their roles as clergy.

This is a somewhat more traditional understanding of the function of practical theology departments than I myself am happy with, but even this would call for significant change in the way we currently conceive practical theology and social ethics. Furthermore, I believe that more radical revision of the current curriculum structure is unlikely, and I am sure that we will not get from where we are to where we might someday be in a single leap. Where these functions and issues do not yet permeate the curriculum as a whole, they must not be left unattended. At present, there may be no other choice than to give them to some particular curriculum area.

Even were it possible to expect these practices—and the understandings and skills intrinsic to them—to be taught within the context of other fields, there still might be some need for something in addition. MacIntyre says that "politics in the Aristotelian sense" is a practice.[33] And what politics in this sense turns out to be is the practice of "the making and sustaining of forms of human community—and therefore of institutions"; it is the practice of "sustaining the institutional forms which are the social bearers of the practice[s]" constitutive of a community's form of life.[34] This is a difficult business, precisely because of the threat already noted that institutionalization can pose to every practice. Thus, the practice of politics requires specific understandings, skills, and virtues intrinsic to itself. And this practice, carried out in the context of the life of a particular Christian community, may well be the particular practice that defines what it means to be clergy.

MacIntyre has said that "a living tradition . . . is an historically extended, socially embodied argument," and that the argument is "precisely in part about the goods which constitute that tradition."[35] I would add that it is also about the shape of the practices in the context of which those goods emerge and the truth and reality on which they are grounded and to which they point. If all this is what a living tradition is, then the shape of theological study and the contours of theological education ought to engage deeply the elements that are vital to it. Eminent among these for the Christian tradition are the practices central to its life.

NOTES

1. With regard to the theological education of clergy, the main focus has been on problems in "practical theology" as a department of teaching or area of study. Some (particularly professors in other departments) say practical theology is too much oriented to teaching people how to carry out certain procedures in church life (such as managing conflict in a group, organizing budgets, teaching a class, giving a sermon, or counseling with a couple having marital difficulties). Others (particularly recent graduates who don't know how to do these things) plead for more of such teaching, not less. Some regard practical theology as far too untheological and overly dependent upon such nontheological disciplines as psychology and sociology and studies in organizational behavior and communications theory. Others say that practical theology is not disciplined enough by the social sciences, is always picking up what has become popularized and out of date, and thus is trailing years behind and is superficial at that.

The confusion regarding these and many other problems is so great that, according to Edward Farley, " 'practical theology' may prove not to be a salvagable term. The term is still in use as a term some seminary faculty members use to locate their teaching in the curriculum of clergy education. As such it functions more as a rubric for self-interpretation and location on the curricular map than a name for a discrete phenomenon. So varied are the approaches and proffered definitions of practical theology in recent literature that it is not even clear what is under discussion." (See "Interpreting Situations: An Inquiry into the Nature of Practical Theology," in *Formation and Reflection: The Promise of Practical Theology,* eds. Lewis S. Mudge and James N. Poling [Philadelphia: Fortress Press, 1987], 1. For a sampling of some of the proposals Farley refers to, including Farley's own, see the various chapters in *Formation and Reflection;* Don S. Browning, ed., *Practical Theology: The Emerging Field in Theology, Church and World* [San Francisco: Harper & Row, 1983]; and the many other articles and books referred to in the bibliographies included in these two works.)

The problems redound not only on practical theology, however. The inadequacy of our current picture of practice also creates problems for other areas of theological study and theological education. When practice means the application of theory to contemporary procedure, biblical studies, history, systematic theology, philosophy, and ethics all become theoretical disciplines in which practice has no intrinsic place. This is a problem not only because of the usual pedagogical complaints heard about such disciplines by those who want from them something immediately usable, but also for reasons intrinsic to the meaning of the disciplines themselves. For when practice is rightly understood, the "academic" disciplines are themselves seen to be practices; it also becomes clear how their subject matter includes practices. Thus, when "practice" is entirely relegated to something called "practical theology," certain features intrinsic to the "academic" theological fields are hidden; they themselves become distorted, fragmented, and overly dependent upon and conformed to university disciplines and their secular, Enlightenment assumptions; and their own point, or telos, as dimensions of theological study is then obscured.

A major problem for congregations, as Farley has pointed out, is that congregations are left without theological study altogether when theological study is identified with "clergy education." (See *Theologia: The Fragmentation and Unity of Theological Education* [Philadelphia: Fortress Press, 1983], chaps. 2 and 7; and esp., *The Fragility of Knowledge: Theological Education in the Church and the University* [Philadelphia: Fortress Press, 1988], chap. 5.) This is a tragic loss. But the answer is not simply to reduplicate clergy education in churches. This is sometimes attempted, but the outcome is almost always the transmission of some of the tips and techniques clergy may have picked up from their own studies of "practice" plus some of the "contents" garnered from their studies in the "academic" fields. And both are watered down and left bereft of the understandings, assumptions, and skills that make theological inquiry sustainable in local church settings. As a result, communities of faith are left with the effluvium of theological study.

The current picture of practice is not, of course, alone responsible for these problems. But it is a major contributing factor that, unless reconceived, will continue to plague communities of faith, theology, and theological education in seminaries and divinity schools.

2. See Farley, *Theologia,* esp. 84–88, 127–35.

3. One attempted solution to problems of practice in the church is the "lay ministry" movement. Movements in this direction are important, but they often lead only to the quasi-clericalization of lay people. This does not solve the problems inherent in our picture of practice; it only abets them.

4. When we think of practice, in fact, we rarely think of someone doing something alone, like praying or meditating on scripture or studying a theology book.

5. See Alasdair MacIntyre, *After Virtue* (Notre Dame: University of Notre Dame Press, 1981), chap. 15, on the necessity of a social and narrative-historical account of any action that is to be rendered intelligible.

6. It is harder to see how they provide content for what is counseled or organized, but attempts along these lines are also made.

7. In a few cases, more sophisticated connections are made, so that ways such studies can indeed provide theoretical guidance to practice become more evident. I have in mind here, as

an example, Marianne Sawicki, *The Gospel in History* (New York: Paulist Press, 1988). Sawicki both rethinks what practice is (though she does not use this language to talk about what she is doing) and uses revisionist historiographical methods to get at it in the Bible and in the Christian tradition. See also her essays: "Historical Methods and Religious Education," *Religious Education* 82, no. 3 (Summer 1987): 375–89 and "Recognizing the Risen Lord," *Theology Today* 44, no. 4 (January 1988): 441–49. The kind of thing Sawicki does requires, however, that we see the "academic" disciplines as involving practice—both as method and subject matter. And this, in turn, presses toward a different understanding of practice than that contained within the prevailing picture. It leads, I believe, to the kind of alternative I will be suggesting.

8. In view of this, some have simply defined the problem away by substituting the single word "praxis" for the phrase "theory and practice." But "thought-filled practice," which is what many seem to mean by "praxis," is what good practice involves anyway, and the regular appearance of the oddity "theory and praxis" proves that nothing is really solved by a name change.

9. Another indication is the inattention to practice that prevails in most history departments in theological schools. Such departments normally do not give systematic attention to the practices of, say, Christian education, homiletics, pastoral care, and so forth. Nor do they seem to attempt systematic connection between the history they teach and the practices their students are supposedly going to be engaged in after graduation. There are several possible reasons for this. One may be that historians simply do not care about practice. Another may be that they assume that it is taken care of by the people in the practical department. More likely, however, the current picture of practice, which both historians and practical theologians assume, keeps each at some distance from the concerns of the other, giving neither group much to think historically about. An alternative understanding of practice may, however, provide a basis for considerable discourse. But it may also imply that the standard rubrics (Christian education, homiletics, pastoral care, etc.) are not really practices.

10. See related comments on this point in Farley, *The Fragility of Knowledge,* 10–11: "Empirical method has stunning success in understanding very specific causal relations. When isolated from all correctives, [however,] it loses the concrete reality in its complexity and, with this, the conditions of criticizing itself. Isolated, it tends to become a paradigm of reality itself, but of reality without the social and political contexts of knowledge, reality dispersed into abstract formulas or causal sequences, reality absented from the deposits of the past's wisdom. . . . Praxis isolated becomes situational abstraction."

11. Important sources of this criticism are: Robert N. Bellah, Richard Madsen, William M. Sullivan, Ann Swidler, and Steven M. Tipton, *Habits of the Heart: Individualism and Commitment in American Life* (Berkeley: University of California Press, 1985); Hans-Georg Gadamer, *Truth and Method* (New York: Crossroad, 1975), and *Reason in the Age of Science* (Cambridge: MIT Press, 1981); Stanley Hauerwas, *Vision and Virtue* (Notre Dame: Fides Publishers, 1974), and *The Peaceable Kingdom: A Primer in Christian Ethics* (Notre Dame: University of Notre Dame Press, 1983); Christopher Lasch, "The Communitarian Critique of Liberalism," *Soundings* 69 (1986): 60–76; Alasdair MacIntyre, *Against the Self-Images of the Age* (Notre Dame: University of Notre Dame Press, 1978), and *Whose Justice? Which Rationality?* (Notre Dame: University of Notre Dame Press, 1988); Michael Sandel, *Liberalism and the Limits of Justice* (Cambridge: Cambridge University Press, 1982); Thomas L. Shaffer, *Faith and the* Professions (Provo, Utah: Brigham Young University Press, 1987); and Jeffrey Stout, *The Flight from Authority* (Notre Dame: University of Notre Dame Press, 1981), and *Ethics After Babel* (Boston: Beacon Press, 1988). The most important single text, however, is Alasdair MacIntyre's *After Virtue.*

12. MacIntyre, *After Virtue,* 175. MacIntyre's understanding of practice comes in the middle of chap. 14 on "The Nature of the Virtues" and is developed in important ways in the next chapter on "The Virtues, the Unity of a Human Life and the Concept of a Tradition." I am not able to discuss all the important connections between these ideas in this brief essay, but they provide an important context for understanding what

this picture of practice involves and implies. For a briefer but extremely helpful presentation of MacIntyre's understanding of practice, see Stout, *Ethics After Babel,* chap. 12.

13. See Stout, *Ethics After Babel,* esp. 276 and 303.

14. MacIntyre, *After Virtue,* 177.

15. Stout, *Ethics After Babel,* 303.

16. MacIntyre, *After Virtue,* 177.

17. Or consider what Stout says about the goods internal to the practice of baseball; they are "what Mattingly achieves, Red Smith appreciated, and Steinbrenner violates." *Ethics After Babel,* 303.

18. MacIntyre, *After Virtue,* 176.

19. Edward Farley, *Ecclesial Man* (Philadelphia: Fortress Press, 1975), 213.

20. Ibid., 214, 215. See also pp. 215–31 for Farley's argument concerning apprehended "realities-at-hand" and the realities they "appresent" that are not accessible to direct apprehension.

21. In raising this point, we are not suggesting that any practice in and of itself provides *sufficient* conditions. As Farley makes clear, these conditions are many and deeply interrelated. They are comprised in what he calls the "faith-world," the key structures of which are its language, the co-intentionalities of its intersubjectivity, and its experience of the redemptive modification of existence. Lacking the category of "practices," however, Farley is forced to leap from these deep-structural levels to institutions and situations or events without benefit of any mediating form of concrete social structure. His accurate awareness of the dangers to the faith-world of institutionalization makes him sometimes pessimistic about the sustainability of the life-world of Christian faith, as well as frustratingly abstract to his readers. The idea of "practices," we would suggest, provides a level of analysis more concrete than "life-worlds," less rigid than institutions, and more sustained and sustainable than situations and events.

22. Sawicki, "Recognizing the Risen Lord," 449.

23. "Practices" names what I believe Lewis S. Mudge tries to lift up as the key to understanding the social fact that "recognizably Christian communities of faith continue to exist" but must be understood as "network[s] of signifying action

and interaction, both scattered and gathered" rather than as an institution or cluster of institutions. (See "Thinking in the Community of Faith: Toward an Ecclesial Hermeneutic," in *Formation and Reflection,* eds. Mudge and Poling, 107, 116–17.) Practices are indeed "networks of signifying action and interaction," and they are not to be identified with institutions. As Stout points out: "Social practices are often embodied in institutions. . . . Without some sort of sustaining institutions, [a] practice would change dramatically for the worse, if not collapse altogether." But institutions also "typically pose significant moral threats to the social practices they make possible" primarily because "institutions necessarily trade heavily in external goods," and such goods "can compete with and even engulf goods internal to [a] practice" (*Ethics After Babel,* 274).

24. See "No Longer Strangers," *Princeton Seminary Bulletin* 6, no. 3 (November 1985): 188–200. A revised version of this listing plus some discussion of the rationale for it appears in a paper adopted for study by the General Assembly of The Presbyterian Church (U.S.A.), which I helped to write. See "Growing in the Life of Christian Faith," *Minutes of the 201st General Assembly* (1989), Part II (Louisville: Office of the Stated Clerk, 1990), 38.087–38.231.

25. Margaret Miles, *Practicing Christianity: Critical Perspectives for an Embodied Spirituality* (New York: Crossroad, 1988), 87–144. Miles's "Introduction to Part Two" contains some very helpful comments concerning the importance of both studying and participating in practices. Although her understanding of practice is usually quite compatible with the one we have been putting forward, it is not well developed, and there is at times a tendency to equate practices with "exercises." This collapses a distinction that it is important to make.

26. See Michael Welker, "Security of Expectations: Reformulating the Theology of Law and Gospel," *Journal of Religion* 66, no. 3 (July 1986): 237–60.

27. See Farley, *Theologia,* 31, 35–36, 151–73. With the word *habitus,* Farley is suggesting a meaning of theology that refers to "a state and disposition of the soul which has the character of knowledge." The nature of this knowledge is "*practical,* not theoretical, habit having the primary character

of wisdom" (p. 35). Later, in *The Fragility of Knowledge,* Farley defines theology as "the reflectively procured insight and understanding which encounter with a specific religious faith evokes" (p. 64). I prefer his earlier understanding of theology as wisdom, which includes, in my view, not only insight and understanding but also the kind of judgment, skill, commitment, and character that full participation in practices both requires and nurtures.

28. Note Farley's discussion of the issue of education in *The Fragility of Knowledge,* 97–100, where he criticizes a current overgeneralizing of the meaning of the word *education* to the point where it encompasses every form of participation in ecclesial life. Farley calls for a more specific understanding of education, which he calls "ordered learning." The focus of ordered learning is not participation, which it presupposes, but interpretation: systematic, linguistically mediated, critical inquiry.

Though Farley is right about the need for ordered learning, he seems to restrict it primarily to the analysis and interpretation of the cognitive products of practices. Significant connections between actual engagements in the practices and inquiry carried out in a context formed through them is vastly underemphasized by Farley. Some criticize Farley's approach as being thereby too cognitive in orientation. That is not my problem with him. I believe theological education ought to be very cognitive. The reason, however, is not that our subject matter is the cognitive products of practices, but that cognition is vitally important to and involved in the practices themselves.

Further, we must be careful not to fall into understandings of cognition (and interpretation) that are too limited in scope, as I believe Farley has. Howard Gardner, in *Frames of Mind: The Theory of Multiple Intelligences* (New York: Basic Books, 1985), articulates seven different kinds of intelligence: linguistic, musical, logical-mathematical, spatial, bodily-kinesthetic, and two personal forms (one, the capacity to have access to the shape and range of one's own feeling life, and the other, "the ability to notice and make distinctions among other individuals and, in particular, among their moods, temperaments, motivations, and intentions" [p. 239]). Each of these intelligences is somewhat distinct, according to Gardner, and each involves modes of insight, interpretation, and expression characteristic of it. Farley seems to identify both cognition and interpretation with linguistic and logical-mathematical intelligence, leaving the others completely unattended to. I would argue that *all* these forms of intelligence are involved in theology-habitus and that all of them must be systematically engaged in theological education at every level.

29. Parallel observations, though couched in terms of "elemental modes of interpretation," are made by Farley, *The Fragility of Knowledge,* esp. 140–41.

30. See n. 1.

31. It would be helpful, in my view, if ethics and church-and-society fields were regularly gathered together with the so-called practical fields under a common departmental umbrella, at least until a more radical reorganization could be configured.

32. In his essay in *Formation and Reflection,* eds. Mudge and Poling, Farley has important things to say about the theological task of interpreting situations. What I am suggesting is that the interpretation of situations be focused and ordered by their relations to practices.

33. MacIntyre, *After Virtue,* 175.

34. Ibid., 181, 182.

35. Ibid., 207.

2

Situating the Structure: Prophetic Feminism and Theological Education

Rebecca S. Chopp

For at least twenty-five years, feminism has offered its resources in North American schools of theological education. The contributions feminism has made in theological education in the period can readily be listed. Yet feminist scholars are among the first to wonder whether or not all these contributions have made a difference, or, more accurately, if feminism has had any significant impact on the structure of theological education.

In this essay I want to examine the status both of feminism and of theological education by suggesting the necessity for adopting the perspective of prophetic feminism as a way of critically situating the roles of knowledge and religion in theological education. I begin by comparing what feminists and researchers cite as the current problems in theological education. I then investigate the way that various formations of feminism address theological education, and I argue for the adoption of a feminist approach of prophetic transformism in relation to theological education. I next examine the relation of this prophetic feminism to current proposals in theological education as I consider how prophetic feminism might respond to one recent proposal for the structure of theological study. I conclude with the critique that prophetic feminism would offer to a proposal such as Edward Farley's by arguing that prophetic feminism is necessary for *any* adequate consideration of theological education in the present situation.

I

It will be helpful to begin by listing, in quite an abbreviated form, the contributions feminism has made to theological education. Certainly, the presence of large numbers of women in theological education has feminist implications, because significant numbers provide a critical mass to start questioning the ideological assumptions about women and the relations between the sexes. The increasing presence of women scholars provides not only much-needed role models, but persons doing research on the neglected or repressed areas of women and the Bible, women in church history, feminist ethics, and so on. The presence of women, then, both as scholars and students, provides the context for the following contributions of feminism in theological education.

1. *The uncovering of new voices and faces in history.* Tremendous work has been done on the role of women in history, including research into issues such as forgotten women leaders, overlooked religious movements among women, and Bible women long neglected. Such research not only provides new historical types of activity by selected persons in certain social positions. It also raises a question in historiography: How do we know the history of those who neither wrote nor read, who had neither a public voice nor a "significant" role in the military, the economic, the aesthetic, or the political production of history?

2. *The defining of new areas of research.* What counts as valid research is generally related to the concerns and issues of the day. An acceptable area of research in the present situation encompasses the numerable issues related to women, including what classical texts such as those by Augustine and Tertullian say about women, and how

their views of women came to influence their notions of sin and salvation.

3. *New resources, new models.* Research on women's experiences has provided us with new models and images of God, community, Christology, and spirituality. These images and models have often fit into contemporary forms of theology, emphasizing God as more loving (more feminine), the church as more caring (more like a family), or even spirituality as more earthly (bodily, like a woman). But increasingly, feminists are questioning the very genre of contemporary theology by seeking to discover new forms of theological reflection.

4. *Inclusive language.* Feminism has had some fair success with insisting on inclusive language, either in the form of substituting nongendered terms for God and humanity or in the form of including feminine terms for God and humanity. Some schools and many journals have required policies of inclusiveness for all writing. Although debates still rage about whether or not one can change the scriptures (debates themselves being dependent upon modern assumptions about reading, authorship, and representation), inclusive language seems to be a fairly standard practice.[1]

These contributions are important and, given the brief history of women in theological education, impressive. Many of us can remember when women, as a rule, were told not to ruin their careers in the academy and the church by being too connected to feminism or women's concerns. That today, in many schools, women and men can study feminism, should they so desire, and, in some of our schools, are required to study feminism denotes major changes in a very brief span of time.

But such applause has to be quickly modulated, for feminists still find themselves and their issues marginalized. Indeed, upon a close survey of material and persons related to feminism and theological education, one wonders whether feminism has a significant voice at all in theological education. In 1980 the Cornwall Collective, composed of women who were working in ongoing projects within theological education, published a book entitled *Your Daughters Shall Prophesy: Feminist Alternatives in Theological Education,* outlining feminist criticisms of theological education and proposing some basic revisions, including some alternative forms of theological education.[2] Yet in spite of, or perhaps because of, their projects and their years in theological education, they could say:

> Questions raised by women, blacks, Hispanics, Native Americans, and the poor are seen as peripheral. New courses may be invented and added to the core curriculum to deal with the interests of current students, but such courses do not alter the structures or assumptions of the disciplines. There are courses in "New Testament" and in "Women in the New Testament," in "Church History" and in "Women in Church History," but basic educational questions are not addressed.[3]

The Cornwall Collective criticized theological education for its division of theory and practice, its organization of disciplines, its reliance on claims of "objectivity," and its use of the model of university education lacking any concern for integration or spirituality. Relying on the resources of women in theological education, the Cornwall Collective called for theological education to be more holistic, more aware of its political nature, more community oriented. Five years later, the Mud Flower Collective produced *God's Fierce Whimsy,* a book dedicated to trying to "help" theological education, because the authors of the book found that Christian seminaries are "arenas in which lukewarm faith and uninspired scholarship are peddled."[4] The Mud Flower Collective offers much the same analysis of theological education as does the Cornwall Collective: "Since the early 1970s, the number of women students in U.S. seminaries has increased 222%. During this period of time, structural changes in seminaries have been minimal."[5]

Indeed, the difference between the 1980 Cornwall Collective and the 1985 Mud Flower Collective could be interpreted as revealing increased frustration at the inability to get feminist issues heard within theological education. The Mud Flower Collective declares that, first and foremost, it is writing to reach other feminist women in theological education who, "as players with us in the grandiose games of misogynist academic gymnastics, . . . have been involved in a lose-lose situation."[6]

Yet the increased frustration depends on the very same issues that the Cornwall Collective found prohibitive to good theological education, for the Mud Flower Collective cites such issues as the politics of education, the role of cultural pluralism, the standards of excellence, the relation of theory and praxis, the role of community, the claims of validity in scholarship, and the definition and structure of theological reflection as the problems for women in theological education. The problems of and for women in theological education, we must conclude, are not merely women's lack of presence, but how theological education is defined, formed, and structured. Once a critical mass of women appear in theological education, problems of the structure of theological education become more and more evident.

What is particularly striking as we turn to consider some recent works on theological education is that these works, none of which has an explicitly feminist agenda, set forward the same set of problems in theological education. Without explicit attention to feminist reflection on theological education, the same issues of fragmentation, validity claims in theology, theory and praxis, and lack of integration occur in recent writings on theological education. Certainly the notion that theological education has to do with issues of justice, both as to the nature of questions asked in disciplines and as to the structuring of theological education, is central to *Christian Identity and Theological Education,* by Joseph Hough and John Cobb.[7] Issues of the relation of theory and praxis, the absence of any material unity in theological studies, the divisions entailed in the fourfold curriculum, and the functionalism of the present clerical paradigm have surfaced in works by Edward Farley, Charles Wood, and Max Stackhouse. Farley, for instance, in his *Theologia: The Fragmentation and Unity of Theological Education* and *The Fragility of Knowledge: Theological Education in the Church and the University,* comes quite close to many of the feminist concerns as he criticizes the present fourfold patterns of studies and as he reconceives the structure of theological study, calling for a habitus that the Cornwall Collective might describe as holistic.[8] And Charles Wood's notion of vision and discernment, in his book entitled *Vision and Discernment: An Orientation in Theological Study,* of the activity that inquires into the validity of Christian witness through seeing the whole and the particulars fits nicely with feminist concerns for the web of meaning in theological education, for asking the necessary, critical questions about what, in our day, counts as Christian witness.[9]

But if feminists identify the same problems as do other recent authors, they have as of yet paid little significant attention to how feminism provides resources for the restructuring of theological education. Likewise, researchers in theological education have not yet paid attention to feminism as a resource for critique and transformation of theological education. In *Theologia,* Farley suggests that feminism may be one of those forms of faith that provides a source for a new habitus, but he does not use feminism as a resource in *The Fragility of Knowledge* for rethinking the structure of theological study. And though Hough and Cobb go out of their way to reformulate the inner circle of Christianity so as to "let" women be identified through Jesus Christ, they never mention any consideration of the potential of feminism to rethink theological curriculum, theory and praxis, or the nature of theological studies.[10]

One might conclude, therefore, that the contributions feminism makes within theological education have to do with correctives of specific aspects, rather than with the nature of theological study itself. But such a conclusion would too quickly pass over the quite interesting fact that feminist writers on theological education identify basically the same set of fundamental problems as do researchers in theological education. If the Cornwall Collective and the Mud Flower Collective succeed in raising the right issues for the well-being of women, then it must be the case that the problems women suffer from in theological education are not just the results of specific patriarchal acts, but somehow intrinsic within the very structure of theological education. Said differently, the problems women face in theological education in some way or another represent the basic problems of the structure of theological education. In light of this intriguing situation, we can make three assumptions: (1) it is widely recognized that feminism has made some contributions to theological education; (2) there is general concern for the nature and structure of theological study, with special attention to the disparate nature of knowledge, the division of theory and praxis, the political nature of interpretation and reflection, and the crisis of validity claims; and (3) feminism shares such problems with the structure of theological study, suggesting that inquiry into how feminism could address theological study might well cast new light on the problems of theological education. If this be the case, then we might ask ourselves if the structure itself is not somehow intertwined with patriarchy or, said differently, if feminism cannot show us something about the very structure of theological education as patriarchal that, in turn, might lead us to a greater understanding of the need of transformation in theological education.

II

What must be asked, then, is what feminism has to say about the structure of theological education. But as a condition for asking this question, we must ask what we mean by feminism itself. It may seem at first glance that feminism can be equated with the movement for the political and civil rights of women, but such advocacy is, itself, only one particular voice or expression of feminism. Upon closer inspection, it is easy to find a variety of definitions of feminism. Three distinguishable historical movements can be discerned in American religious feminism, as it has been active in theological education: (1)

the use of democratic principles and liberal rights theories to get women into the ministry and theological education; (2) the focus on what it is women bring to religion and theology; and (3) the critique and transformation of religion and theology using feminist critical theory.[11] These three historical movements can also be identified as three ways of understanding feminism's contribution to theological education. These three ways are all historically based, are interrelated in their political and social dimensions, and yet each formulates feminism in its own particular fashion.

The first way to understand feminism is as a theory of equal rights, a theory in which women are viewed as human first and foremost, and thus deserving of the same rights as men under the laws of the government, of the church, or of universal morality. This perspective developed out of Enlightenment liberalism and the movements for revolution testified to in the American Declaration of Independence (1776) and the French Declaration of the Rights of Man (1789). Josephine Donovan has listed the following basic tenets of this type of feminism: a faith in rationality, a belief that women's and men's souls and rational faculties are the same, a belief in education as the most effective way to change society, a view of the individual as an isolated being, and subscription to a doctrine of natural rights.[12] This perspective is helpful in theological education, because democratic consensus is the reigning practice in most of our schools. Thus we can argue for equality in hiring, special programs, recruitment, even time devoted in class to feminist issues. But, as Zillah Eisenstein has pointed out, this perspective is flawed in that it fails to pursue the depths of sexism, seeing it correctible by simply adding women.[13] We might also call liberal equalitarianism a quintessentially humanist perspective, denying all differences as nothing more than secondary expressions of the same human posited underneath. This perspective prevents us from talking about what women bring, or making any special claims for women, or offering a critique of liberalism itself. To deal with what it is women bring to theological education, we must move to another perspective.

The second perspective considers the uniqueness of women based in biology, culture, religion, or ontology. In its purest form, this perspective might be called romantic expressivism, which maintains that women, as a sexual class, have special gifts, talents, abilities, values. This has been formulated through a wide variety of theories and literature, from Jungian psychology to literature about goddesses.[14] This perspective assumes that women really are, in essence, different from men, and that either women should separate from the reigning order or that women can join the order, adding their necessary qualities and values to improve public life. This position is helpful in capturing forgotten or distorted traditions; it is helpful in raising the questions of the resources women bring; and, depending upon its particular formulation, it can be the most palatable and the most offensive form of feminism to the dominant order. As a palatable form of feminism, this perspective adds the special contributions of women to the social order. According to many historians, this perspective won the right to vote for women under the guise that women were the natural housekeepers of society and needed to vote to clean house in society.[15] As offensive to the dominant social order, this position tends to see history as irredeemably faulted and calls for the formation of a new separate space for women. For instance, in Mary Daly's reading of Christianity in her feminist classic *Beyond God the Father,* a special ontology of women allows her to read Christianity as inherently distorted and holding no value for women.[16]

Whether offensive or palatable, this position is important for surfacing gender-related questions, values, and readings. Daly's reading of the Christian patriarchy and her pursuals of patriarchal logic through aphorisms (such as "if God is male then male is God") break through the denial and trivialization that occur on issues of women and religion.

In theological education, this perspective of feminism

has also contributed new images and resources to speak about God and the world. Though no long-standing separatist movement has emerged within theological education, the belief that women contribute special gifts to the ministry, to moral reasoning, and to counseling is fairly widespread. If the liberal equalitarian perspective in theological education could be summarized "add women," the romantic expressivist perspective could be summarized "add women and stir," because, in the view of this perspective, women will add to the greater good of the whole. The problem with this perspective is that it assumes that "women's experience" can be separated out, and thus buys into the patriarchal ideology that women are, and should continue to be, different from men. This perspective is always in danger of reifying the very dualism that creates the reason for its existence; it fails to address the causes and reasons for this dualism, thereby failing to question why it is that women should bring these specific gifts and talents to theological education and ministry.

But if the romantic expressivist perspective of focusing on the difference between women and men is problematic, and if the opposite, liberal equalitarianist perspective of relegating difference to a secondary status and assuming a fundamental identity between men and women is also problematic, is there a third way to view feminism? I believe there is, if we view feminism as a way to understand and transform both the relations between men and women and also the way those relations define gender values and roles.[17] This view, which I will call prophetic transformism, or prophetic feminism, argues that gender analysis is necessary for an adequate understanding of the present situation of theological education.

Prophetic transformism opposes any "essence" approach, including the "essence of human being" approach in liberal equalitarianism and the "essence of woman" approach of romantic expressivism. Rather, prophetic transformism assumes that gender identity, what it is to be a man or a women, is a matter of social construct, or, as Simone de Beauvoir said, one is born female but becomes a woman. Gender, at least in our culture, is a fundamental determination of the social order: men and women define different roles, spaces, values, language, ways of knowing, forms of social practices. Women are "woman" because of the position they occupy in the social order.

It is this position that requires "woman" to be raised in a certain way, to represent "feminine" values, and to occupy the private realm. Likewise, "man's" position insures a different set of child-rearing patterns, a different group of values to represent, and a different space to occupy in the public realm. But these two positions are not equal, for woman's position is marginal to man's position, both in the sense that it is valued as borderline, not as important as man's position, and as faulted, not as good as man's position.

Yet the marginality of woman's position is the fundamental possibility for the continuation of the social order: woman's physical body allows the perpetuation of social order, whereas woman's otherness masks the dependency needs of the independent, autonomous agent. Analyzing woman's position involves trying to understand not only what it is to be a woman, but also the gender rules of the social order.[18] If woman represents and constitutes the public realm, understanding what it is to be a man and woman will involve analyzing the rules of gender as they form the public and private realms and the values, roles, and practices consigned to each realm.

In addition, prophetic feminism maintains, these gender divisions operate for whatever is identified as located primarily within the public or private realms. In reference to theological education, gender divisions form the definitions of both knowledge, as located primarily in the public realm, and religion, as located primarily in the private realm.

Poststructuralist theorists have already pointed out how modernity defined knowledge through what can be called the normative gaze, a gaze that defines itself as an idealized self who can classify according to observable and measurable differences.[19] Cornel West has examined the normative gaze through the correlation of three historical processes: the scientific revolution putting forth knowledge as observation and evidence; the Cartesian transformation of philosophy giving the controlling notions of the primacy of the subject and the preeminence of representation; and the classical revival privileging Greek ocular metaphors and ideas of beauty into modern discourse. West understands the modern discourse of knowledge and truth, relying on these three historical processes, as "governed by an ideal value-free subject engaged in observing, comparing, ordering, and measuring in order to arrive at evidence sufficient to make valid inferences, confirm speculative hypotheses, deduce error-proof conclusions, and verify true representations of reality."[20]

But the normative gaze, prophetic feminism argues, also defines knowledge by placing it in the masculine subject position. Knowledge is defined not only in a certain way, through the normative gaze, but also in a certain subject position, through its location in the masculine realm. If knowledge, in modern discourse, is forced to accept the standards of neoclassical beauty and thus designates the idea of black equality as irrational, it is also constituted as masculine and forced to identify anything in the feminine subject position, such as religion, art, or tradition, as prior to or outside of the realm of knowledge. In sum, knowledge is to men as religion is to women: knowledge is figured as masculine and defined through an understanding of reason as objective, universal, autonomous; whereas religion is feminine and defined through an understanding of the affections as irrational, chaotic, impulsive.

Religion is thus separated from knowledge, and reason from the affections, as women are separated from men in the gender definitions of modernity.[21] Religion, like the gender construct of woman, serves the needs of private individuals that arise at the limits of the public: birth, death, suffering, linkages to nature and transcendence, aesthetic values, tradition. All such needs are seen as nonnecessary and thus reside in the private realm, ordered and controlled with no claims to public knowledge. As a number of feminist critical theorists have pointed out, this division of masculine and feminine constitutes a particular view of the "unencumbered" self and universal reason that requires the separation of theory and practice, the division of disciplines of study, the normativity of "objective" knowledge, and strict adherence to rules of privacy in areas such as religious beliefs and sexual identity. Iris Marion Young has captured the modern gender definitions of masculine and feminine in the following manner:

> Impartial civilized reason characterizes the virtue of the republican man who rises above passion and desire. Instead of cutting bourgeois man entirely off from the body and affectivity, however, this culture of the rational public confines them to the domestic sphere which also confines women's passions and provides emotional solace to men and children. Indeed, within this domestic realm sentiments can flower, and each individual can recognize and affirm his particularity. Because virtues of impartiality and universality define the public realm, it precisely ought not to attend to our particularity. Modern normative reason and its political expression in the idea of the civic public, then, has unity and coherence by its expulsion and confinement of everything that would threaten to invade the polity with differentiation: the specificity of women's bodies and desire, the difference of race and culture, the variability of heterogeneity of the needs, the goals and desires of each individual, the ambiguity and changeability of feeling.[22]

Theological education, from the perspective of prophetic transformism, has been caught in the continual confusion of the subject positions of masculine and feminine, the rules of knowledge and religion, the public and private realms. The ordering of theological education has been largely that of the normative gaze of modernity: classifying, dividing, separating. But this ordering has not fared well, for problems such as the split of theory and praxis are but symptoms of the underlying clash of modern rules and practices of knowledge and religion, of masculine and feminine, that theological education cannot resolve according to the divisions between genders. This perspective of feminism forces us to understand that the problems of theological education are deeply embroiled with the politics of knowledge and piety in modernity, the division of the public and private realms, and the very reality of what it is to be a man and a woman in modernity.

Such an analysis helps us understand why it is that feminists and researchers in theological education list essentially the same set of problems in their respective criticisms of theological education. For problems such as the relation of theory and praxis or the division of the disciplines are caused not merely by internal problems in the ordering of theological education nor by some essentialist bias against women, but by the forms of religion and knowledge, which are forced to follow the divisions of the feminine and masculine subject positions in modernity. A thorough critique of theological education from the feminist perspective of prophetic transformism would consider the following areas:

1. *The definition and form of modern Christianity.* Feminism assumes that modern theological education served specific interests of modern Christianity that could not resist the modern definition of knowledge wherein piety became prelinguistic or other than linguistic, and theology was a second-order, abstract analysis of piety.

2. *The form of theological education within the educational practices of modernity.* Modern educational practices depend upon classificatory schema, the internalized norm of the idealized spectator, and the definition of knowledge as observation and classification, which are formed through modern gender divisions.

3. *The way knowledge is classified.* The way knowledge is classified enables both a subjectivity and politics in modernity, which divides public and private interests, thereby limiting certain forms of practices and subjectivity to men and certain forms to women.

III

Because prophetic feminism understands itself not only as a form of critique but also as a form of transformation, it might be well to consider what this perspective might suggest for the transformation of theological education. Furthermore, because feminist works in theological education have agreed with researchers in theological education as to the basic problems in theological education, we might take one such proposal and ask what prophetic feminism might contribute to it.

The most thoroughly formulated proposal to date for the revisioning of theological education and the reordering of the structure of theological study is that of Edward Farley in *The Fragility of Knowledge: Theological Education in the Church and the University*. Farley defines theology as habitus, the reflective wisdom of faith, as the cognitive dimension of faith.[23] Reformulating the aim of theological education from the training of clergy to teaching the activity of ordered learning, Farley proposes that all ordered learning of theology begin with foundational studies and then be conceived around faith's elemental modes of interpretation: the interpretation of events and texts of tradition; the interpretation of the vision or content of these things under the posture of truth and reality; the interpretation of these things under the posture of praxis or action; and two "synthetic" hermeneutical modes, situational hermeneutics and the hermeneutics of vocation.

Prophetic feminism would find much to applaud in Farley's foundational studies. Farley suggests three basic areas for foundational studies: the comprehensive cultural context of religion and the church, an account of human reality and human being, and some knowledge of Christianity as a historical reality. The emphasis in prophetic transformism on the social location of knowledge and the historicity of religion could be served through Farley's foundational studies. But prophetic transformism would want these foundational studies done in a particular fashion, a fashion we might call pragmatist because it has basic affinities with the philosophy of Charles Sanders Peirce and John Dewey.[24]

A pragmatist approach would render these foundational studies as themselves only readings, fallible in status, dependent upon present material conditions and the social order. And, because the feminist perspective of prophetic transformism is quite aware of the fallible assumptions of discourse, it would demand that all assumptions be labeled as explicitly relative to social conditions.

The next part of Farley's proposal, concerning the primacy of hermeneutics, would be very congruent with prophetic feminism, though again, feminism would want to be specific about what is meant by hermeneutics. For Farley's insistence on five dimensions of hermeneutics does not in itself define the nature of hermeneutics, an activity that has known many forms and shapes. In many regards, it could be said that modern hermeneutics is the dominant approach in many of the disciplines in theological education. Phrases such as "what I hear you saying, what I really mean is, what the text says is, the point of this book is" are all used to identify the primacy of modern hermeneutics in theological education. A certain methodological self-consciousness of modern hermeneutical practice is required of all students, and the process of forming students is the process of making them self-critical interpreters in the modern figuration of knowledge.

Hermeneutics, as formulated through modern knowledge, tends toward foundationalism; that is, it posits an origin or essence of meaning that is in the text, the event, the person. Though modern hermeneutics depends on ambiguity or openness for its activity, it tends to repress ambiguity in the process of uncovering the real meaning of a text or situation. The feminist perspective of prophetic transformism questions foundationalist assumptions by suggesting that hermeneutics should be formed through rhetoric, the historical boundedness of text, and interpretation.[25] Rhetoric considers the relation of text to social practices and underscores the persuasiveness of discourse in both the text and its interpretations. A good example of this in feminist scholarship is the work of Elisabeth Schüssler Fiorenza, who formulates the status of scripture as prototype and not archetype, as a way of suggesting that truth is in the community's ongoing activity and discourse.[26]

Hermeneutics, as formulated in relation to rhetoric in feminist theology, assumes that interpretation is also an aesthetic act as much as an analytical one. In this regard, some works in contemporary hermeneutics come close to a feminist perspective. Hans-Georg Gadamer, for instance, indicates that every interpretation is a new construction, a new interpretation.[27] Feminism radicalizes this insight, forcing us to understand the process of theological education as one of forming interpreters who look not only to the past and to the present, but to the future, using their interpretive activity as also providing new resources and visions for human flourishing.[28]

In sum, prophetic feminism finds much to agree with in Farley's proposal about the structure of theological reflection. Indeed, the refinements of Farley's fundamental terms through pragmatism, rhetoric, and aesthetics could well be pursued within the confines of Farley's own project, given Farley's continual insistence on the historicity of faith.

IV

Despite prophetic feminism's ability to contribute and revise the structure of theological education, prophetic feminism argues that reordering the structure of theological education will not adequately reform theological education. From the perspective of prophetic transformism, Farley's goal of habitus, or wisdom, requires addressing not one, but *three* problems in theological education. First, the structure of theological education must be addressed in light of prophetic feminism's revisions of Farley's proposal. Second, the process of education, that is, the fundamental assumptions about what education is and how it works, must be theologically considered. Third, the material form of habitus, the nature of wisdom in this time and place, must be located and envisioned. Prophetic feminism, based on its gender analysis of religion and knowledge, contends that the problem of the practice of education and the problem of the material form of habitus must be addressed and transformed along with the problem of the structure of education.

The contemporary structure of education depends upon a practice of education in which the objective knowledge of specialized fields is handed on by expert professionals to students understood to be empty receptacles. Such a process has been the educational practice correlate with the contemporary structure of theological education. Farley's goal of habitus, or wisdom, not only requires a shift in the structure of learning, but also a reformation of the practice of education, a shift from merely imparting information to the process of forming persons. Prophetic feminist theology, like other forms of liberation theology, shares with Paulo Freire the assumptions about the nature of education as a practice of freedom (see his *Pedagogy of the Oppressed*). Freire maintains that education, in a liberation perspective, is a process of making persons fully active in their particular situations.[29] Education as a liberating practice emphasizes what persons bring to education and their own processes within the practice of education. In this liberating practice of education, the educator becomes an enabler who, with resources, empowers persons in their own practice of freedom. In prophetic feminism, great emphasis is placed on the community in the education process, because the practice of freedom, theologically understood, grows out of and is enabled through the community of emancipatory transformation.[30]

Perhaps prophetic feminism can address the problem of the practice of education because of feminist insight into the second problem, the material concreteness of what habitus requires. Prophetic feminism suggests that Farley's formal claim for habitus, as helpful as it is, will not be enough to reform education, for habitus requires historical formations, including particular emotions, virtues, claims of knowledge, concrete practices, and social organizations.[31] The problems of theological education are not, as the gender analysis of prophetic feminism demonstrates, merely problems of ideas about knowledge but also of the historical organization, including political, cultural, and psychological forms of religion and knowledge.

Prophetic feminism invokes not an abstract goal of habitus but a historical goal of emancipatory transformation represented by the presence of liberation theologies in our current schools of theological education. The contemporary forms of liberation theology, such as feminist theology, African American theology, and Hispanic theology, criticize the systematic oppression of groups of persons and offer new ways of Christian faith, new ways of knowing, and new practices of education for all. These liberation theologies and their respective movements in churches and religious communities are contemporary expressions of the American tradition of prophetic movements of emancipatory transformation, including civil millennialism in the eighteenth century, social purity movements in the nineteenth century, and social gospels movements in the twentieth century.[32] This long and diverse tradition has questioned, in many different ways, the division of theory and practice, public and private, religion and knowledge, and has worked for the transformation of the oppressive political, cultural, and psychological practices in American culture and Christianity.

Though prophetic feminism continues a long tradition in American theology, it as yet has not produced a complete vision of theological education. Feminist theologians, along with African American, Hispanic, and other theologians of marginalized groups, still struggle to gain the critical mass necessary to produce systematic works on theological education. Indeed, the writings of such scholars need continued and even increased support in their efforts to work on the problems of theological education. But the lack of a full vision for the transformation is not due simply to the present struggle of these movements; it is also due to the radical critique that prophetic feminism suggests is necessary to understand adequately the present problems of theological education. Prophetic feminism contends that problems of theological education will not be solved by simply reordering the structure, but only through the difficult task of reformulating the assumptions, rules, forms, and practices of Christianity, education, and knowledge. Although it is easy to propose a vision when one is reordering a structure, it is a much more difficult task when one judges that a reformation of structure, process, and the material form of habitus must occur.

Although prophetic feminism does not yet have some "complete" vision of what the reformation of theological education should look like in relation to the three problems of structure, practice of education, and material form of habitus, two areas invite immediate attention along with Farley's suggestions of rearranging the structure of theological education. First, not only must the structure of theological education be reordered, but the practice of education must be reformed as a practice of freedom where persons are formed and empowered. Such a reformation will include attention to the resources persons bring to student attention in order to enable their activity in the process of ordered learning. It will also require theological education to attend to the process of learning in community, to switch to pedagogical styles of empowerment instead of impartation, and to explore spiritual and aesthetic as well as cognitive dimensions of habitus. Second, because persons are not formed into habitus in some abstract fashion, attention must be paid to the material form of habitus, which for prophetic feminism has to do with prophetic movements of emancipatory transformation. This will include "mainstreaming" contemporary expressions of liberation theology and reorienting courses such as congregational studies, pastoral care, and systematic theology to ask about the material forms of contemporary Christian practice.

In conclusion, the perspective of prophetic transformism is essential to understanding the problems of theological education. I have suggested that although prophetic feminism can use much of the critique and proposal of Edward Farley's recent work, it offers to all of us an additional, necessary analysis of the problems of theological education, and it provides resources for constructing a concrete vision of the formation of habitus in theological education.

NOTES

1. Studies abound on modern practices of reading and writing. See, for instance, Wayne Booth, *Critical Understanding: The Power and Limits of Pluralism* (Chicago: University of Chicago Press, 1979); Terry Eagleton, *Literary Theory: An Introduction* (Minneapolis: University of Minnesota Press, 1983); and David Tracy, *Plurality and Ambiguity: Hermeneutics, Religion, Hope* (San Francisco: Harper & Row, 1987).

2. The Cornwall Collective, *Your Daughters Shall Prophesy: Feminist Alternatives in Theological Education* (New York: Pilgrim Press, 1980).

3. Ibid., 5.

4. The Mud Flower Collective, *God's Fierce Whimsy: Christian Feminism and Theological Education* (New York: Pilgrim Press, 1985), 3.

5. Ibid., 29–30.

6. Ibid., 27.

7. Joseph C. Hough, Jr., and John B. Cobb, Jr., *Christian Identity and Theological Education* (Chico, Calif.: Scholars Press, 1985).

8. Edward Farley, *Theologia: The Fragmentation and Unity of Theological Education* (Philadelphia: Fortress Press, 1983), and *The Fragility of Knowledge: Theological Education in the Church and the University* (Philadelphia: Fortress Press, 1988).

9. Charles M. Wood, *Vision and Discernment: An Orientation in Theological Study* (Atlanta: Scholars Press, 1985).

10. Hough and Cobb, *Christian Identity and Theological Education,* 27–28.

11. For further development of these three movements in relation to feminist theology, see my *The Power to Speak: Feminism, Language, God* (New York: Crossroad, 1989).

12. Josephine Donovan, *Feminist Theory: The Intellectual Traditions of American Feminism* (New York: Frederick Ungar Publishing, 1985), 8.

13. Zillah R. Eisenstein, *The Radical Future of Liberal Feminism,* The Northeastern Series in Feminist Theory (Boston: Northeastern University Press, 1986).

14. For an excellent cross section of this approach, see Carol P. Christ and Judith Plaskow, *Womanspirit Rising: A Feminist Reader in Religion* (San Francisco: Harper & Row, 1979).

15. Aileen Kraditor, *The Ideas of the Woman Suffrage Movement 1890–1920* (Garden City, N.Y.: Anchor, 1971); and Donovan, *Feminist Theory.*

16. Mary Daly, *Beyond God the Father: Toward a Philosophy of Women's Liberation* (Boston: Beacon Press, 1973).

17. For an excellent introduction to poststructuralist feminism, see Chris Weedon, *Feminist Practice and Poststructuralist Theory* (Oxford: Basil Blackwell, 1987).

18. Julia Kristeva, "Women's Time," in *The Kristeva Reader,* ed. Toril Moi (New York: Columbia University Press, 1986), 187–213.

19. See, for instance, Cornel West, *Prophesy Deliverance!: An Afro-American Revolutionary Christianity* (Philadelphia: Westminster Press, 1982).

20. Ibid., 53.

21. For a variety of approaches to this topic, see Seyla Benhabib and Drucilla Cornell, eds. *Feminism as Critique: On the Politics of Gender* (Minneapolis: University of Minnesota Press, 1987).

22. Iris Marion Young, "Impartiality and the Civic Public," in *Feminism as Critique,* eds. Benhabib and Cornell, 67.

23. Farley, *The Fragility of Knowledge.*

24. Charles Hartshorne and Paul Weiss, eds., *The Collected Papers of Charles Sanders Peirce.* 5 vols. (Cambridge: Harvard University), vol. 5; and John Dewey, *Reconstruction in Philosophy* (Boston: Beacon Press, 1949).

25. Eagleton, *Literary Theory,* 206–12.

26. Elisabeth Schüssler Fiorenza, *In Memory of Her: A*

Feminist Theological Reconstruction of Christian Origins (New York: Crossroad, 1983), pp. 26–36 and *Bread Not Stone: The Challenge of Feminist Biblical Interpretation* (Boston: Beacon Press, 1984), pp. 9–11.

27. Hans-Georg Gadamer, *Truth and Method* (New York: Seabury Press, 1975).

28. For further development of aesthetics, hermeneutics, and feminism, see my *The Power to Speak.*

29. Paulo Freire, *Pedagogy of the Oppressed,* trans. Myra Bergman Ramos (New York: Herder & Herder, 1970).

30. The historical development of liberation theology, at least in part, is related to education movements understood in distinctly theological terms. See, for instance, Rebecca S. Chopp, *The Praxis of Suffering: An Interpretation of Liberation and Political Theologies* (Maryknoll, N.Y.: Orbis Books, 1986), 21–22.

31. One of the rich insights of Edward Farley's *The Fragility of Knowledge* is his analysis of the three critiques of knowledge in modernity: romanticism, theology, and the radicalizing of critique (pp. 6–9). Despite the potential of this insight as a resource for reformulating knowledge in relation, for instance, to the affections, the virtues, and aesthetics, Farley has not yet turned to this topic and given us a new definition of knowledge. The reader has to assume, therefore, that when Farley is calling for a habitus, as the cognitive dimension of faith, he is calling for a new definition of cognition along with a new structure of learning.

32. Contemporary texts on theological education are generally silent about the particular history of North America, especially the republican government, the separation of church and state, the role of religion as morality, and the religious imagery used to speak of the mission and destiny of the United States. Likewise, the present works in theological education largely fail to mention the professionalization of American culture since World War II and the relationships such professionalization had to the organization of knowledge in America.

3

The Historical Consciousness and the Study of Theology

Walter E. Wyman, Jr.

We are children of time, not masters of time, and can only act upon time from within time.

—Ernst Troeltsch[1]

Christian theological studies have for some time been organized in a conventional fourfold pattern: biblical studies, church history, systematic theology and practical theology. Historical studies occupy a prominent place in this classical organization of theological education. Yet the fourfold pattern has recently been subjected to a sharp, perhaps even devastating, critique. Edward Farley argues that this pattern, which is the uncriticized outcome of a process of development, is so problematic that it needs to be reformed. Among other defects, it obscures the unity of theological study, fragmenting it into guilds or disciplines that not only bear little relation to each other, but also threaten to lose their identity as theological disciplines. Moreover, the fourfold structure that emerged in the time of Protestant scholasticism embodies precritical, pre-Enlightenment assumptions no longer appropriate to the modern, let alone the postmodern, world. So Farley urges us to begin a reform-oriented conversation, and he has his own suggestions as to the pattern and structure of theological study, and a carefully articulated, systematic rationale for it.[2]

It is my thesis that any rethinking of the structure and pattern of theological study needs to take into account the historical consciousness. By the historical concious-ness I mean, first, a critical attitude toward history and a consequent method ("the historical-critical method"); and second, the acknowledgment of the historicity of human existence ("we are children of time") and consequent worldview ("historicism"). The historical consciousness is itself a product of history; it appears in the great watershed in Western culture, the Enlightenment. So decisive was the impact of this historical moment that Ernst Troeltsch saw it as the dividing line between "old Protestantism," the religion of the Reformers and Protestant scholastics, and "New Protestantism," the religion of the modern world.[3] If it is the case that the modern world arose with the Enlightenment, no account of theology or of the structure of theological study may be said to be adequate that fails to come to terms with it. That means, among other things, that such an account must come to terms with the historical consciousness.

The agenda for this essay follows from my central claim about the historical consciousness. First, how should "the historical consciousness" be understood? Section II provides an analysis and characterization. Second, what are the implications of the historical consciousness for theology? What issues does it raise; what conditions does it impose upon theological thinking? Sections III and IV will address these issues. Finally, what follows from this analysis for the structure, the pattern, of theological study? Should historical studies occupy as central a position in whatever new pattern of studies that emerges as they did under the old fourfold pattern? Or should they be de-emphasized, considered at best a matter for persons with historical interests or the concern of the guild of historians, but not something to be inflicted on seminarians primarily interested in the pastoral ministry? What other considerations besides the place of historical studies are implied by the historical consciousness? Section V is devoted to these problems. Because reflection on the pattern of theological study necessarily presupposes some understanding both of theology and of the purpose and goal of theological study, section I will briefly state my assumptions on these matters.

I

Christian theology may be defined as critical reflection on the meaning and truth of the Christian faith. Its task is both to interpret the Christian tradition and to articulate what it is reasonable to believe in the present. As *reflection*, theology is distinct from the life of faith itself: it is second-order thinking that makes faith its object. Insofar as faith itself does not exist in atomistic isolation, but is the inheritance of preceding generations appropriated in the present, theology entails reflection on tradition. As *critical*, theology raises the question of meaning and truth—how the ideas of faith (the doctrinal dimension of religion) ought to be interpreted and whether and in what sense those ideas may make good their claim to be true.

It is Edward Farley's disturbing observation that "the typical product of three years of seminary study is not a *theologically* educated minister. The present ethos of the Protestant churches is such that a theologically oriented approach to the preparation of ministers is not only irrelevant but counterproductive."[4] If Farley's pessimistic analysis is warranted, the situation is indeed critical, for a theologically sophisticated clergy is of vital importance. My assumption is that among their many roles, clergy are public interpreters of the meaning and truth of the Christian faith. Being able to think theologically, being able to mediate between theological scholarship on the one hand and the congregation on the other, is crucial to the intellectual vitality of the Christian faith in the closing decade of the twentieth century. Accordingly, it follows that the telos of theological education ought to be the fostering and disciplining of theological thinking.[5]

Therefore, the central questions for this essay are:

What is the significance of the historical consciousness for theology understood as critical reflection on the meaning and truth of faith? What are the consequences of the historical consciousness for theological education, understood as the disciplining of theological thinking and the training of a learned clergy? In light of the conditions imposed upon theology by the historical consciousness, how should the study of theology be conceived and structured so as to fulfill its telos?

II

The first step in understanding the implications of the historical consciousness for theology and for the study of theology is to understand what it is. It is helpful to begin by distinguishing two interrelated dimensions or aspects: a historiography, the modern historical-critical method, and a worldview, which I will label historicism.

The historical-critical method, as the characteristically modern form of historiography, entails what Troeltsch called a "scientific attitude to facts."[6] It is not possible in this essay to probe the extensive literature in the philosophy of history exploring the question of whether and in what sense history is a science, or what constitutes a historical explanation. For the purpose of characterizing the historical-critical way of thinking, Ernst Troeltsch's classic definition of the three principles of historical method—criticism, analogy, and reciprocity—will have to suffice.[7]

Troeltsch's first principle, criticism, makes the point that knowledge of the past is possible only through criticism of the sources.[8] Historical reports are not to be taken at face value. Embedded in this notion of criticism is what Van Harvey has called the Enlightenment's "will to truth" and its "morality of knowledge."[9] A product of the Enlightenment's emphasis on autonomy, this attitude was classically expressed in David Hume's dictum "the wise man apportions his belief to the evidence."[10] In other words, the historian confers authority on his or her sources; he or she does not treat them as authorities.[11]

But how is the historical evidence to be assessed? That is, on what basis is the probability of reports about the past and thus the authority to be conferred upon the sources to be decided?

This question is answered by Troeltsch's second principle of the historical method: the basis for judgments of probability about the past is the analogy of present experience.[12] The principle of analogy means, in effect, that our present state of knowledge, including the conclusions of natural science and the insights of the social sciences, is the only basis we have for deciding upon the credibility of traditions about the past. The reason for this is aptly stated by Gerhard Ebeling in his claim that modern historical thinking "cannot simply set aside the understanding of reality as that has been acquired by the modern mind." Thus the historian is "compelled to take the sources of the past and set them, too, in light of the new self-evident assumptions."[13] To interpret the past by means of the analogy of present, critically interpreted experience is to use what we presently hold to be true about reality (nature, society, historical causation, and so on)—that is, Ebeling's "self-evident assumptions"—as a critical canon for interpreting the past. Van Harvey, in his very careful exploration of the role of present experience in historical judgments, develops a carefully nuanced argument to the same conclusion.[14]

What is at stake, then, is fundamentally a method of inquiry intimately related to convictions about what constitutes a historical explanation. Analogy is a principle with far-reaching ramifications. Troeltsch expressed them in terms of "homogeneity": history is homogeneous, not in the sense that it knows no unique events, but in the sense that those processes we recognize as functioning in the present functioned in the past.[15] For Troeltsch, this clearly ruled out supernaturalism as an explanation for past events; he labeled his position "antisupernaturalist."[16] Ebeling agrees: for the modern world, "all that is metaphysical and metahistorical has entered the dimension of the problematical."[17] Just as the natural sciences have their canons for what constitutes a scientific explanation, so too historiography has its canons as to what constitutes a legitimate historical explanation. However much the eyes of faith may perceive divine causality at work in events of the past, the invocation of a divine cause does not constitute a historical explanation, whether it be for the Confederate loss of the Battle of Gettysburg or the Exodus from Egypt. Historical claims must be adjudicable by public criteria; ever since the Enlightenment, any appeal to divine causation as a warrant or backing for a claim counts as a private, not a public appeal.[18]

Troeltsch called the third principle of the historical method "reciprocity" or "correlation" (*Wechselwirkung*).[19] The point is that all events occur within a web of cause-and-effect relations; history forms an interconnected stream. This, too, is a principle that rules out divine interventions that break the causal chain from the historian's tool kit of acceptable explanatory hypotheses. Similarly, it rules out the assertions of any "absolute" beginning points in the historical stream. All events are preceded by previous, conditioning events, and as soon as they occur, they become antecedents or causes influencing the subsequent course of events. For Troeltsch, this meant the exclusion of the absolute from history.[20] If the "absolute" means that which is unconditioned, without relation to others, the absolute in history is inconceivable to the historical consciousness.

In Section III, I will track some of the implications of the historical-critical method, so understood, for theology. But first I will turn my attention to the second aspect of the historical consciousness, historicism as a worldview. Of course, historicism and the historical-critical method are closely intertwined; in my discussion of the principles of the historical method, I have already begun the discussion of the historicist worldview. As is the case with historical method, the literature dealing with historicism is enormous; I cannot undertake to discuss it here, but must present a schematic, programmatic characterization.

The historical consciousness as a worldview is, to put

it simply, the consciousness of the historicity of human existence—that human beings exist in space and time.[21] This simple idea has such wide-ranging ramifications that it gives rise to a worldview. When Karl Mannheim speaks of historicism as a worldview, he means that the *object* of historical cognition has been historicized. The historicist mode of thought and living experiences "every segment of the spiritual-intellectual world as in a state of growth and flux."[22] In a word, the historicist worldview sees all of human reality—institutions, ideas, even religions—as the product of processes of development. This is the "historicizing of all our thinking and knowing" that formed the center of Ernst Troeltsch's intellectual concerns:

> The word "historicism" . . . signifies the historicization [*Historisierung*] of our entire understanding and experience of the spiritual [*geistigen*] world, as this came into existence in the course of the nineteenth century. Here we see everything in the river of becoming, in endless and always new individualization, in determination by the past towards an unrecognizable future. The state, law, morality, religion, and art are dissolved in the flow of historical becoming and are comprehensible only as ingredients of historical development.[23]

A second aspect of historicism as a worldview is the historicizing of the *subject*. H. Richard Niebuhr spells out this aspect in this way:

> It is not enough to say that men live in time and must conceive all things as temporal and historical. Doubtless it is true that all reality has become temporal for us. But our historical relativism affirms the historicity of the subject even more than that of the object; man, it points out, is not only in time but time is in man.[24]

Niebuhr here makes a point about the historicity of the human subject. To say that time is in us means that our categories of thought and interpretation, our beliefs, have been historically conditioned, and "no observer can get out of history into a realm beyond time-space; if reason is to operate at all, it must be content to work as an historical reason."[25]

Out of historicism in the sense of the insight into the historicity of the human subject and the historical development of institutions and ideas results the "crisis of historicism." The insight into the relativity of all creatures of history gives rise to skepticism about norms of truth and value: "Every worldview is conditioned historically and therefore limited and relative. A frightful anarchy of thought appears."[26] Here *relativity* gives rise to *relativism*. Now clarifying exactly what is meant by the global term *relativism* and specifying what the problems really are is itself a difficult philosophical task with important theological ramifications.[27] It is not my intention here to enter into such an analysis; my intention is only to characterize the historical consciousness and to sketch out some of its implications and problems. As Sarah Coakley has pointed out, relativism involves issues of method, metaphysics, epistemology, and ethics. It is sufficient for our purposes to give the problem of relativism a bit more precision by reference to her discussion of "epistemological relativism," which she calls "relativism proper." This position holds that "proposition p is actually 'true' . . . relative to, or in virtue of, framework f."[28] If this is so, then Christian doctrinal claims are actually "true" only in the context of Christianity, not for all human beings; first-century Christian claims are only "true" in the context of the first century, and so on. My point is a modest one: without making a judgment as to the merits of such epistemological relativism, or distinguishing (as Coakley helpfully does) the various strengths with which it may be held, I want only to claim that relativism in this sense has in fact been one of the issues raised by the historicist worldview, and thus constitutes one of the problems that modern theology must reflect on and respond to.

To sum up, then, the modern historical consciousness consists of at least the following elements: (1) a historiography, the "historical-critical method," which operates with the principles of criticism, analogy-homogeneity, and reciprocity; (2) an awareness of the historicity of all human cultural creations, including worldviews and religions, as the product of processes of development extended over time; (3) an awareness of the historicity of the human subject, as one whose worldview and reason is historically conditioned; and (4) the consequent problem of relativism—the suspicion, justified or not, that because one's own convictions about truth and value are the contingent product of where one stands in the historical flux, their claim to truth must be very modest, that is, "true for me."

III

The historical consciousness that I have so briefly characterized has far-reaching implications for theology. Ernst Troeltsch was by no means exaggerating when he called the historical method "a leaven which transforms everything and finally bursts the entire previous form of theological methods."[29] In this section, I will draw out some of the implications of the historical consciousness for theology by taking up each of the four characteristics delineated in the preceding section and indicating the impact each makes on theology and the theological issues that result. In this way, a rough portrayal of the conditions that the modern historical consciousness imposes on theology may be sketched out.

The most obvious impact of the historical consciousness as historiography (the historical-critical method) on theology is in biblical studies. Biblical texts are treated analogously to all other historical texts as objects of historical criticism. The impact was already felt during the Enlightenment; it is symptomatic that both Albert Schweitzer and Werner Kümmel begin their overviews of the history of New Testament research with Enlightenment thinkers (Reimarus and J. S. Semler and Michaelis, respectively).[30] It is not necessary or desirable here to retrace the long march of critical biblical studies through "lower" and "higher" criticism to the twentieth-century development of source, form, and redaction criticism to the present explosion of methods in biblical study, only some of which are strictly speaking historical-critical methods. Nor do we need to review the accomplishments of the heroes of the long march, from Strauss to Weiss, Bultmann, and Perrin, or from Wellhausen to von Rad and Gottwald. Rather, what is crucial to my argument is the range of theological issues generated by this impact.

The first is the issue of the theological and religious authority of the biblical texts. Once viewed as historical documents analogous to other texts of the past, the problem of the authority of that text or, better, of those collections of texts for present thought and life becomes acute. Are they not documents reflecting the consciousness of a bygone age? If so, can they have the kind of absolute authority that the *sola scriptura* principle accords to them? Are they not rather to be accorded the status of the first chapter in the unfolding story and thus have at best the status of relative priority? The solution of Old Protestantism, of viewing the text as the locus of a divinely revealed word, retains its popularity even now, but it has become incredible to those who have drunk deeply of the modern historical ways of thinking.

Second, aside from the problem of the formal authority of the texts is the hermeneutical problem: how are these ancient texts to be interpreted and understood? Assuming some positive answer is given to the preceding issue that determines these texts to be significant, the problem of the hermeneutical gulf between the ancient horizon of the text and that of the modern interpreter remains.

> I can understand a past text (through an effort of sympathetic imagination) but I find I cannot, because of my different cultural framework, share the precise meaning that the original author intended. I find I have to add to the meaning, reinterpreting the text from my new context or framework, bringing new issues to the text, and at the same time extracting new layers of insight from the text. . . . [T]he hermeneutical process is one of a continuous

> creation of new meaning from the texts, as a particular temporal and cultural "horizon" meets and engages with the various biblical horizons.[31]

Third, the historical consciousness generates a budget of issues that may be grouped under the heading "faith and history." As the issue of faith and historical events, this is the issue of the connection of the content and truth of faith to claims about certain historical events having happened, and having happened in a particular way. As the problem of God and history, this is the issue of whether and in what sense God may be said to act in history. As the problem of the historical Jesus, this is the question of whether faith's content and certainty rest on knowledge of or particular claims about the historical Jesus, which are always judgments of probability open to revision. In each case, difficult theological problems are generated by the historical consciousness; many were clearly seen in the nineteenth century, and two centuries of theological thought have generated a variety of responses.

Corresponding to my threefold analysis of historicism as a worldview, a threefold impact on theology may be discerned. First, the historicity of the object of historical knowledge gives rise to the developmental perspective on Christianity. Here church history and historical theology, which are, of course, also influenced by the historical-critical method as historiography, must be considered. The classics of the developmental perspective are the historical works by F. C. Baur and Adolf von Harnack. But once again it is not crucial to rehearse the contributions of the heroes, but to see the theological ramifications of this way of thinking.

The most important ramification of this awareness of the historicizing of theology came to expression in the discussion of the essence of Christianity. As Harnack put it in his classic book on the problem: "What we are and what we possess, in any high sense, we possess from the past and by the past—only so much of it, of course, as has had results and makes its influence felt up to the present day." Thus Harnack sets out to answer the question, What is Christianity? by means of the "methods of historical science": "We cannot form any right estimate of the Christian religion unless we take our stand upon a comprehensive induction that shall cover all the facts of its history."[32] The issue posed for theology by the developmental perspective, then, is the question, What is Christianity? that is, What are its central claims and values, given its long history of development and the various forms that it has assumed over time?

Second, as the historicity of the historical subject (Niebuhr's "time is in man"), the historical consciousness points out the limitations of one's standpoint as relative and conditioned. For Mannheim and Niebuhr, this problem was above all an epistemological problem, solved for the former by a perspectival theory (*Standortsgebundenheit*), for the latter by a confessional perspective ("inner history" as the community's confession of its history). A further dimension is added to this problem by the critique of classical theology by Latin American, feminist, and black theologies. Classical Western theology, it has been disapprovingly been pointed out, has been produced by white males in the First World; its pretensions to universality are to be rejected, for they merely universalize a partial standpoint. A "hermeneutics of suspicion" operates, suspecting the classical theology of the past of ideological distortion; that is, its positions not only reflect but tend to justify a particular social order, set of assumptions about gender, race, and class, and so on.[33] One of the theological issues generated by this aspect of the historical consciousness is the problem of the universality of theological claims: can inescapably particular (historical) beings make universal claims? However universal the subject matter of theology, are theological claims not irreducibly particular? Beyond this theoretical issue lies the far-reaching constructive issue—can Christian theological claims be critically reconstructed so as to free them of their ideological distortion? In what ways does such a critical reconstruction transform Christianity?

This last set of considerations is closely related to the specter of historical relativism, the third aspect of historicism's worldview. Here we have to do with the problem of relativism and norms of truth and value. In theology, this sorts out as several distinct problems. On the one hand is the pluralism of Christian doctrinal claims: Protestant, Catholic, and Orthodox, evangelical and liberal, and so forth. What is to be made of the competing claims to truth? Are they all equally valid developments of the Christian spirit, all equally a mixture of truth and error? Or are some forms and some answers to be decisively rejected as distortions? What criteria decide such questions, and how are the criteria themselves to be justified? How does one draw the boundary line between the "still appropriately Christian" and the "no longer Christian" interpretations?

On the other hand is the problem of the pluralism of religions. It follows from the principles of analogy and homogeneity that the historically conscious thinker views Christianity as analogous to other religions. The grounds upon which rested the older conviction of Christianity's uniqueness as the locus of God's singular revealing activity have been decisively undercut. Similarly, Jesus of Nazareth is seen as analogous to other founders of religions, such as Muhammad or Siddhartha Gautama. In Troeltsch's pithy expression, primitive Christianity "had already taken Jesus out of history and made him logos and God, the eternal Christ appearing to us in historical form. . . . But historical criticism . . . has returned him to history where all is finite and conditioned."[34] Ultimately, then, the historicizing of Christianity, perceiving it as a product of historical development analogous to other, similar products, throws into question the epistemological privilege of Christianity.

The analysis of the implications of the historical consciousness for theology has generated a rather full budget of issues. What the historical consciousness offers for theology is a method for understanding the past, a perspective on what it means to be historical, and a series of complex problems. The central theological question that is generated has to do with the meaning and truth of this complex historical heritage, the Christian tradition. Given the multiple issues that have been analyzed in this section, what can this heritage be said to mean for us and for now? And in what sense, if any, can its claims to truth be sustained? These questions point to the juncture of the historical and the systematic tasks. They arise out of historical thought; and however continuous their answer may be with historical thought, they cannot be answered out of history alone. What this means is that the historicist worldview makes an impact not merely on the historical disciplines (biblical studies, church history), but on the normative disciplines (systematic theology, ethics). The attempt to formulate the meaning of the gospel in the present cannot be just a handing-on of tradition or a restating of the eternal truth, whether enshrined in Bible or creed; it must recognize and come to terms with the developmental character of all thought.

IV

These reflections point to the main methodological consequence of the historical consciousness—the historicizing of the theological task. One of the first of the post-Enlightenment attempts fundamentally to rethink the character of theology (and of theological education) in the modern world carried out just such a historicizing of theology—Friedrich Schleiermacher's *Brief Outline on the Study of Theology*. A consideration of Schleiermacher's organization of theological studies is germane at this point, for although we would not want (for reasons be explained below) to attempt to repristinate the *Brief Outline* in our own day, Schleiermacher's reshaping of the theological disciplines under the impact of the historical consciousness remains nonetheless instructive.

For Schleiermacher, the study of theology is organized into three branches: philosophical theology, historical theology, and practical theology. Historical theology, consisting of exegetical theology, church history, and church statistics and dogmatics, constitutes the "actual corpus of theological study."[35] In the very structure of theological study, Schleiermacher acknowledges the historical consciousness: Christianity, as a distinctive way of believing, cannot be understood speculatively, that is, through philosophical reflection alone. Nor can it be understood by studying the Bible alone, for the New Testament is evidence of the religious consciousness of the first century, not of the "essence of Christianity" per se. Christianity can be understood only through grasping the present "as product of the past and kernel of the future."[36] Thus historical theology constitutes the actual body of theological study, whereas two other disciplines, philosophical theology and practical theology, make connections to philosophical speculation and to practice, respectively.

The logic underlying Schleiermacher's threefold scheme is explained in the introduction to his *Entwurf eines Systems der Sittenlehre*, where his philosophy of science is unfolded in a series of propositions "borrowed" from dialectics. If we are to grasp fully Schleiermacher's organization of the branches of theology, we must attend to that text.[37] Reasoning from the "highest antithesis" accessible to thought, that of being as material and being as spiritual, Schleiermacher concludes that there are two manifestations of being: nature and reason. It follows that there are two principal sciences: those of nature and of reason. But there are two forms of knowing: the speculative knowledge of essence and the empirical knowledge of existence. Combining the two forms of knowing with the two manifestations of being results in four sciences: the speculative knowledge of nature (physics); the empirical knowledge of nature (natural science); the speculative knowledge of reason (ethics); and the empirical knowledge of reason (historical science [*Geschichtskunde*]).[38]

In addition to these four sciences, Schleiermacher deduces the "critical" and "technical" disciplines. These "hover," as he says, between empirical and speculative disciplines. The critical disciplines connect what has appeared in history with speculation; for, as Schleiermacher says:

> Everything constructed in ethics contains the possibility of an infinite variety of appearances. Besides the empirical grasping of the latter arises the need of a closer connection of the empirical with the speculative presentation, namely in order to judge how the individual appearances hold as presentations of the idea, both as to grade and as to characteristic limitation. This is the essence of criticism, and therefore there is a circle of critical disciplines which are connected to ethics.[39]

Whereas the critical disciplines make the connection to the speculative deliverances of ethics, the technical disciplines connect the empirical historical reality with practice. Technical disciplines are "rules of art" that provide the theory of practice.[40]

This brief excursus was necessary to clarify the architectonic of the *Brief Outline*. Historical theology falls under historical science; it is empirical knowledge of the appearance of reason in history, namely, the appearance of reason in the form of a specific way of believing, the Christian faith. Philosophical theology is a critical discipline, connecting the empirical data of history with the speculative knowledge of the essence of reason developed in the famous "propositions borrowed from ethics." And practical theology is a technical discipline, providing the "rules of art" for church service and church government.

Schleiermacher is instructive because his *Brief Outline* represents one model of how a thorough historicizing of theological study can be carried out. The study of theology consists largely of the empirical study of history. Even the normative disciplines, doctrinal theology (*Glaubenslehre*) and Christian ethics (as distinct from philosophical ethics, which is entirely speculative), fit under the empirical study of history, for they provide accounts of the doctrine and ethics current in the church at the present time. For Schleiermacher, the study of history can be no wooden or mechanical undertaking; in fact, he complains that from a merely mechanical study of history the confused state of the theological disciplines has followed. It is only through historical study that the present development of doctrine can be understood and, where necessary, criticized. Historical study is always a process of making judgments: "In historical theology must appear what was held as the essence of Christianity at different times, and how the view of the same has been modified; from it each [student] forms his own impression (*Vorstellung*) of the essence of Christianity, and then he possesses the foundation for himself, on which he can build."[41]

If Schleiermacher's *Brief Outline* has taken into account the necessity of historicizing the theological task, does it provide the outline we need for the present constitution of the theological disciplines and the pattern for theological study? Formidable objections to the adequacy of Schleiermacher's program for the present have recently appeared. It has been argued that he has set up a movement that leads from theory to practice along a one-way street; there is no way in which concrete practice can affect theory, and thus no way empirically to learn and modify one's understanding.[42] Moreover, it has been held that Schleiermacher's "clergy paradigm" for the constitution of theological studies is far too restrictive, for it limits theology and theological education to the professional training of ministers.[43]

It would take us too far astray to assess the merit of these particular criticisms of Schleiermacher's *Brief Outline*.[44] Neither criticism, though, touches upon what I have argued is the essence of Schleiermacher's contribution—his *historicizing* of theology. But I would certainly agree that, from the perspective of the historical consciousness itself, it would be self-contradictory to suggest that all that is needed is to model contemporary theological education along the lines of the *Brief Outline*. Schleiermacher's scheme, after all, was developed to fit the conditions of his own day; he was wrestling with problems of the early nineteenth-century German university and had at his disposal philosophical resources (in the form of the idealistic philosophy of science) that are hardly appropriate to our very different age. Our conditions, problems, and resources are much different. Yet I would contend that Schleiermacher remains instructive, and reflection on his organization of theology may guide us as we attempt our own solutions. Specifically, by making historical theology the "actual corpus" of theological studies and by showing (by means of their inclusion under a single rubric, "historical theology") that there are no sharp breaks between biblical studies, church history, and systematic theology and ethics, Schleiermacher may be held to point the way toward a contemporary, historically conscious organization of theological studies.

V

What does the historical consciousness imply, then, for the pattern of theological study in our day? In particular, what does it imply about the place of historical studies (biblical studies, church history, historical theology) in the curriculum? The following theses sum up my own conclusions.

Thesis 1: The mere presence of historical subjects in the curriculum of theological studies does not by itself ensure that the historical consciousness will be taken into account.

The reason for this is that it is quite possible to study history without reflecting explicitly on historiography as a method, historicism as a worldview, or the theological ramifications of either. Mere mechanical or wooden historical studies, consisting of chronicles of Israel's history, important events in church history, or information about the setting and authorship of texts in the canon, as well as intensive study of the ideas of dead thinkers would not entail any coming to terms with the historical consciousness or its implications. Such historical study could only be dreaded as a hurdle to be surmounted, a set of required courses to be successfully negotiated.

Thesis 2: The historical consciousness is adequately taken into account only if the historical-critical method and historicism as a worldview, with their theological implications, become explicit themes of theological reflection.

This does not mean that either the believer as such or the student for the ministry must become professional philosophers of history. It does mean that a mere aggregate of historical studies is not adequate. Historical studies must be informed by (1) a critical awareness of the method of historical studies and its assumptions, and (2) a critical and informed awareness of the historicist worldview. This does not necessarily imply "methods" courses in the curriculum, but attention to such questions in the very process of historical study. Thus students of the Bible need to reflect upon the historical-critical method—how they are proceeding and why they are doing so. Through historical and systematic studies, they need to confront the question of the authority of these texts for the present and the hermeneutical gulf between these ancient texts and the modern world. The lack of historical-critical and hermeneutical sophistication will become all too painfully apparent in their future preaching practice. Students of the history of Christian thought need not be told from the lectern that Christianity develops over time, but they should be given the occasion to discover the truth of that thesis as their own inductive generalization. In this way, they too will have the occasion to confront the problem of "development of doctrine" and the "essence of Christianity" in an informed and self-critical manner, and will form their own judgments as to what the Christian message is through a "comprehensive induction." In this way, they will own the tradition of which they are a part. What is essential, in short, is that the theological implications of the historical consciousness become explicit in the course of study.

Thesis 3: Historical studies are theological only insofar as critical reflection on the meaning and truth of the Christian tradition is their telos.

This thesis is intended to explicate further the meaning of thesis 2. Without this proviso, historical studies, even if carried on in the context of a seminary, lose their theological character, becoming the history of institutions and ideas. The budget of issues distinguished in Section III is obviously crucial to contemporary reflection on the meaning and truth of the Christian tradition. Not every theological student will become a professional historical or systematic theologian. But every theological student needs to wrestle with problems of hermeneutics, faith and history, the development and pluralism of Christian doctrine, and Christianity's place among the religions of the world, as well as with the problems of universalism, particularism, and ideological distortion. Otherwise, how can she or he speak publicly to the meaning and truth of the Christian faith?

Thesis 4: Indispensable to wrestling with the meaning and truth of the Christian tradition is a firm grasp of what that tradition has been; specifically, how it has developed. Thus biblical studies (as study of the originating witness) and church historical studies (including especially the history of theological ideas) constitute the body of theological studies.

Herein lies the enduring validity of Schleiermacher's *Brief Outline:* historical theology constitutes the core of theological studies. Here much of the traditional subject matter, if not the traditional pattern or rationale, has its continuing place. Biblical studies and historical studies, understood in this moment of study as historical theology, belong together as constituting studies in the Christian tradition. Just as Schleiermacher grouped exegetical theology and church history under the same heading, I would argue that biblical studies and the history of Christian thought form part of historical theology. The intention is not to create a "book binder's synthesis," but rather to see the organic connection of the biblical period (and its documents) with the subsequent unfolding history. As has been argued above, for the historical consciousness the Bible can have but a relative priority vis-à-vis tradition. That church historical studies means here the history of theological ideas follows from the telos of theological education, understood as the disciplining of theological thinking, and from the definition of theology as critical reflection on the meaning and truth of faith.

This proposal is likewise not intended as a rationalization for the activities of the guild of historians. Rather, the rationale for the centrality of historical studies lies in the historically conscious understanding of Christianity as a product of history that evolves over time. The tradition is studied in order to understand how we got to where we are, and to provide orientation for critically appropriating the tradition in order to hand it on to the next generation. Such study is both appreciative (to grasp what the tradition held and why), but also critical. There is ample room in this understanding for the hermeneutics of suspicion, critical feminist hermeneutics of the Bible, and similar proposals. To study the tradition for the sake of wrestling with its meaning and truth and ultimately handing it on does not mean to adopt an uncritical stance toward tradition: "What you do with tradition is to learn it well—and criticize it." This follows from the conviction that "appropriating and transforming the past—in short, the development of doctrine—is what theology is all about."[45]

Thesis 5: The historical consciousness is adequately taken into account only if it informs all of the theological specialties in the educational program.

The historical consciousness has to do not only with the study of history itself; as a worldview in addition to a historiography, it is an understanding of reality as historical. Thus, whether the task be analyzing the contemporary cultural, social, and political context, formulating a contemporary practical theology, engaging in ethical reflection, participating in interreligious dialogue, or wrestling with a particular doctrine, historical thinking will be involved. Historical subjects per se do not wrestle with all the issues; to say that they constitute the "corpus" of theological studies (to use Schleiermacher's word) is not to say they constitute *all* of theological study. Critical reflection on contemporary praxis, or normative proposals concerning the meaning and truth of Christianity for us and for now, although making use of history and historical thinking, are not themselves historical subjects.[46]

A conversation directed at the reform of theological education will have to take many factors into account. My argument in this essay points to two central contentions regarding the structure of theological study: (1) historical studies themselves (the traditional disciplines of biblical studies and historical theology) ought to constitute the core of theological study; and (2) the historical consciousness ought to pervade all areas of study, not just the explicitly historical subject areas. My argument is based on an understanding of the telos of theological study (as the disciplining of theological thinking) and upon an analysis of the historical consciousness. To be historically conscious is to understand reality as historical. The Christian faith itself does not merely have a past; it is an evolving creature of time. Christian believers are historical, standing in one moment of an ongoing process. If theological education is to discipline theological thinking, if it is to foster responsible grappling with the meaning and truth of Christianity, it must address not only the problems and possibilities of the present but the heritage of the past. We need not remain imprisoned in the categories of the past; but as long as we claim for ourselves the name "Christian," we are confronted with the task of "creative fidelity" to that heritage.[47] For we are children of time; and if we are to act responsibly upon time from within its stream, we must understand where we have come from and where we are.

NOTES

1. Ernst Troeltsch, *Gesammelte Schriften*, 4 vols. (Tübingen: J. C. B. Mohr [Paul Siebeck], 1912–1925; reprint, Aalen:

Scientia, 1961–1966), 4:337. Cited hereafter as *GS*.

2. For his criticisms of the fourfold pattern, see Edward Farley, *Theologia: The Fragmentation and Unity of Theological Education* (Philadelphia: Fortress Press, 1983), 127–46; for his constructive proposals, see *The Fragility of Knowledge: Theological Education in the Church and the University* (Philadelphia: Fortress Press, 1988), 133–91.

3. Ernst Troeltsch, "Protestantisches Christentum und Kirche in der Neuzeit," in *Die Kultur der Gegenwart*, ed. Paul Hinneberg, Teil I, Abt. IV.I, II Hälfte (Berlin: B. G. Teubner, 1922), 600–743, and *Protestantism and Progress: The Significance of Protestantism for the Rise of the Modern World*, Fortress Texts in Modern Theology (Philadelphia: Fortress Press, 1986), 35–36.

4. Farley, *Theologia*, 4.

5. I have appropriated the notion of theological education as "disciplining" from Farley, applying it to the disciplining of theological thinking as defined here. See *The Fragility of Knowledge*, 136. I might add that although I agree with Farley's concern that theology not be restricted to the clergy, and theological education not be restricted to clergy education, the argument of this essay is focused on seminary training as clergy education. I believe, however, that my understanding of theology does not restrict it to a clergy activity, and that my conclusions apply, *mutatis mutandis*, to contexts other than clergy education, such as lay and university education.

6. James Hastings, ed. *Encyclopedia of Religion and Ethics*, 13 vols. (New York: Charles Scribner's Sons, 1908–1922), 6:718, s.v. "Historiography."

7. Ernst Troeltsch, "Über historische und dogmatische Methode in der Theologie," *GS* 2:729–53.

8. Ibid., 731–32.

9. Van A. Harvey, *The Historian and the Believer* (New York: Macmillan, 1966), 38–48, and "The Alienated Theologian," in *The Future of Philosophical Theology*, ed. Robert A. Evans (Philadelphia: Westminster Press, 1971), 118–21.

10. David Hume, *An Inquiry Concerning Human Understanding*, The Library of Liberal Arts (Indianapolis: Bobbs-Merrill, 1955), 118.

11. Harvey, *Historian*, 42.

12. Troeltsch, *GS* 2:732–33.

13. Gerhard Ebeling, *Word and Faith* (Philadelphia: Fortress Press, 1963), 43, 47.

14. Harvey, *Historian*, 68–99.

15. Troeltsch, *GS* 2:732. The paragraph in question is, as Sarah Coakley points out, "notoriously difficult" (*Christ Without Absolutes* [Oxford: Oxford University Press, 1988], 24). Consequently, interpretations of Troeltsch's actual meaning vary considerably. My intent is not to make a contribution to Troeltsch scholarship on this vexed point, but to make use of him as a point of entrance to understanding historical thinking.

16. Ernst Troeltsch, "Geschichte und Metaphysik," *Zeitschrift für Theologie und Kirche* 8 (1898): 1–69.

17. Ebeling, *Word and Faith*, 47.

18. On the public character of theological argument, see David Tracy, *The Analogical Imagination: Christian Theology and the Culture of Pluralism* (New York: Crossroad, 1981), xi, 3–82. On warrants and backings, see Harvey's use of Toulmin in *Historian*, 49–54.

19. Troeltsch, *GS* 2:733–34.

20. Ernst Troeltsch, *The Absoluteness of Christianity and the History of Religions* (Richmond: John Knox Press, 1971), 85: "the historical and the relative are identical."

21. This is the deceptively simple starting point for B. A. Gerrish's reflections in "Theology and the Historical Consciousness," *McCormick Quarterly* 21 (1968): 199.

22. Karl Mannheim, *Essays on the Sociology of Knowledge* (London: Routledge & Kegan Paul, 1952), 86.

23. Ernst Troeltsch, "Die Krisis des Historismus," *Die neu Rundschau* 33 (1922): 573, cited by Robert Rubanowice in *Crisis in Consciousness* (Tallahassee: University Presses of Florida, 1982), 50–51.

24. H. Richard Niebuhr, *The Meaning of Revelation* (New York: Macmillan, 1960), 9–10.

25. Ibid., 12.

26. Wilhelm Dilthey, "The Dream," in *The Philosophy of History in Our Time*, ed. Hans Meyerhoff (New York: Doubleday, 1959), 41.

27. See Sarah Coakley, "Theology and Cultural Relativism: What Is the Problem?" *Neue Zeitschrift für systematische*

Theologie und Religionsphilosophie 21 (1979): 223–43, for a helpful analysis.

28. Ibid., 227.

29. Troeltsch, *GS* 2:730.

30. Werner Georg Kümmel, *The New Testament: The History of the Investigation of Its Problems* (New York and Nashville: Abingdon, 1972); Albert Schweitzer, *The Quest of the Historical Jesus* (New York: Macmillan, 1968).

31. Coakley, "Theology and Cultural Relativism," 239.

32. Adolf von Harnack, *What Is Christianity?* Fortress Texts in Modern Theology (Philadelphia: Fortress Press, 1986), 4, 6, 11.

33. The literature on this problem is enormous. See Juan Luis Segundo, *The Liberation of Theology* (Maryknoll, N.Y.: Orbis Books, 1976); James H. Cone, *God of the Oppressed* (New York: Seabury Press, 1975); Rosemary Radford Ruether, *Sexism and God-talk* (Boston: Beacon Press, 1983). For a recent formulation of the methodological significance of a feminist perspective, see Rebecca S. Chopp, "Feminism's Theological Pragmatics: A Social Naturalism of Women's Experience," *Journal of Religion* 67 (1987): 239-52. That the application of Marxism's suspicion of ideology to Christian theology predates contemporary liberation theologies may be seen in Reinhold Niebuhr's 1935 *An Interpretation of Christian Ethics* (New York: Seabury Press, 1979). See p. 75 and esp. p. 99, where Niebuhr speaks of "the degree to which Christianity became the [witting] as well as the unwitting tool of class interests."

34. Robert Morgan and Michael Pye, eds., *Ernst Troeltsch: Writings on Theology and Religion* (Atlanta: John Knox Press, 1977), 182.

35. Friedrich Schleiermacher, *Kurze Darstellung des Theologischen Studiums zum Behuf Einleitender Vorlesungen*, critical ed. by Heinrich Scholz (Darmstadt: Wissenschaftliche Buchgesellschaft, 1973), 9–12.

36. Ibid. 11, author's translation. (This formulation comes from the first edition.)

37. Of the Schleiermacher literature with which I am acquainted, only Hans-Joachim Birkner has taken into account Schleiermacher's system of the sciences in interpreting the *Brief Outline*; see *Schleiermachers Christliche Sittenlehre in*

Zusammenhang seines philosophisch-theologischen Systems, Theologische Bibliothek Töpelmann, vol. 8 (Berlin: Verlag Alfred Töpelmann, 1964), 30–64.

38. Friedrich Schleiermacher, *Entwurf eines Systems der Sittenlehre, Friedrich Schleiermachers Literarischer Nachlass*, ed. Alexander Schweitzer, Teil III, Band 5 (Berlin: G. Reimer, 1835), 13–84.

39. Ibid., 68–71; the quotation is from pp. 70–71.

40. Ibid., 69–70; Friedrich Schleiermacher, *Christian Caring: Selections from Practical Theology*, eds. James O. Duke and Howard Stone, Fortress Texts in Modern Theology (Philadelphia: Fortress Press, 1988), 88–103.

41. *Friedrich Schleiermacher Theologische Enzyklopädie (1831/32): Nachschrift von David Friedrich Strauss*, ed. Walter Sachs, Schleiermacher Archiv, Band 4 (Berlin: Walter de Gruyter, 1987), 29.

42. John E. Burkhart, "Schleiermacher's Vision for Theology," in *Practical Theology: The Emerging Field in Theology, Church and World*, ed. Don S. Browning (San Francisco: Harper & Row, 1983), 52–56.

43. Farley, *Theologia*, 84–94, 130; *The Fragility of Knowledge*, 143–44.

44. James Duke and Howard Stone have provided a convincing answer to the former critique. As Christian practice transforms Christianity, a new reality appears to be known by historical theology and critically analyzed by philosophical theology (Schleiermacher, *Christian Caring*, eds. Duke and Stone, 23–24). As to the latter critique, it might be noted that Schleiermacher's sense of "ecclesial interest" provides a broader basis for construing the unity of theology than the "clergy paradigm": persons other than clergy may have such an "ecclesial interest" combined with a "scientific spirit."

45. B. A. Gerrish, *Tradition and the Modern World: Reformed Theology in the 19th Century* (Chicago: University of Chicago Press, 1977), 169 (referring to A. E. Biedermann's position), 183.

46. Thus I would not follow Schleiermacher in including contemporary constructive theology under historical theology, because I think a distinction must be made in the constitutive questions of each. Although both wrestle with ques-

tions of meaning and truth, the former critically assesses past thoughts, whereas the latter makes constructive proposals for the present. See Schubert M. Ogden, *On Theology* (New York and San Francisco: Harper & Row, 1986), 8–13. Nevertheless, as should be apparent, although the constructive task is to be distinguished from the historical task, it is nevertheless *continuous* with it. This is what I take B. A. Gerrish's term "constitutive historicism" to imply constructively. See John P. Clayton, ed., *Ernst Troeltsch and the Future of Theology* (Cambridge: Cambridge University Press, 1976), 123.

47. Mary Potter Engel, "A Call to Creative Fidelity: Reflections on Christian Tradition in Light of Feminism," *Prism* 4, no. 1 (Spring 1989): 13–24.

4

Theological and Religious Studies: The Contest of the Faculties

Francis Schüssler Fiorenza

The relation between theological studies and religious studies is a basic issue affecting the academic study of religion today. The definitions of the very terms are often ambiguous. This ambiguity often clouds any discussions of their relation to each other. In discussing the relation between religious and theological studies, some preliminary clarification of the terms is necessary.

"Religious studies," the current term in English, has a broader meaning than the German *Religionswissenschaft* (science of religion) or the designations "comparative religion" and "history of religions," which often refer to very specific schools and methods in the study of religion.[1] "Religious studies," as a broad term, is often used as a title for programs or departments of religion. As such, it refers primarily to a program of studies that has religion as its subject matter rather than to a single discipline or a particular approach to the study of religion. Its unity comes not so much from a particular method as from a common subject matter. Quite often, disciplines that only indirectly study religion, for example, sociology and theology, are included under the umbrella of programs of religious studies, when a particular study, investigation, or course includes the study of religion. Broadly conceived, religious studies covers the range of disciplines that are studying religion. More narrowly conceived, religious studies refers to the explicit and direct study of religion for its own sake rather than indirectly in relation to another dimension of human life, such as sociology of religion or psychology of religion.

Theological studies can also be understood broadly or narrowly. Narrowly defined, theological studies, referring to the single discipline of theology often called systematic theology, designates a single discipline of theological studies that deals systematically with the meaning and truth claims of a particular religious or denominational tradition. Broadly defined, theological studies refers to the whole gamut of theological disciplines; besides theology, it includes other theological disciplines, such as New Testament studies, church history, and so forth.

The title of this essay, therefore, can be understood in a broad as well as a narrow sense. Understood broadly, it deals with the relation between theological studies, as carried out within a department of theology or a divinity school, and religious studies, as carried out within a department or program of religious studies. More narrowly understood, it contrasts theology as a systematic discipline with the study of religion in which the religious question is systematically raised and analyzed.

Because of these terminological ambiguities, I will begin this essay by surveying diverse conceptions of the nature of religious and theological studies and their relation to one another. Moreover, I will examine the reasons given for contrasting religious studies and theological studies as two opposing disciplinary approaches that constitute contesting faculties. Then I will analyze attempts to relate religious studies and theological studies in ways that either reduce theological studies to religious studies or transform religious studies into theological studies. Finally, I will propose a way to understand theological and religious studies as neither contrasting nor identical. Instead, I will argue that each is distinctive and yet complementary insofar as both are cultural and human disciplines.

The Contest of the Faculties
The Myth of a Contrast

Often one relates theological to religious studies in a way that contrasts them.[2] One contrasts subjective faith with objective knowledge, epistemic privilege with scientific neutrality, and advocacy claims with disinterested impartiality. These contrasts constitute a current "contest of the faculties."[3] Such a contest between religious studies and theological studies, however, should be located within the broader context of current debates on the cultural and human sciences.

Today, a contest of the faculties exists that is much more radical than at the time of the Enlightenment. No longer is it an issue of a justification before the court of a transcendental reason. No longer is it an issue of legitimation before the court of a Neo-Kantian scientific objectivity. Instead, what is debated is rationality itself. What is contested is scientific objectivity, and what is claimed is the intertwinement of structures of civilization, science, and culture with those of domination, exploitation, and oppression. Standards of scientific rationality do not exist apart from the web of history and society. The issue of the relation between theological and religious studies, therefore, stands within the context of these broader debates.

Subjective Faith Versus Objective Knowledge

Many consider theological studies and religious studies as contrasting disciplines. Theological studies presupposes a faith stance. Religious studies aims for objectivity of knowledge. Hideo Kishimoto expresses this view when he claims: "Theological and philosophical studies both belong to the subjective standpoint. Of these theology is based on the standpoint of faith. It accepts without condition the given premises of a particular religion and always works from within the framework of the presuppositions of that religion."[4]

Joachim Wach makes a similar argument: "Theology has its own task in identifying its own confessional norms, and none may take this task from it. Theology is concerned with understanding and confirming its own faith."[5] In contrast, the study of religion does not presuppose the subjective faith of the individual, but impassioned objectivity. It does not rule out that the individual scholar might be a person of faith. What it excludes is that personal faith can intrude into the study of religion. Theological studies, however, often views personal faith not as an intrusion but as integral to the theological task.

Contemporary hermeneutical theory challenges this contrast. A so-called double hermeneutic exists in the human sciences, *Geisteswissenschaften,* and social sciences.[6] This double hermeneutic underscores the distinctiveness of the cultural and human sciences. They are hermeneutical not just because the models or categories chosen to organize and explain the data affect the interpretation and application of that data. They are hermeneutical because the world of human meaning constitutes their object domain. As hermeneutical, they require a preunderstanding, or life-relation, to the world of meaning as a prerequisite of the very attempt to interpret.

This appeal to a double hermeneutic is not the same as the theological appeal to personal faith, for the preunderstanding that is essential to the study of the human sciences does not entail the claim of epistemic privilege. It does not make personal faith into a stance of an unquestioned epistemic privilege, nor does it necessarily transform preunderstanding into an advocacy position. It does, however, emphasize the importance of a life-relation to the subject matter. In addition, it underscores that this life-relation is embedded in the historical, societal, and cultural traditions. Such a life-relation requires critical scrutiny because, as a preunderstanding, it often influences, if not determines, interpretation. The necessity of such a preunderstanding and the need for a critical examination of it is common to both theological and religious studies.

Because of this double hermeneutic, one must carefully nuance any distinction between religious studies and those studies that indirectly deal with religion, for example, sociology of religion or psychology of religion. Not only religious and theological studies but also the study of religion in sociological and psychological approaches to religion need to take this double hermeneutic into account. These disciplines become "scientific" not by claiming objectivity, but by becoming more "critically self-conscious."[7]

Epistemic Privilege Versus Scientific Neutrality

One often contrasts theological and religious studies insofar as one claims that theological studies, as compared with religious studies, is grounded on claims of epistemic privilege. This claim is not the claim of an individual's personal faith, but the claim of access to special knowledge and insight that possesses an epistemic privilege. Just as in Lessing's "Parable of the Three Rings" each son claimed to possess the unique ring, so too every theology claims the epistemic privilege of foundational texts, dogmas, creeds, history, and so forth. The theological task thus consists in explicating the truth claims of these sources of epistemic privilege. In this view, theological argumentation seems to be based on privileged criteria and precritical authorities that have a foundational significance for the discipline. As such, its method contrasts with the critical inquiry and scientific neutrality of religious studies.

This understanding of theological studies follows a Western and even Christian view of theology in its reliance upon the epistemic privilege of a foundational revelation or foundational religious documents. Not every religious tradition makes such exclusive claims of epistemic privilege. In addition, the critique of foundationalism within contemporary epistemology has important implications for such an understanding of theological studies—implications that also extend to religious studies. This critique maintains that data, experience, and method do not have independent epistemic privilege status. They stand within a holistic framework. They are not only interrelated with each other, but are interrelated within a complex network of interpretations.[8]

For theological studies, what counts as foundational data in terms of appeals to a set of scriptures or traditions or to a set of experiences cannot in isolation warrant interpretation or truth claims without a host of other considerations. Religious studies, however, faces the same problem not only for its historical or experiential data, but also in its use of diverse methods. A holistic approach that takes seriously how theory formation, interpretative frameworks, and societal practice are intertwined excludes any conception of theological or religious studies based upon the epistemic privilege of data, experience, or method.[9]

This complex issue has been well formulated by Helmut Koester in his analysis of the crisis of theological and historical criteria. "The structure of our question," he notes, "is identical with the problem of systematic theology today. Since no generation of Christian theologians has direct access to the criterion of its own legitimacy, the result of historical research should never be presented as an abstract and timeless norm. It is impossible to isolate this kind of criterion, be it a priori, be it in retrospect."[10]

Committed Advocacy Versus Disinterested Impartiality

A third contrast between theological and religious studies is often seen in the dimension of advocacy that religious studies shuns. Such advocacy often appears to be a form of apologetics. As such, theological studies seems to be concerned with the demonstration of the truth of its beliefs and the legitimacy of its claims to epistemic privilege. Religious studies, however, with its disinterested impartiality, appears to be more capable of studying the subject matter with an openness that allows scientific objectivity and neutrality to have their rightful place within the academy.

To equate theological studies with advocacy and religious studies with disinterested non advocacy is to make a questionable assumption. First, current philosophical analyses have shown the intertwinement of knowledge and interest, of knowledge and advocacy: Foucault has stressed the interrelation between discursive relations and nondiscursive practices. Philosophy of science has shown the significance of diverse paradigms (Kuhn) or styles of reasoning (Crombie).[11] The Frankfurt School, from Max Horkheimer to Jürgen Habermas, has highlighted the relation between knowledge and interest.[12] The importance of Habermas's linkage of theory and interest is that it links the cultural sciences to the practical intent of the communication of a life-praxis. Therefore, religious studies as a cultural science has a constitutive interest in the communicative application of a cultural tradition to a life-praxis. Not only theological studies, but also religious studies, is constituted by an interest.

Second, in addition to these formal epistemological considerations, liberation theologies (feminist, black, Latin American, African, and Asian) raise political and practical issues that have epistemic import for academic method. These liberation theologies criticize as illusory the academic claims to neutrality and objectivity. What the Frankfurt School raises formally with the category of interest, they raise concretely. They argue that allegedly disinterested theory formation betrays the claim to interests of economic, racial, and gender domination. They thereby challenge the alleged neutrality of religious as well as theological studies.

Third, the analysis of religious pluralism indicates the degree to which neutral categories and methods are embedded within traditions of specific historical civilizations and within life-practices of distinct cultures. Insofar as religious studies recognizes the religious pluralism of diverse cultures, it recognizes that beliefs, symbols, and ideas are embedded in concrete sociocultural relations. This acknowledgment should lead to the self-understanding that abstract disinterested theories do not exist.

Theological and religious studies are thus "interested" disciplines. Each needs to take seriously the relation between knowledge and interest, theory and advocacy. Harvey Cox has argued that considerations of practice have "pushed the academic study of religion toward a frank acknowledgment that no one can study religion merely descriptively. This in turn makes the modern myths of neutrality and objectivity increasingly implausible. . . . Ironically the momentum of current academic studies in religious pluralism is pushing it toward an approach which is similar to more praxis-oriented theologies."[13]

In sum, three contemporary philosophical considerations (the double hermeneutic of all humanistic studies, the critique of foundationalism, and the dialectical relation between knowledge and interest) contest the usual contrasts between religious and theological studies. Instead, the three considerations pose challenges that religious studies and theological studies have to face in developing an adequate disciplinary self-understanding.

Religious Studies as Theological Studies

Religion as the Generic Expression of Human Faith

Schubert Ogden argues that theology relates to religious studies in a way analogous to the difference between religious studies and all other studies of religion, such as sociology of religion or psychology of religion. Religious studies differs from these studies because it raises the question of faith as the constitutive question of the discipline. Religious studies does not require that the scholar have faith. It does, however, require that the scholar explicate the question of faith as a question of the meaning and truth of religion. If the scholar of religion does not raise this question, then she or he does not raise the constitutive question of religious studies.

Christian theology relates to religious studies in two ways: as the specific to the generic and as answer to question. First, religious studies raises the question of the truth and meaning of religion in general. Christian theology raises the question of the truth and meaning implied in the Christian witness.[14] The notion of a common human faith grounds the relation between religious studies as the generic to theology as the specific. Schubert Ogden reformulates Tillich's statement that "faith is the substance of culture, while religion is the particular cultural form in which this substance is first of all made explicit."[15] In his reformulation, religious studies examines the question of faith as the substance of the culture. Christian theology studies Christian religion as a particular cultural form of this substance.

Second, Christian theology raises "the reflective question as to the meaning and truth of the Christian witness as an answer to our own question of faith as human beings."[16] Ogden distinguishes between appropriateness and adequacy, and between what constitutes the meaning of Christian religion and what constitutes its truth. The earliest Christian testimony provides the criteria of "appropriateness" and specifies the meaning of the Christian religion. Contemporary experience provides the criteria of truth.[17]

The criteria of appropriateness determining the meaning of Christianity stem from the earliest Christian witness, or what the New Testament exegete, Willi Marxsen, calls the "Jesus Kerygma." This focus on the earliest Christian witness is in my opinion questionable, given Walter Bauer's analysis of the second century in terms of the relation between orthodoxy and heresy.[18] But of most importance, this conception does not allow the study of other religions to influence the specification of the meaning of Christianity. Religious studies needs to raise the question of the truth of human religiousness, but theology does not need for its criteria of appropriateness the study of other religions. The earliest Christian testimony is the prime criterion for specifying what is Christian and the appropriateness of theology as Christian.[19]

David Tracy concurs with Ogden's distinction between criteria of appropriateness and criteria of truth, but he modifies it in typical Roman Catholic fashion. First, he does not limit the criteria of appropriateness to the earliest Christian witness or to a "canon within a canon." Instead, he opts for a "working canon" and sets as normative the classics of the whole range of the Christian tradition. Second, he further explicates the relation to contemporary experience through transcendental analysis and argumentation. Third, he logically extends Ogden's notion of common faith through his proposal that a hermeneutics of religion be the mediating and foundational link between the specific claims of Christian theology and those of religious studies.[20] To perform this function, the hermeneutic of religion must raise the question of the meaning and truth of religion.

Tracy's appeal to a hermeneutics of religion can also be questioned. It appears to presuppose that religion exists as some common universal underlying all particular religions. It tends to overlook the critique that Schleiermacher had already made of the Enlightenment's concept of natural religion when he argued that only positive religions exist. It overlooks the fact that the concept of religion is a modern and Western concept.[21] Edward Farley has noted the inadequacy of referring to religion in general in view of the three dimensions constitutive of and pervasive in all religion: transcendent, experiential, and institutional.[22] Nevertheless, Farley agrees with both Ogden and Tracy that religious studies is a general form of theological studies. Because religious studies must deal with the distinctiveness of religious truth claims, it requires a theological hermeneutics in order to be genuinely religious studies. It must include "the engagement with those faiths at the point of their reality claims and their experiential dimensions (of theological hermeneutics)."[23] These affirmations approximate the second approach to be discussed.

Religionswissenschaft Als Theologiewissenschaft

Wolfhart Pannenberg develops a conception of theology that takes up the issue of the relation of theology to the problem of religion. He writes that "a theology which, because it is a theology of Christianity, is in our terms a branch of theology, would need at least to be based on a fundamental theology. This would attempt to define the particularity of the Christian revelation in the context of the general problematic of religion."[24]

Yet, in analyzing Christian particularity within the context of religion, Pannenberg seeks to reform the "science of religion." There is, however, one condition to be met before the science of religion can acquire the status of a foundational theological discipline," he writes, "and in its present state of development it does not meet it. That is that the science of religion should . . . also investigate the reality experienced in religious life and its history."[25] Consequently, he concurs with Heiler's affirmation that "all science of religion is ultimately *theo*logy because it is concerned not only with psychological and historical phenomena but also with the experience of other-worldly realities."[26]

Because the study of religion should be a theology of religion, Pannenberg argues that it should have the foundational theological task of comparing the diverse religions in order to specify Christianity. It should raise the truth claims of Christianity and the diverse religions. Pannenberg emphasizes the relevance of truth claims both for religious and theological studies.[27]

Pannenberg's conception is provocative, yet it is in some respects questionable. First, Pannenberg operates very much out of the Western conception of religion that defines religion by its object—God. Consequently, the only adequate study of religion is a theology of religion constituted by the question of God. Second, the issue of the truth claims raises the question of how these truth claims are to be adjudicated. In raising truth as a hypothesis, Pannenberg refers to the object of religion and assumes that one examines its claims about the truth of reality. Third, comparative analyses presuppose an overarching framework to judge them. Yet in asking how theology can be a science, he answers the question somewhat with a trick of the hand. Theology can be the academic study of religion, but the academic study of religion should properly be a theology of religion that raises truth questions.[28]

In many respects, the Roman Catholic theologian Bernard Lonergan comes close to Pannenberg's thinking. Lonergan argues that the comparative study of diverse religions belongs to the functional specialty of dialectics that immediately precedes the truth issue that is raised in foundational theology.[29] Like Pannenberg, he appeals to Friedrich Heiler to justify religious studies as theological studies. Lonergan attributes "a preparatory function for the history of religions" in the cooperation among religions.[30] He suggests that religious studies serves a function similar to philosophy for the medieval theologian. This implies, as Charles Davis has criticized, that religious studies is reduced to the handmaid of theology.[31] Lonergan maintains that if religious studies raises questions of meaning, it is doing theology: "They [religious studies] are borrowing the techniques of theologians if they attempt to say what the equivalent symbols literally mean and what they literally imply."[32] Both Pannenberg and Lonergan argue that if religious studies fulfills its proper task of investigating the truth and meaning of religion, then it raises theological issues. In short, both transform religious studies into theological studies.

Critical Reservations

Both of the above positions, Christian theology as a specific instance of the more generic religious studies or religious studies as authentic only insofar as it raises theological questions, bring important considerations to the issue of the relation between religious and theological studies. Nevertheless, I have basic reservations about both approaches.

First, both overcome the dichotomy between theological and religious studies in a somewhat one-sided manner. They contend that the dichotomy is overcome or lessened insofar as religious studies is given a theological orientation. Unconsciously, they make Christian or

Western conceptions of theology and religion covertly normative for what constitutes religious studies. They insist that religious studies has to raise the issue of truth. For Pannenberg, religious studies is properly religious studies when it becomes a theology of religion and raises the truth of the God question.[33] For Schubert Ogden, religious studies takes into account the basic foundational trust implied in religious faith.[34]

Moreover, when both positions claim that Christianity is the specific of a general study of religion universal (Ogden, Tracy), they downplay the distinctiveness of Christianity and minimize the historical otherness and distinctiveness of other religions. They relate Christianity to an anthropological universal. One can question whether the Christian religion or any religion is merely a concrete instance of an anthropological universal, but rather a radically diverse and historically concrete particular. Moreover, one can question whether this position shows how the study of diverse religious traditions affects Christian theology as the hermeneutic of Christian institutional Christianity.

Second, these theologians seek to change the self-understanding of religious studies more than the self-understanding of theology. They insist that religious studies raises issues of truth, yet they do not also emphasize that theology must radically revise its way of dealing with issues of truth and issues of meaning. Either the earliest Christian testimony or the Christian classics determine the meaning of Christianity and the appropriateness of Christian theology. The location of theology within a religiously diverse context does not seem to change the criteria for theology. Religious studies is made either preparatory to theology (Lonergan) or is identified with theology (Pannenberg).

Third, in raising the issue of the status of theology within the university, Lonergan and Pannenberg do not take up the epistemological challenges to the nature of academic study. Here I refer to the critique of foundationalism within American philosophy or the critique of "scientific objectivity" within liberation theology.

Pannenberg seeks to retrieve the Roman Catholic discipline of foundational theology for contemporary Protestant theology in the context of the German university. He can easily show the relevance of nineteenth-century foundational theology because his epistemology is much more closely attuned to the epistemology of German idealism than to that of current critiques of foundationalism.

Theological Studies and the Interpretation of Religion

The questions remain: What is the nature of theology in particular and theological studies in general in relation to the academic studies of religion? What constitutes theology as a discipline within the academy in comparison to religious studies? Does theology have a distinctive self-understanding as an academic discipline? In my opinion, contemporary hermeneutical theory provides some insights that help us answer these questions and avoid a one-sided response.

Explanation and Understanding

Contemporary hermeneutical theory maintains that the interpretation of the cultural tradition should be much more than empathetic appropriation. Interpretation needs to consider the dialectic between the dual modes of explanation and understanding. This dialectic has been the center of the philosophical reflection of Georg Hendrik von Wright, Karl-Otto Apel, Paul Ricoeur, and Calvin Schrag.[35] Each of these authors insists that both explanation and understanding are essential to interpretation.

An example of such a dialectic is David Tracy's use of Gadamer's notion of the classic and his modification of it through Ricoeur's conception of explanation and understanding. Tracy maintains that theological studies should engage not only in the mode of understanding, that is, in the hermeneutical retrieval of the classics of tradition. It should also engage in the ideological critique of a tradition's distortions through modes of explanation.

His conception thereby seeks to balance retrieval and critique.[36]

The relation between theory and practice, however, suggests that such a conception should be broadened in two ways. First, that which determines which works are our classics depends upon what practices we have, what communities we are, to which communities of discourse we belong. Our life-practices and communities of discourse likewise determine our interpretations and critical evaluations of these classics.

Second, Ricoeur's conception of the dialectic of explanation and understanding, as John Thompson has noted, relates explanation primarily to a "text that is treated as a self-enclosed entity." It primarily examines the "internal constitution, the ways in which its constituent elements relate to one another," but not the social-historical production of the text.[37] Consequently, for David Tracy the major problem of hermeneutics is the ambiguity of the text and the plurality of disclosive possibilities rather than the relation between the text and societal practice.

Yet the dialectic of explanation and understanding includes issues of the social-historical production of texts as well as the social-historical consequences of certain texts. It thus needs to examine the reasons for their selection and endurance as normative classics within dominant communities. This emphasis on the life-praxis that produces texts and on the life-praxis that flows from texts raises the issue of the relationship between diverse life-practices and the meaning and truth of religious classics. It raises a problem that affects theological as well as religious studies.

Interpretation should therefore take into account the complementary dialectic of explanation and understanding with reference to the social, historical, practical location. Interpretations of religious classics, whether within religious or theological studies, must take into account all these elements of the dialectic of understanding and explanation. If religious studies would overemphasize the explanatory element, then it would run the risk of becoming reductionistic in its interpretation of religion.

It would risk neglecting the ideal content and semantic potential of religion. If theological studies would neglect the explanatory modes of analysis, it would run the risk of overlooking the embodiment of religious traditions within the forces, dynamics, and influences of social life-practices. Theology would risk abstracting the ideality of the religious tradition from the facticity of its concrete embodiment.

Life-Praxis and Meaning

The relation between life-praxis and meaning poses a further challenge to religious as well as theological studies that goes beyond the dialectic of explanation and understanding. It is the problem of understanding diverse forms of religious faith. These diverse forms of faith exist, in Wittgenstein's terminology, as "forms of life" with diverse shared practices, customs, and institutions.[38] The meaning, significance, and truth of religious beliefs are integral to these forms of life and shared practices. Both religious and theological studies must, therefore, ask, How does one understand a religious faith when it is integral to distinct practices and forms of life? The theologians surveyed rather quickly in this essay proposed that religious studies should raise the question of truth if religious studies seeks to remain religious studies. Yet if one seriously considers that religious beliefs are intertwined with diversely shared practices, customs, and institutions, then the issues of meaning and truth become exceedingly complex. How is understanding of other religions possible when one does not share the practices, customs, and institutions of those beliefs?

Before one can even raise the question of truth, one must face the question of the understanding of meaning. The intertwinement of beliefs and life-practices confronts us with the problem of ethnocentricism. Often one's own life-praxis does not help but obstructs understanding. Often, it becomes the standard by which one views and interprets other life-practices and their corresponding faiths, thereby causing one to fail to understand them.

Theological studies in the context of religious studies must raise the question, How does one understand those patterns of behavior and shared human practices that constitute diverse religious institutions? If one views these beliefs merely as expressions of a generic anthropological universal question, then one neglects the particularity of these beliefs. One overlooks their intertwinement in concrete narratives. Concerning this point, George Lindbeck has rightly criticized the pretension to universalism of some forms of transcendental theology and has highlighted the role of story and narration within religion and theology.[39]

This critique brings up the problem of sectarianism and incommensurability. Several philosophical attempts seek to bridge the gap between relativism and objectivism, between conceptual incommensurability and an objectivistic realism.[40] The recent philosophical work on the cutting edge of this problem attempts not to opt for one or the other but to look for bridges. Donald Davidson refers to the implicit knowledge that makes possible conversation about incommensurability. Such conversation requires some types of common reference points, making dialogue possible.[41] Joseph Margolis refers to a pragmatic transcendental analysis that proceeds by way of salient exemplars rather than universal rules and by the meta-analysis of the transcendental argument.[42] Hilary Putnam's transcendental pragmatic approach develops the notion of rationality as a "limit concept."[43] Richard Bernstein and Jürgen Habermas seek to deal with the problem of rationality and relativism with reference to communities of discourse.

An examination of these attempts to bridge the gap between incommensurability and objectivistic standards suggests that the problem is much more complex for religious beliefs. These attempts refer to implicit reference points, paradigms, and types of argumentation that can serve as bridges for dialogue. But religious beliefs differ from nonreligious beliefs. Religious beliefs have a transcendent reference that unifies our experience of the world. Therefore, religious beliefs, despite all historical and experiential grounding, point to a transcending and unifying dimension of our worldviews. As such they exercise a significant influence on how we understand ourselves and the world, and as such they affect our practice in the world.[44] For religious beliefs, the type of realism that makes dialogue possible and overcomes incommensurability is not as easily available.

Philosophers advocating critical realism can argue that realism in science best explains "the continued success of a theoretical research program" because "its associated model gives an approximate 'fit' to the structure of nature itself."[45] They can, for example, argue for a fit between Einstein's theory of relativity and certain experimental measurements on the distortion of light through gravity. They can show that the truth conditions of a theory are constitutive to its meaning and interpretation. Religious and theological studies do not have such an easy and realistic "fit." Issues of meaning and truth cannot be resolved simply by references to objective, expressive, or social human nature. The way religious beliefs integrate objective, expressive, and social nature affects human practice. Practice becomes what I would like to call a "hermeneutical link."

In facing shared problems of human practice, such as nuclear peace, political oppression, economic domination, race and gender exploitation, as well as death, isolation, and loneliness, we encounter issues that retroductively make possible areas of communicative discourse and even agreement possible. These common issues, even though viewed quite diversely, require a dialogue so that in facing them we strive to surmount elements of incommensurability that prohibit dialogue. What I am suggesting is that precisely where humanity is threatened, the challenge emerges for diverse religious beliefs and practices to bring the resources of their religious traditions to bear on these threats to humanity. In confronting these challenges, possibilities for religious self-transcendence and for conversation exist. For example, when we face issues of the exploitation of other races, nations, or the world of nature, then the voices of non-Western and non-Christian religions enter into the conversation and bring criticisms of Christian images of God, ourselves, and the world.

The suggestion that praxis is a hermeneutical link within a religiously diverse world applies equally to religious studies and to theological studies. Quite often one understands practice in a narrow sense. One views practice as proper to theological studies, as, for example, in the view that "the primary purpose in studying a religion is to practice it."[46] Nevertheless, within the broader context of the human sciences, both religious and theological studies share a relation to practice. Philosophical and literary texts are often incorporated into the canon of required reading because they provide opportunities for normative reflection in relation to life practice. Religious texts provide similar opportunities for normative and practical reflection within religious studies as a human discipline, not just within theological studies.

Conversation and Theological Pluralism and Identity

In addition to praxis, the role of community is relevant to the issue of incommensurability without foundationalism.[47] The community of inquiry has from Peirce to Habermas and Bernstein been conceived somewhat abstractly. They often overlook the fact that ideal communities of discourse do not exist, even when they acknowledge that communities consist of individuals embedded in similar or diverse practices. To the extent that the community of discourse has become broadened so that it includes more persons—for example, blacks, women, Third- and Fourth-World persons—to that extent the practices by which religious symbols and beliefs are understood and evaluated become broadened.[48]

Communities of discourse have a significant impact on human practice and identity. Personal identity is not simply a given, but is also achieved. Through social and communicative interaction, what is given is reconstructed, and identity is formed. Likewise, the identity of societies and institutions is not simply given but results from communicative interaction and reconstruction. Identity involves given and constructive dimensions. Identity does not simply grow or mature, as in vegetative life, but must be reconstructed within historical, social, and communicative interaction.[49]

This reconstructive and communicative nature of identity applies especially to religious traditions. For example, Christian theology previously may have understood Christian identity as a given contained in a scriptural or dogmatic essence. Today, it is increasingly clear that much of Christian identity is European, white, male, and so forth. As Christianity spreads and encounters other communities of discourse, Christian theology will increasingly reconstruct the identity of Christianity as it seeks to achieve a reflective equilibrium between the givenness of its tradition and the challenge of its encounter with other communities of discourse and practice.

A parallelism exists between theological and religious studies. Contemporary Christian theology faces the reconstruction of its identity in the face of contemporary crises. Faced with issues of the Jewish Holocaust, nuclear war, world hunger, oppression of human rights, extreme poverty in the Third Word, ecological crises, sexism and racism, and so forth, the constructive theological task is to ask, How can the image of God or Christ or of community be reconstructed so that the Holocaust is not repeated, so that exploitation, racism, and sexism are eliminated?

Such a reconstructive task may seem far removed from religious studies. The approach of religious studies does not at first glance appear to be primarily concerned with the reconstruction of identity. Religious studies investigates Christianity as one religion within antiquity, studying it alongside of other Greco-Roman religions, each in its own right. In its approach, religious studies may examine equally the leadership of women in Jewish synagogues, mystery religions, and Gnosticism. Or a religious studies approach might seek not simply to explicate the fourth-century Donatist controversy as a debate about belief, but instead to explain it as one of social difference and then strive to appropriate the Donatist viewpoint. Or it may approach early medieval Christianity not just from the perspective of Christianity but also from that of Islam. In all these cases, an academic analysis of religion examines stories of the victims of the "Great Church" or of those who have lost out or have been marginalized by the church that came to dominate European civilization.

Such a religious studies does not eschew the issue of identity, but actually challenges theological studies and itself. It steps outside of the narrow focus of Christianity's self-reflection. It retrieves viewpoints of those marginalized or victimized by Christianity. It highlights neglected elements that critique and even oppose Christianity's self-understanding. Religious studies challenges Christianity to reconstruct its identity. The foundational theological task to reconstruct Christian identity does not stand in opposition to religious studies but is thereby radically challenged by it.

What then is the difference between theological studies and religious studies? In my conception, theological studies is oriented toward the reconstruction of identity of a specific tradition in relation to practice. Religious studies, as well as studies of religion, engages in interpretation with a practical intent insofar as it is a human science, but its practical intent does not have the same identifiable reconstructive task that it does in theological studies. Through its practical function, theological studies is a constant reminder to religious studies of its status as a human discipline. At the same time, religious studies, through its representation of diverse religious traditions and disciplines, provides a critical challenge to the self-understanding of theological studies.

The relation is dialectical; religious studies challenges theological studies to become critically self-conscious, to move critically and creatively toward its goal of the practical reconstruction of identity. Theological studies challenges religious studies to realize its role as a human science that interprets cultural traditions with a practical intent. In short, religious studies challenges theology to overcome its danger of dogmatism. Theology challenges religious studies to overcome the danger of historicism.

This suggestion defines theology not in relation to a specific conception of transcendence or some universal concept of religion of which it is only the particular. Instead, it defines theology in terms of a broad reflective equilibrium among diverse elements.[50] Theology seeks to specify the ideal potentials and paradigms of identity within its tradition. It seeks to consider the demands of diverse practices. It seeks to reflect on appropriate background theories of contemporary worldviews. Theology seeks to achieve this reflective equilibrium within a community of discourse that is in conversation with other communities of discourse, representing distinct traditions of religious and social practice.

By describing theology as the reconstruction of religious identity within a broad reflective equilibrium that, in addition to the tradition and background theories, gives a constitutive role to praxis as a retroductive warrant, my account takes seriously Schleiermacher's view of practical theology as the crown of theology. At the same time, my account avoids the criticisms that Pannenberg, Farley, and others have brought against this functional orientation as ecclesial or clerical,[51] insofar as it relates practice to a reflective equilibrium of diverse elements and it locates practice in relation to broader societal and political issues.[52] My account thereby points to practice as a hermeneutical link significant for the reconstruction of identity and for the encounter with distinct religious traditions, and even with nonreligious traditions. Such a theology is not based upon epistemic privilege, but is ordered to practice and to dialogue. Only such a theology deserves its place within the academy.

This conception of the relation between theological and religious studies has implications for theological education. It suggests that theological education must be shaped in a way so that theological and religious studies are neither sharply contrasted nor reduced to one another. Instead, the curricula should bring to the fore their complementarity and distinctiveness so that they can challenge each other through their similar but different practical intents. By contrasting theological and religious studies, one accentuates further the fragmentation of theological education. The split of theological curricula into fourfold specialties becomes reinforced and extended by a further split into religious and theological studies. The fragmentation of the fourfold disciplines becomes intensified as a fragmentation of approach and method, which leads to the negative consequences and fragmentation for theological education that Edward Farley has so clearly profiled.[53]

My proposal underscores the complementarity of the modes of understanding and explanation. It also emphasizes the practical intent for both theological and religious studies as interpretive disciplines. Yet it argues that religious and theological studies exercise the dialectic between understanding and explanation as well as the practical intent in similar but distinctive ways. Therefore, the development of curricula should encourage and intensify a crisscrossing of theological and religious studies. If the curriculum and institutional arrangement relegates theological studies to the divinity school and religious studies to the university, then the contrast between the two becomes institutionalized. It impedes religious studies from challenging theological studies and vice versa.

My proposal also points to the importance of hermeneutics within the contemporary curriculum. The last two centuries have witnessed the broadening of hermeneutics as a discipline. Previously, hermeneutics concentrated on the interpretation of texts. It often focused exclusively on religious texts. Today, hermeneutics extends beyond texts. It extends to the method of the cultural sciences. It examines the relation between theory and practice. It explores the interpretive nature of rationality and experience. This more extensive focus enables hermeneutics to provide a unity. Previously, in theological education individual disciplines served as the unity of theological education. Scripture studies, systematic theology, foundational theology, and philosophical theology or philosophy provided resources for this unity. The development of religious studies alongside of theological studies within the academy took place at the same time as the development of hermeneutical theory. This dual development points to the importance of hermeneutical theory to elaborate the unity in difference of theological and religious studies.[54]

My proposal also has implications for graduate and doctoral studies. Under the impact of professionalized training and specialization, some disciplines, especially historical and empirical disciplines, develop a technocratic rationality in which questions of value, significance, and application are often excluded or bracketed out. Questions of hermeneutics are left to the philosopher of religion or to the systematic theologian and are not considered to be integral to the specialized discipline. Such doctoral training then affects how these individual disciplines are taught. The specialized training in limited issues is transferred to theological education as well as to the study of religion, resulting in a truncated dealing with the material in which substantial issues are not raised. My proposal about the relation between theological and religious studies, therefore, bears on the very practice and teaching of the individual disciplines within the whole gamut of religious and theological studies.

Conclusion

I have argued three theses. First, the academic status of theological studies today is a question of the relation between theological and religious studies. Some resolve this issue by arguing that religious studies should be a generic form of theological studies. I have argued instead that this worthwhile suggestion does not adequately address the foundational theological task of rethinking theological studies according to contemporary standards of rationality.

Second, I have suggested that both religious and theological studies need to consider the double hermeneutic of the cultural sciences; the implications of the critique of foundationalism for claims of epistemic privilege for data, experience, and method; and the interrelation between advocacy and objectivity based upon the interestedness of knowledge.

Third, I have argued that theology as an academic discipline within a religiously plural context should take into account not only the dialectic between explanation and understanding, but also the degree to which the meanings of religious beliefs become objects of discourse insofar as they intersect with praxis. I have not suggested that religious studies is a discipline within theological studies or that theological studies simply incorporate features of approaches from religious studies. Instead, I have sought to describe theological studies with a very specific intent. Theological studies is not so much the interpretive discovery of identity as it is the interpretive reconstruction of a specific tradition's integrity and identity with reference to retroductive warrants drawn from practice and to appropriate background theories within a community of discourse, with participants of other disciplines and religious traditions.

NOTES

1. For the latter, see Gerd Lüdemann, "Die Religionsgeschichtliche Schule," in *Theologie in Göttingen,* ed. Bernd Moeller (Göttingen: Vandenhoeck & Ruprecht, 1987); and Kurt Rudolph, *Historical Fundamentals and the Study of Religions* (New York: Macmillan, 1985).

2. For a recent defense of a similar contrast, see Ninian Smart, *Religion and the Western Mind* (Albany: State University of New York, 1987).

3. For a survey of problems of deconstruction and philosophical rationality, see Christopher Norris's *Contest of Faculties: Philosophy and Theory After Deconstruction* (New York: Methuen, 1985). See Immanuel Kant, "Der Streit der Fakultäten," in *Werke,* vol. 6 (Darmstadt: Wissenschaftliche Buchgesellschaft, 1964), 275–393. As the third contest indicates, the issue also concerned the nature and progress of humanity.

4. Hideo Kishimoto, "Religiology," *Numen* 14 (1967): 81–86; here p. 84.

5. Joachim Wach, "Introduction: The Meaning and Task of the History of Religions *(Religionswissenschaft),*" in *The History of Religions: Essays on the Problem of Understanding,* ed. Joseph M. Kitagawa (Chicago: University of Chicago Press, 1967), 1.

6. Anthony Giddens, *Profiles and Critiques in Social Theory* (Berkeley: University of California Press, 1982), 1–17.

7. Wilfred Cantwell Smith has advocated "corporate critical self-consciousness" rather than objectivity as the goal of the human sciences. See his "Objectivity and the Human Sciences: A New Proposal," in *Transactions of the Royal Society of Canada* (Ottawa, Royal Society of Canada, 1975), 81–102. Reprinted in abridged form in Willard G. Oxtoby, ed., *Religious Diversity: Essays by Wilfred Cantwell Smith* (New York: Harper & Row, 1976), 158–80.

8. It is this critique of foundationalism that undermines the medieval conceptions of the scientific nature of theology. In relating theology to the other sciences, medieval theologians argued that communality exists because the source, goal, and object of all was God. Nevertheless, it differed from other sciences because it appealed to principles of revelation known through inspiration or illumination. (For a description of these medieval theories, see Ulrich Köpf, *Die Anfänge der theologischen Wissenschaftstheorie im 13. Jahrhundert* [Tübingen: J. C. B. Mohr, 1974], 226–47.) The critique of foundationalism, however, radicalizes the insight of post-Enlightenment hermeneutics in its focus on the common problem of the understanding of all texts.

9. Frank Reynolds, "Maps, Models and Boundaries: Some Reflections on the Historical and Normative Elements in Religious Studies," *Criterion* 20 (1981): 26–31, argues that *Religionswissenschaft* has a distinctive normative approach that studies religion as a universal phenomena in contrast to parochial theological and historical studies (the traditional theological studies). The decisive questions are, of course: According to what standards does one adjudicate such "universal" normativity? and, Can theological studies still be done in such a parochial fashion and still be valid? Reynolds has recently drawn out the implications of his approach for theological education. See "Diversification Without C? Some

Reflections on the Future of the Divinity School?" *Criterion* 25 (1986): 14–18; see also Hans Dieter Betz, "Response to Frank Reynolds," ibid., 19–20.

10. James M. Robinson and Helmut Koester, *Trajectories Through Early Christianity* (Philadelphia: Fortress Press, 1971), 118.

11. See Michael Foucault, *Language, Counter-Memory, Practice* (Ithaca, N.Y.: Cornell University Press, 1977); Thomas S. Kuhn, *The Structure of Scientific Revolutions,* 2nd ed. with postscript (Chicago: University of Chicago Press, 1969), and *The Essential Tension: Selected Studies in Scientific Thought and Change* (Chicago: University of Chicago Press, 1977); and for a discussion of Alistair Crombie's notion of styles of reasoning, see Ian Hacking, *Representing and Intervening: Introductory Topics in the Philosophy of Science* (Cambridge: University of Cambridge Press, 1983).

12. Jürgen Habermas, *Knowledge and Human Interests* (Boston: Beacon Press, 1968).

13. Harvey Cox, *Religion in the Secular City* (New York: Simon & Schuster, 1984), 224; see also 216–29.

14. One might say that in its generic sense, which corresponds to the generic sense of "religion," "theology" designates a higher level of reflection to which the claims of a particular religion may possibly be subjected. This would seem to indicate that theology, in the specific sense of "Christian theology," must be reflection on the claims expressed or implied by the Christian theology—or, as one might prefer to say, "the Christian witness of faith." See Schubert M. Ogden, "Theology and Religious Studies: Their Difference and the Difference It Makes," *On Theology* (New York and San Francisco: Harper & Row, 1986), 116.

15. Ibid., 109.

16. Ibid., 118–19.

17. See the critical remarks by Owen C. Thomas, "Theology and Experience," *Harvard Theological Review* 78 (1985): 179–201.

18. Walter Bauer, *Orthodoxy and Heresy in Earliest Christianity,* 2d ed. (Philadelphia: Fortress Press, 1971).

19. For my criticism of Ogden on this point, see "Reflective Christology," *Cross Currents* 32 (1982): 373–76.

20. David Tracy, "Is a Hermeneutics of Religion Possible?" in *Religious Pluralism,* ed. Leroy Rouner (Notre Dame: University of Notre Dame Press, 1984), 116–29, and "Religious Studies and Its Community of Inquiry," *Criterion* 25 (1986): 21–24. See also Judith Berling, "Response to David Tracy," ibid., 25–27.

21. Wilfred Cantwell Smith, *The Meaning and End of Religion* (New York: Harper & Row, 1962). Smith suggests that the notion of religion should be replaced with personal religiousness and corporate tradition as two dimensions of the human religious response. Whether such a proposal takes sufficiently into account the distinctive particularity and historicity of concrete religions is debatable.

22. Edward Farley, "The Place of Theology in the Study of Religion," *Religious Studies and Theology* 5 (1985): 9–29. The first, the transcendent dimension or the principle of reality, is the concern in religions with truth and a reality, with the ultimate horizon of human existence. The second, the anthropological dimension or principle of experientiality, is the distinctive way religions express the possibilities of human existence. The third, the dimension of institutionality or principle of concreteness, is the corporate and constitutional way that religions create continuity over a period of time. For Farley, these three pose requisites or criteria for the study of religion. A study of religion that does not pose the issues of truth, distinctiveness, and concreteness is not an adequate study of religion.

23. Ibid., 26. For this very reason, Farley comes close to Ogden and Tracy and maintains that "there appears to be some coincidence between the hermeneutics of a specific religious faith represented by this seriousness and the hermeneutics required by the study of religion" (p. 25). See Farley's further development in *The Fragility of Knowledge: Theological Education in the Church and the University* (Philadelphia: Fortress Press, 1988).

24. Wolfhart Pannenberg, *Theology and the Philosophy of Science* (Philadelphia: Westminster Press, 1976), 325.

25. Ibid., 363.

26. Friedrich Heiler, *Erscheinungsformen und Wesen der*

Religion (1961), 4–5. Quoted in Pannenberg, *Theology and the Philosophy of Science*, 364–365.

27. Pannenberg, *Theology and the Philosophy of Science,* 326–45. See also Wolfhart Pannenberg et al., *Grundlage der Theologie—Ein Diskurs* (Stuttgart: Kohlhammer, 1874), 29–57.

28. Bernard Lonergan's proposal is similar, except that, as a representative of Roman Catholic transcendental theology, his conception is much more anthropological. Pannenberg uses the category in the broad sense that bridges the gap between the philosophy of religion and history of religion. See his discussion of C. Colpe's position in *Theology and the Philosophy of Science,* p. 368.

29. Bernard J. F. Lonergan, *Method in Theology* (New York: Herder & Herder, 1972), 101–24 and 235–93. See also the three lectures in Part 2 entitled "Lectures on Religious Studies and Theology," in Frederick E. Crowe, ed., *A Third Collection: Papers by Bernard J. F. Lonergan* (New York: Paulist Press, 1985). See also P. Joseph Cahill, *Mended Speech: The Crisis of Religious Studies and Theology* (New York: Crossroad, 1982).

30. Crowe, ed., *A Third Collection,* 163. See also Friedrich Heiler, "The History of Religions as a Preparation for the Cooperation of Religions," in *The History of Religions: Essays in Methodology,* eds. Mircea Eliade and Joseph M. Kitagawa (Chicago: University of Chicago Press, 1959 and 1962), 132–60.

31. For a view giving much more weight to religious studies, see Charles Davis, "The Reconvergence of Theology and Religious Studies," *Sciences Religieuse/Studies in Theology* 4 (1974/5): 205–36.

32. Crowe, ed., *A Third Collection,* 164.

33. Pannenberg, *Theology and the Philosophy of Science,* 358–71.

34. Ogden, *On Theology,* 102–20.

35. Georg Hendrik von Wright, *Explanation and Understanding* (Ithaca, N.Y.: Cornell University Press, 1971); Karl-Otto Apel, *Understanding and Explanation: A Transcendental-Pragmatic Perspective* (Cambridge: MIT Press, 1984); Paul Ricoeur, *Critical Hermeneutics and the Human Sciences: Essays on Language, Action, and Interpretation,* ed. and

trans. John B. Thompson (New York: Cambridge University Press, 1981); and Calvin O. Schrag, *Communicative Praxis and the Space of Subjectivity* (Bloomington: Indiana University Press, 1986).

36. Ricoeur, *Critical Hermeneutics and the Human Sciences.*

37. John B. Thompson, *Studies in the Theory of Ideology* (New York: Cambridge University Press, 1984), 196.

38. For the problem of comparing diverse forms of life in Ludwig Wittgenstein's conception of meaning, cf. Paul Seabright, "Explaining Cultural Divergence: A Wittgensteinian Paradox," *Journal of Philosophy* 84 (1987): 11–27.

39. George Lindbeck, *The Nature of Doctrine: Religion and Theology in a Postliberal Age* (Philadelphia: Westminster Press, 1984).

40. See Richard J. Bernstein, *Beyond Objectivism and Relativism: Science, Hermeneutics, and Praxis* (Philadelphia: University of Pennsylvania Press, 1983), and *Philosophical Profiles: Essays in Pragmatic Mode* (Philadelphia: University of Pennsylvania Press, 1986).

41. Donald Davidson, *Inquiries into Truth and Interpretation* (New York: Oxford University Press, 1984).

42. Joseph Margolis, *Pragmatism Without Foundations: Reconciling Realism and Relativism* (New York: Blackwell, 1986).

43. Hilary Putnam, *Realism and Reason: Philosophical Papers,* vol. 3 (New York: Cambridge University Press, 1983).

44. Gordon Kaufman has consistently developed this point. See *An Essay on Theological Method,* rev. ed. (Chico, Calif.: Scholars Press, 1979), and *Theology for a Nuclear Age* (Philadelphia: Westminster Press, 1985).

45. Ernan McMullin, "Realism in Theology and in Science: A Response to Peacoke," *Religion and Intellectual Life* 2 (1985): 39–47; here p. 43. The issue of realism is strongly debated. See the essays representing diverse positions in Jarrett Leplin, ed., *Scientific Realism* (Berkeley: University of California Press, 1984).

46. Smart, *Religion and the Western Mind,* 25. He calls this model the traditional Christian theological model.

47. See Francis Schüssler Fiorenza, "Foundations of Theology: A Community's Tradition of Discourse and Practice,"

Proceedings of the Catholic Theological Society of America 41 (1986): 107–34. See also his "Theory and Practice: Theological Education as Reconstructive, Hermeneutical, and Practical Task," *Theological Education* 23 (Supplement 1987): 113–41.

48. See Margaret Miles, "Hermeneutics of Generosity and Suspicion: Pluralism and Theological Education," *Theological Education* 23 (Supplement 1987): 34–52; and Diana L. Eck, "Hinduism and Incarnation Theology," and Ronald F. Thiemann, "Toward a Critical Theological Education," *Harvard Divinity Bulletin* 18 (1986).

49. See my development of the conception of identity in "Critical Social Theory and Christology," *Proceedings of the Catholic Theological Society of America* 30 (1975): 63–110.

50. See Francis Schüssler Fiorenza, *Foundational Theology: Jesus and the Church* (New York: Crossroad, 1984), 301–11, for a discussion on the important difference between narrow and broad reflective equilibrium within the contexts of the debates surrounding John Rawls' *A Theory of Justice* (Cambridge: Harvard University Press, 1971).

51. Pannenberg, *Theology and the Philosophy of Science,* 250–56; Edward Farley, *Theologia: The Fragmentation and Unity of Theological Education* (Philadelphia: Fortress Press, 1983), 73–98.

52. Ronald Thiemann, "Piety, Narrative, and Christian Identity," *World and World* 3 (1983): 148–59, perceptively uses the critique of foundationalism to show how Schleiermacher's claim that "practical theology is the crown of theological study" can be much more consistently achieved.

53. Farley, *Theologia* and *The Fragility of Knowledge.*

54. See Francis Schüssler Fiorenza, "Thinking Theologically About Theological Education," *Theological Education* (Supplement 2, 1988): 89–119, and "Theory and Practice."

5

Beyond a Mono-religious Theological Education

Paul F. Knitter

In this essay, I will try to explain and ground a conviction that I share with many colleagues in the Christian theological community: that if, as many contend, there is a growing awareness in seminary and divinity schools that theological education is not doing its job of enabling Christian ministers and laypersons effectively to "reflect" on their "existence and action in the world"[1] or to "reconstruct Christian identity . . . in relation to practice,"[2] one of the reasons for this failure is that theological education has been and remains so *mono-religious.* Theological educators are going about their job of reflecting and reconstructing on the basis of an exclusive, or too restrictive, use of Christian tradition and experience. They are not able effectively and engagingly to reflect on and reconstruct Christian tradition and identity because they have closed themselves to, or are not sufficiently open to, other religious traditions and identities.

The Problem of Theological Education: New Patterns, Open Patterns

This opening statement is more than another facile liberal twist on Max Müller's dictum that to know only one religion is to know none. The criticism of a mono-religious theological education is rooted in Edward Farley's careful analysis of the malaise in theological education today. Farley contends that the needed reforms in "the overall pattern or structure of theological study" will, like a slippery fish, constantly evade our grasp until we face the more disturbing question of the "deep presuppositions" that sustain theological education today. After critically analyzing these deep presuppositions, Farley concludes that the foundational nature and purpose of theology can better be realized not as a collection of loosely linked "specialty fields" (biblical, systematic, historical, and practical theology) that examine or apply a determined body of knowledge (that is, the Christian fact or tradition), but rather, as a dynamic, fluctuating process by which Christians respond to "modes of interpretation"—that is, to the hermeneutical demands confronting the community. Theology is the community's response to the issues that call for reflection and action as those issues arise both within and beyond the community. According to Farley's proposal, what we need is a "shift from theology as a cluster of sciences . . . to theology as historically situated reflection and interpretation. The outcome of that shift is that the structure of theological study or pedagogy is recognized to be determined by basic modes of interpretation rather than by sciences."[3]

When Farley goes on to delineate the basic modes of interpretation that confront Christian identity, he reflects the current revisionist model of the two sources that are to sustain the theological task. His "primary hermeneutic modes"—*traditio,* or the sweep of Christian experience; *veritas,* or the truth of the gospel; and *praxis,* or Christian life and action—might fit David Tracy's and Schubert Ogden's notion of "the Christian fact." His "synthetic hermeneutic modes"—*mundus,* or our general world context; and *vocatio,* or our particular way of acting in the world—match the broad category of "human experience."[4] Farley's understanding of the "modes of interpretation" are more nuanced than the revisionists' notion of the two sources. He goes on to level an even more tell-ing criticism of the revisionist model: insofar as it is applied within the traditional structure of the fourfold specialty fields of biblical, systematic, historical, and practical theology, even the revisionist model can hardly escape the confines of neoorthodoxy.[5] The reason for this is that this fourfold structure—or its deeper presupposition—is itself locked within what Farley calls "the house of authority": "The essential feature of the house of authority is its presumption that the historical vehicles through which the community of faith preserves its tradition (Scripture, dogmas, magisterium) have *as such,* a priori, the character of truth."[6] I would say that the presuppositions undergirding theology today have bestowed a much too facile or naive "character of truth" not just on the "historical vehicles" of tradition "as such" (I prefer, "by themselves") but also on the experiential criteria used to interpret that tradition. Christian theological education today is ailing because it has locked itself within—or is fearful of stepping outside of—the house of its own aggrandized and isolated authority.

To render this claim more comprehensible and persuasive, I prefer to follow the recent lead of Mark K. Taylor and view the "modes of interpretation" differently and, I think, more disturbingly than Farley does. Rather than envision theological education according to the revisionist two-source model as a delicate balancing of tradition and experience, Taylor describes the theological task as an effort that is expressly aware of its *cultural-political* context (both of its past and of its present situation) and that seeks to respond, with as much balance as possible, to the *postmodern trilemma.*[7] Our postmodern consciousness, at least in North America, is shaken and enlivened by three different concerns, or three different awarenesses, that all together demand our attention and press our conscience as we try to understand and act within the world.

In large part responding to the "liberal" dangers of reducing or selling out the Christian witness, postmodern awareness is held, first, by a *sense of tradition.* We need to acknowledge and keep hold on who we are; though we don't want to be locked in our own house, neither can we forget that it is our home. At the same time, our postmodern cultural-political context feels bound to acknowledge and even celebrate *pluralism*. This is the impelling awareness, articulated theologically by Francis Schüssler Fiorenza and George Lindbeck and philosophically by Richard Rorty and Richard Bernstein, that there is no one, abiding foundation for the search for truth, no one touchstone located outside the play of relativizing forces. As Fiorenza has put it: "No external standard, be it history or human experience, exists independent of cultural traditions and social interpretation that can provide an independent foundation for either faith or theology."[8] But having lost the one foundation, we are still given and called by the many culturally limited perspectives. It is within this play of the many, not outside of it, that theology must find and fashion its criteria and carry on its interpretative task. Thus, although we cannot forget that tradition is our home, we do have to venture out of it to meet the many others.

But when we venture out, we find not just diversity but also domination and oppression—needless human and ecological suffering. This third horn of the postmodern trilemma, perhaps more urgently than the others, also demands a hermeneutical response—one that will lead not just to understanding but to resistance. In view of the domination that is sapping the lives of peoples and of the planet, the affirmation of either tradition or of pluralism cannot be absolute. An interpretation of tradition that does not respond to the domination outside or within itself is felt to be effete, even immoral. The same must be said about a celebration of pluralism that takes place amid starvation and death squads and a diminishing ozone layer. We are in a "postmodernism of resistance."

This trilemma of tradition, pluralism, and domination—all calling for interpretation and engagement—is claiming, more and more, the minds and sensitivities of Christians in general and of theology students in particular, at least within the mainline churches. Unless theological education can blend and balance all three of these ingredients of postmodern consciousness, it will not be "claiming" students either in their own subjectivity or in the role they must play as ministers and theologians in the postmodern world. The problem is that such a blending is not possible within the present structure of specialty fields dominating theological education. And because theology is not responding to all the elements of the trilemma, theological education finds itself, as Farley maintains, captured in its own house of authority. This captivity applies to both sources held up by the revisionist model.

Speaking out of an experience of the third ingredient of the postmodern trilemma, liberation theologians have been reminding representatives of the so-called dominant theology (European–North American, white, male, middle-class) that in trying to work out a correlation between tradition and "common human experience," the experience that has counted most, or been used most, is not at all that "common." It has indeed excluded, or at least neglected, the vast majority of humankind who, caught in a variety of oppressive structures, have not had a voice in the assemblies of government, church, or academy. So the voices and experience of the "wretched" of the earth (who populate more than the so-called Third World), who because of class, gender, or race have been excluded, must also be given "authority" in the hermeneutical task of theology. Because this has not yet really come about, the experiential sources for theological criteria are still locked in a middle-class house of authority.

Expressing awareness of the second element in the postmodern trilemma—pluralism—others, especially those speaking out of non-Western cultures (again, such cultures are present within the West), protest that the other source of the revisionist model, tradition, has also been understood too restrictively. Tradition is caught in a house of authority not just because, as Farley explains, it is viewed too uncritically (as possessing a priori truth) but also because it is viewed too isolatedly. The claim being made here is that although Christian tradition is certainly the focal content of Christian theology, it cannot be the only content. Indeed, one effective way of unlocking the door of the house of authority that confines the current notion of Christian tradition is to recognize that there are other traditions that also claim us. The Christian house is not the only house on the block! There is no better challenge to abusive authority than to recognize other authorities. This means, therefore, a better balance between tradition and pluralism.

The criticism of theology and theological education from the awareness of domination and oppression has been made by others, including contributors to this collection.[9] In the remainder of this essay, I would like to draw out and analyze the criticism coming from those who are struggling to restructure theological education by a better blending of an awareness of pluralism, on the one hand, and a commitment to tradition and a resistance to domination, on the other. I would like to show first why a marriage between theology and religious studies is necessary, and then why such a marriage is difficult, yet possible and fruitful. I will conclude with some practical suggestions on how such a marriage can be "arranged" in the educational structures of seminary and divinity schools.

As I hope will be evident, my use of the terms *theology* and *religious studies* does not signify two approaches or methods that can be identified simply as "subjective vs. objective" or "advocacy vs. scholarship." Rather, I am speaking of two different areas or contents for study, both of which include advocacy *and* scholarship, subjective engagement *and* objective data. Both theology and religious studies seek to mediate between religion and culture. Religious studies does so with an understanding of religion as a pluralistic phenomenon and so recognizes the possible "truth" or " validity" of many religious traditions and forms of religious experience; religious studies, therefore, does not operate with a priori criteriological preferences for any one religious tradition. Envisioning a more modest goal, theology seeks to mediate between the Christian religion and culture, convinced that this mediation can take place from within the Christian tradition *by itself*. By calling for a marriage between theology and religious studies, I am questioning this "by itself."

Theology and Religious Studies: A Necessary Marriage

A New Awareness of Other Religions

The awareness of pluralism that goes to make up what we are calling a postmodern consciousness has been brought about through a variety of factors. One of them is what can be called the *new* experience of religious pluralism. Those who would diminish the impact of this experience by arguing that it is not at all new and that Christianity from its cradle was aware of and struggled against a variety of religions are missing, I suspect, the significant differences between the two ages.[10] Certainly, the early Christians were aware of the religious panorama that colored the Roman Empire, but they saw these religious others either as a state religion that threatened to dominate their own newborn identity or as a syncretistic force that would throw their unique experience of Jesus the Christ into a religious boiling pot made up of "a little bit of everything." Given both the rampant syncretism of the time and the fragile, minority self-awareness of the Christian churches, one can understand that a conversational encounter between Christianity and other religious paths was not then possible.

Today it seems that such an encounter is possible, indeed is taking place. We are aware today not only of the enduring existence of other spiritual paths (after centuries of Christian missionary efforts!); we are aware not only of their richness and beauty; today many Christians are also coming to perceive what Langdon Gilkey has termed the "rough parity" of other religious ways. It is an undeniable reality that other religious paths and religious figures have played, and continue to play, as valid and engaging a role in the lives of others as Christianity has played for Christians. And it looks like this is the given, the enduring, state of affairs. There are many religions, and if we hesitate to speak of a "rough parity" between them, at least we must recognize "equal rights" among them. This, as Gilkey himself has experienced, is "a monstrous shift indeed . . . a position quite new to the churches, even to the liberal churches . . . [a move that] has devastating theological effects." It means that "no one revelation is or can be the universal criterion for all the others."[11]

Such an awareness of religious pluralism makes heavy demands on our traditional ways of interpreting Christian tradition. Wilfred Cantwell Smith's oft-quoted declaration is a challenge that has not yet penetrated most programs of theological education: "We explain the fact that the Milky Way is there by the doctrine of creation, but how do we explain the fact that the Bhagavad Gita is there?"[12] Traditional explanations that either condemn other religions as pagan, or ignore them as irrelevant, or affirm them as stepping stones to the gospel *(praeparatio evangelica)* just do not fit the experience and awareness that many Christians have of other believers. As David Tracy, himself wary of simplistic responses to this new awareness, has admitted: "For many of us, as the dialogues become more serious and more a part of thinking religiously and theologically, some envisionment of radical religious pluralism becomes a live option."[13]

Shift from a Foundationalist to a Conversational Model for Interpreting Tradition

But the new awareness and its demands are leading theologians and the faithful not merely to *affirm* the "rough parity" of other religions, but also to *engage* it. As part of a broader development in hermeneutical theory, the experience of religious pluralism has helped generate the conviction that the way to interpret reality in general, and one's own religious tradition in particular, must follow the path of *conversation.*[14] If the early arguments of Ernst Troeltsch for a historical consciousness and the recent case of philosophers such as Richard Rorty and Richard Bernstein for antifoundationalism have confirmed the experience of many of us that indeed there are no absolute, unchanging foundations for our pursuit of the real, we have also come to realize that this does not leave us with no place to go or nothing to do, awash in a sea of relativism. Rather, deprived of our absolutes, we are invited to conversation—to affirm our own limited views and to present them to others.

Every interpretation of the world, every truth claim, is both, as it were, "sadly" relative and, at the same time, "happily" related. In its finitude and limitations, it is related—or relatable—to other interpretations, and through this relationship it can, partially but really, overcome its own limitations. Truth, therefore, must be both "critical" (the result of our efforts to be, as Lonergan counsels, attentive, intelligent, reasonable, and responsible) and "corporate" (the result of our conversations with others who are also seeking to be critical).[15] So our stumbling affirmations of what is true and good are not simply the result of our ideas "corresponding" to reality, nor solely of their coherent order; rather, truth has the quality of a happening, an almost miraculous disclosure, resulting from conversing with others. Our search for truth is thus based, in the words of Charles Sanders Peirce, on a trusting to "the multitude and variety of arguments rather than to the conclusiveness of any one."[16]

We need conversation with others not only in order to *affirm* our own truth but also in order to be *saved from it*. Another quality of our postmodern consciousness, not mentioned above, is the awareness of the distortion or unavoidable corruption that creeps into our pursuit or affirmation of truth. With the help of masters of suspicion such as Nietzsche, Freud, Marx, Foucault—especially as those suspicions have been given a feminist application—we have grown aware of the need for a "hermeneutics of suspicion"—the need constantly to be on the lookout for the worm of ideology that can penetrate our noblest affirmations of the true and the good.

For whatever reason, we bear the ever-lurking proclivity to use our truth as a means of assuring our own advantage or control over others.[17] As Walter Benjamin has said, "Every work of civilization [we could add, every work of religion] is at the same time a work of barbarism."[18] Such ideological abuse of religion is not just an "error" that can be pointed out and neatly removed. It is, rather, a "systemic distortion."[19] And we cannot defend ourselves against such distortions by ourselves. We need conversation with others—the insights and perspectives of others who look at the world differently than we do, who can look at our visions of truth from a critical standpoint outside our circle, who perhaps can tell us how our "truth" has excluded or victimized them. To carry out a hermeneutics of suspicion, we must, then, converse with others so that they can point out our distortions, our self-centered abuse of the truth we have claimed. Combining the insights of Max Müller and Walter Benjamin, we can say, "Those who know only one, turn that one into a work of barbarism."

By Itself, Christian Tradition Cannot Function as Tradition

If some such conversational model is indeed part of the hermeneutical task, there will have to be a major rehauling in the structure of theological education. More precisely, the revisionist method of theology will have to recognize explicitly that "tradition" as a source for the theological task cannot be understood only as Christian tradition. By itself, Christian tradition is both incomplete and inaccessible for the work of theology.

To recognize that Christian tradition is incomplete means that revisionist theologians cannot simply place other religions within the category of "common human experience" that is to be brought into correlation with "God's Word." In the conversational approach to truth, based on our new awareness of pluralism, we recognize that the Christian truth that we have discovered, or that has been given to us by God, can be neither "the whole truth" nor "nothing but the truth." Our conversational awareness of other religions enables us to repossess the traditional Christian assertion that God is a power of universal and self-communicating love and that therefore there is a universal revelatory presence of God within all creation. If Christian belief includes an affirmation of a "universal revelation"—as even the later Karl Barth seems to have admitted—if we claim that God has indeed "spoken in sundry forms" to all our brothers and sisters (Heb. 1:1), then what has been made known to others must be respected by us, and it must have meaning for us too.

If we believe that God has spoken to others, we must enter into a conversation with that Word. To affirm only Christian tradition as the source or sole norm for divine revelation is to disrespect what God has revealed elsewhere. The Christian Word is incomplete without other Words. Or, in more contemporary terms, if it is the nature of any classic, including religious classics, to speak "publicly" and not just to members of its parent culture or religion, then this applies to all religious classics. If Christians would hold that the Bible can also, in some analogous form, be a classic for Hindus, they must also recognize that the Upanishads can be a classic for them.

In a conversational hermeneutic, furthermore, Christian tradition, by itself, is inaccessible. Again in terms of the revisionist model, this means that theologians must expand their procedure for establishing the "appropriateness" of a theological interpretation. As Francis Schüssler Fiorenza argues in his contribution to this volume, Christian theologians can no longer draw the criteria for establishing "the appropriateness determining the meaning of Christianity" by making use only of the earliest Christian witness (Ogden) or traditional Christian classics (Tracy). This is so not simply for the general reason that we can understand ourselves and the meaning of our own kerygma only in conversation with others and their kerygmas. As Fiorenza points out, it is also because the meaning of a text can be grasped not only through an "explanation" and "understanding" of the text itself; texts must also be grasped within the socio-historical life-practice that produced them and that resulted *and results* from them. "This emphasis on the life-praxis that produces texts and the life-praxis that flows from texts raises the issue of the relationship between diverse life-practices and the meaning and truth of religious classics." Such life-practices involve others, especially other believers, then and now. Thus we cannot understand the meaning and truth of our religious classics unless we also analyze and evaluate the life-practices that they produce—including those practices that affect, positively and negatively, other religious communities and their classics. And we will be able truly to comprehend such practices only if we hear directly from those religious communities. This means that only in a conversation with other religious communities, not only about the meaning of their classics but also about how the life-practices produced by our classics have affected them—perhaps excluded or subordinated or marginalized them—only then can we move forward to an appropriate interpretation of the meaning of our classics and tradition.[20]

Under pressure from this new awareness of the validity of other religious paths and of the necessity to converse with them, we have recently heard rousing, daunting calls for a marriage between theology and the study of other religions. Paul Tillich was one of the first to voice the invitation when in the last lecture of his life he expressed his desire to rewrite his *Systematic Theology* "oriented toward, and in dialogue with, the whole history of religions."[21] Wilfred Cantwell Smith has gone even further and disturbed many a comfortable theology professor with his call for a "world theology."

> The true historian [of religions] and the true theologian are one and the same. . . . To speak truly about God means henceforth to interpret accurately the history of human religious life on earth. . . . The new foundation for theology must become the history of religion.[22]

With such a world theology, Smith means more than the already unsettling claim made by John Cobb that Christianity can and must reinterpret and even "transform" itself through conversations with other traditions.[23] Smith envisions a Christian theology so transformed that it would have a certain universal validity: "No statement about Christian faith is valid to which in principle a non-Christian could not agree." A global theology—that is, one married to religious studies—"should be acceptable to, even cogent for, all humankind."[24] Raimundo Panikkar seems to agree when, in his Indian context, he envisions "a genuinely valid theology for both Hindu and Christian."[25]

One has a distinctly uneasy feeling that with such proposals and visions, one might be rushing into the marriage of theology and religious studies much too quickly, or expecting too much of it.

Theology and Religious Studies: A Difficult Marriage

Spouses or Just Friends?

Any new romance between theology and religious studies must be "interrupted" by warnings from antifoundationalist philosophers and hard-nosed cultural anthropologists. If one takes these warnings seriously, one finds almost as many reasons for the impossibility of a healthy marriage between theology and religious studies as one has found for its necessity. Like many a modern marriage that claims to be based on equality but in reality is still caught in patriarchal structures, many theologians who endorse pluralism and a new relationship between Christian theology and religious studies actually end up with a relationship of subordination. The criticism that Fiorenza levels in this volume against Schubert Ogden, David Tracy, Wolfhart Pannenberg, and Bernard Lonergan has been posed, *a fortiori,* to the more hardcore pluralists such as John Hick, W. C. Smith, and Paul Knitter: "Unconsciously, they make Christian or Western conceptions of theology and religion covertly normative for what constitutes religious studies."[26] In one way or another—either via a singular *Theos* or Ultimate Reality, or a universal faith or basic trust, or a falling in love unrestrictedly, or an openness to the future—such pluralists presuppose some kind of common ground on which they live out the marriage of theology and religious studies; that is, by which they understand and adjudicate all religious reality. The common ground, of course, is found in their own backyard. And so, well-intentioned pluralists become anonymous imperialists. It is one thing to affirm the lack of absolute foundations; it is quite another to live and act without them.

There are those who say it is impossible to live without such foundations. I am not speaking of fundamentalist believers for whom there is but one, unchanging truth in light of which all other claims are either valueless or evil, to be tolerated or obliterated. I refer, rather, to a response to pluralism that has called itself "postliberal." Recognizing the reality of pluralism and perhaps even the "rough parity" of other religions, these theologians are equally sobered by the antifoundationalist claims and the consequent specter of incommensurability between religious perspectives. For them, there is no common experience or common goal or common anything within the world of religions; rather, religions are different "cultural-linguistic" systems that determine whatever experience is had within the different traditions. To think, as people such as Hick or Smith or Knitter seem to, that we can transcend these cultural-linguistic traditions and understand and even pass judgment on others is to begin the descent down the slippery slope of imperialism.

So, rather than rush into a marriage between theology and religious studies, postliberals propose a kind of "good neighbor policy," according to which Christians realistically resist any appeals to understand themselves and their tradition through conversations with others and realize that their identity is to be established within their own house or system; and yet, they are not to ignore their neighbors, as if they and their neighbors didn't have anything to say to each other. Though there is no intrinsic need to converse with others—and no given foundations to do so—Christians are to give witness of what they believe and how they address the life-threatening issues of our age. How that witness is received, how its reception affects others or Christians themselves, is not for them to know in advance. William Placher has called such postliberal realism an "unapologetic theology" according to which he maintains "that Christians ought to speak in their own voice and not worry about finding philosophical 'foundations' for their claims. . . . Christians must remain faithful to their own vision of things for reasons internal to Christian faith, and if, in some contexts, that means intellectual isolation, so be it."[27]

There is no doubt about the validity and importance of postliberal concerns that a marriage between theology and religious studies, required by a conversational model of truth, can easily lead either to a loss of Christian identity or to an exploitation of other religions. Yet the postliberal option for what we have called a good-neighbor policy seems exposed to serious dangers as well. As others have pointed out,[28] it can lead to a new form of fideism by which one has no grounds to criticize one's own cultural-linguistic system, or to a type of isolationism in which one is protected from criticisms and suspicions of others, or to a political toothlessness brought about by the lack of any basis on which validly and coherently to resist what appear to be intolerables in other cultural-linguistic systems. More fundamentally, the postliberal position seems to rule out any possibility of really testing or verifying whether the conversational model of truth just might be correct. Maybe the marriage between theology and religious studies, difficult though it be, can work—and bear abundant fruit.

Working At It

Like many a young (or old!) couple trembling before the apparent impossible possibility of a healthy, happy marriage but nonetheless believing or trusting that it can work, so too do many philosophers, anthropologists, historians, and theologians confront the complexity and dangers of a genuine conversation with another culture or period or religion. Such conversations, they feel, are among those forced options that cannot be ignored without incurring even greater dangers or harm. Well aware of the incommensurability gaps between cultures and religions, well aware that one always views another cultural-linguistic system through one's own, many people today are also convinced that if they are to save and transform the world, they must interpret it, and that such interpretation calls for conversation and joint efforts. Therefore, they find themselves responding with a basic trust—or better, a Kierkegaardean leap of faith—that interpretation through conversation *is* possible and that it *can* bear fruit.

Our experience somehow tells us that though complex and dangerous, conversations, like marriages, do work. Incommensurability, though real and painful, should not be made into an absolute any more than any particular religious claims should be absolutized: "We cannot find an Archimedian point, a universal standard of rationality. On the other hand, we are not utterly imprisoned within our own current horizons."[29] In other words, like any real conversation or marriage, a relationship between theology and religious studies can work—but only by being worked at, carefully, daily.

How do we actually enter into and carry on the conversation? How do we hear new questions and open ourselves to new answers? How do we state our case so that others can understand? How can we not just understand but also judge each other? Here we face again the delicate and thorny question of the need for some kind of common ground for the task of mutual understanding and judging. In order to respond to this need without slipping into imperialism, one must keep in mind that such common ground must be established mutually; it must be discovered—or created—within the conversation itself by all the partners, not beforehand by any one. Also, if we do find such common ground that will enable us to speak and listen and act together, we must also bear in mind that it will be the kind of terrain on which we can build—not concrete structures, only tents. As Mark K. Taylor has stated, it will be "shaky" common ground, which will shift and reform as the conversation stumbles on.[30]

Another guideline in stumbling on and trying to create the common ground of understanding is to proceed with something like an analogical imagination. In trying to converse with another believer in a face-to-face encounter or in trying to interpret another religious classic in the classroom, we first affirm and allow the otherness of the other to confront us and make itself known. This will require an embracing of the otherness through some form of "passing over" to and entering into the world of that other; this process engages our intellect but is energized and directed especially by the imagination. We allow the images of the other world to lead us where they will and to stir our own imaginations to see and feel things differently and so to come to insights into reality that we perhaps never entertained before; we then seek to test these insights by applying them to our own previous understandings and way of being in the world. In such an effort to pass over via the analogical imagination, there is required a letting go, a trustful following of the images and insights, a conversation that, like a game, ends up playing us more than we play it. And in this effort, we experience the analogical nature of the process when we discover that, after having affirmed and felt the other to be genuinely different, we realize that what is different can become for us a genuine and new possibility of understanding and living. Analogy wins out over incommensurability. The incommensurable becomes the possible. Conversation has taken place and borne fruit.[31]

In this process of creating common ground through the analogical imagination, there is a mystical ingredient. However, it is not the battered claim of a common mystical core within all the religions of the world, which can be discovered when mystics of different traditions slough off their externals of doctrine and ritual, and enter, nakedly and silently, into the one Still Point within all traditions. The process of passing over makes no claims about a "common essence" or "core-religious experience" for all religions. But it does, at least implicitly, require all participants in the interreligious conversation to take the mystical step of letting go of previous concepts and patterns and of embracing the other in the trust, even the expectant hope, that there is something that makes it possible and worthwhile and necessary to embrace the other and to discover with the other the possibility of common ground. We find ourselves trusting that there is such common ground to be created and that on it we can, together, grow in mutual understanding and efforts to transform this world. Without such trust, the conversation would never really be taken up. But in such trust, we are not trusting a predefined "one God" or "Ultimate Reality." Genuinely mystical, it is more a trust in a "known Unknown."[32]

The Hermeneutical Link: Pluralism and Oppression

But more can, and must, be said about how theology and religious studies can carry on their relationship and conversation. In our present-day world, especially as experienced in a postmodern consciousness, there is a starting point or a context for creating the common ground of understanding and criticism between religions. It is a context that both obligates and facilitates the interreligious conversation. I am speaking of the necessary link between the elements of pluralism and oppression in the postmodern trilemma.

Some postliberal theologians suggest that the conversation between Christians and others might use an "*ad hoc* apologetics." "All that we ever have is the common ground that *happens to exist* [emphasis mine] among different particular traditions . . . By 'ad hoc apologetics' . . . [is meant] that we should let the common ground we share with a given conversation partner set the starting point for the particular conversation, not looking for any *universal* rules or assumptions for human conversation generally."[33] Such advice makes sense but is vastly understated. As Barbara Wheeler, in the introduction to this volume, states, there is a common situation facing all humankind that can (and must?) guide the general task of reforming patterns of theological education and the specific task of relating theological studies to religious studies; Wheeler describes the common situation as the "new critical self-consciousness" prompted by "global ecological imbalance, recalcitrant racism and patriarchalism, unstable and unjust political arrangements, the possibility of nuclear destruction."[34] In other words, there is a general, universal *ad hoc* situation that can provide the starting point for establishing the common ground of religious discourse and the "raw material," as it were, for the analogical imagination—the specter of universal domination and oppression; that is, human and ecological suffering brought about by human choices.

Pluralism and oppression, then, are not just two realities weighing equally upon our postmodern consciousness; they are interrelated in the responses that they elicit from us. This interrelatedness can be demonstrated in a variety of ways. First, the oppression that may afflict the participants in interreligious discourse must become part of the discourse itself. In order genuinely to converse with the other, it is not sufficient to recognize his or her *difference.* Before we can recognize and affirm a person's difference, we must first affirm, or make possible, his or her *freedom.* How can I respect and hear from someone else's otherness if that otherness is not permitted to be what it seeks to be or to express itself? Therefore, it would seem that a condition for the possibility of real conversation with an other whose identity is dominated by structures of socioeconomic or racial or gender oppression is first to resist actively and act to overcome that domination. "Celebrating difference" and "resisting domination," therefore, become dipolar phases of the same act of discourse. As Mark K. Taylor has observed, "This brings the struggle for liberation and justice and the struggle for knowledge amid relativity much closer to one another than we often think."[35]

But the conversation must include resistance not only

to the oppression of the participants themselves, but also, and especially, to that of others outside the immediate conversation. Participants in religious conversations must listen to the anguished voices of oppressed groups in their immediate environment, their nation, and the community of nations, and of the oppressed earth. Certainly, not all these issues can be embraced in every conversation, but neither can the interreligious dialogue take place without in some way responding to the *ad hoc* reality of oppression and suffering that racks our world. If there is any context in which the airy expression "common human experience" might be concretized, it is in these frightening faces of ecological devastation, death-dealing poverty and starvation, and threatened nuclear holocaust that confront all human beings cross-culturally and cross-religiously.

One must be careful of speaking of the ethical imperative to confront such issues, because morality is so cultural bound. And yet, it does seem evident that today followers of almost all the religious paths—from Eastern to Western to so-called primal spiritualities—are recognizing that their own spiritual traditions require them to respond to the reality of human and planetary oppression. (Perhaps Marx was right in describing religion as "the sigh of the oppressed creature.")[36] Various, vastly different "theologies of liberation" are aborning among religious communities throughout the world. If Tracy is right in describing the religions as "exercises in resistance" and as revealing "various possibilities for human freedom . . . whether seen as Utopian visions or believed in as revelations of Ultimate Reality,"[37] if, as I have argued elsewhere, within all religious traditions there seems to be a "soteriocentric core" of concern for human well-being in this world,[38] then a commitment to "liberation from" or "resistance to" the myriad forms of oppression that bind our world not only can but must function as a starting point (certainly not the only one) or as the "*ad hoc* context" for creating the common ground of understanding and mutual cooperation.

We can expect that the shared praxis of resistance to

domination, recognized as a shared ethical imperative, can become a hermeneutical link by which religions are able to bridge the chasm of incommensurability. Certainly, each religion will have its different forms of praxis, based on its different analysis of the cause of oppression; but in sharing and acting together out of these various forms of praxis, religious believers will open new possibilities of reflective sharing. Interreligious dialogue and the wedding of theology and religious studies will be infused by a shared praxis of trying to overcome domination and suffering. As the base Christian communities of Latin America have been enriched by grounding their interpretation of Christian tradition on a praxis of justice, so might communities of interreligious discourse and study be enriched by basing their efforts to interpret each other on a shared praxis of resistance to oppression.[39]

Some Practical Suggestions

In this essay we have been criticizing and attempting to revise some of the presuppositions that undergird and determine the structures or patterns of theological education. The central claim has been that theology can no longer do its job mono-religiously. If it is going to perform its task effectively of preparing Christians to continue interpreting and reconstructing Christian belief and praxis, it will have to do so multi-religiously; that is, through a close relationship with other traditions and other believers. We further suggested that such a "marriage" between theological and religious studies can best be "worked at" as a conversation in which mutual differences are scrupulously affirmed and respected and yet turned into opportunities for mutual understanding and transformation, especially through a shared commitment to overcoming oppression and suffering. If there is any validity to this revision of presuppositions for theological education, then it will demand revisions in the structure and organization of theological programs in seminaries and divinity schools. Such practical restructuring can, of course, best be worked out *in situ,* according to varying contexts. The following are a few concluding practical, though still general, suggestions.

Clearly, as has often been noted, the restructuring of theological education requires much more than tinkering with the curriculum; yet my first suggestion has to do with curricular changes. If the conversation with other traditions has to enter into the theological process in some significant degree, then there will have to be more opportunities for taking up that conversation than are presently available in most seminaries and divinity schools. Simply put, theological students need opportunities to learn about traditions that, given their traditional Western, Christian background, are for the most part foreign to them. This will call for courses, *required courses,* in traditions other than Christianity, and such courses will have to form an integral part of the educational program.

Such courses will require a special and demanding methodology. As stated earlier in this essay, they must meld both scholarship and advocacy and so enable students not only to understand but also to be challenged by other religious ways of being in the world. It would be ironic to teach other religions in a theology program with a method that is increasingly recognized as outmoded within "religious studies" programs. Even teachers of comparative religions in secular universities are admitting that to present the contents of religious traditions in a detached, objective, and nonjudgmental way is both impossible and, for most students, a waste of time. Religions make claims about reality, and we don't respect those claims unless we ask questions not only of their meaning but of their truth.[40] In like manner must religions be taught in theological curricula—in a conversational rather than a purely informational mode, and in an attempt to mediate between the religions and contemporary culture.

This, of course, is more easily said than done. If such courses must avoid a purely disinterested approach, they must also steer clear of the other extreme, more common in seminaries, of forming Christian judgments before one has been attentive to and intelligent about what the religions are really saying. Such an approach is usually predetermined to see the religions as either inferior to or as a preparation for Christ and Christianity. The multi-religious model we are calling for must enable conversation, not monologue.

But such conversation requires more than the careful, sensitive, involved study of another religious tradition; it also calls for a personal entrance into the other's world of experience. Earlier in this essay, I referred to this as a process of "passing over" via the analogical imagination. To carry out this process, seminary courses in other traditions will have to provide their students with opportunities genuinely to feel and to experiment with the truth of other ways. In a sense, students are to be encouraged, provisionally and always in a limited sense, *to be* Hindu or Buddhist or Muslim. How this can be done will depend on the ingenuity and boldness of the teacher. Passing over to another religious world can be facilitated, for instance, through some form of actual conversation with followers of other faiths, whether this takes place in the classroom or coffee shop. Christian theology students can be greatly helped by the I-Thou experience of existentially hearing the personal witness and feeling the committed praxis of someone who is following a different way of being religious. Besides such personal encounters, passing over to another religious world can also be fostered through "trying out"—or at least observing—the spiritual practices of other religions. This can best take place in zendos or ashrams or temples where students are enabled to participate in forms of meditation, or chanting, or the puja sacrifice, or daily prayers. Religions must be studied as lived realities, not only as cherished teachings.

Another form of passing over to other religious ways of being in the world can be realized though the praxis-oriented methodology suggested earlier. After a basic introductory course in "comparative religions," further courses, rather than dealing simply with more specific areas (e.g., the "history of Zen" or "Islamic mysticism") could be issue oriented. They could combine the ingredients of pluralism and oppression, and use areas of needed liberation as the starting points or shared context for establishing the common ground of genuine conversation. Courses on "Religions and Peace" or "Buddhism, Christianity, and Ecology," or "Feminist Voices in Muslim-Christian Dialogue" would be both more engaging of student interest and would provide a more effective hermeneutical link for both entering into and being challenged by other religious worlds.

Merely to add quality, theologically oriented courses on other religious traditions to the curriculum will not, in itself, achieve the intended goal of a multi-religious restructuring of theological education. If the conversation with other religions cannot, understandably, be the exclusive or dominant concern in theological reflection, neither can it be shunted off to the side track of a few required courses. What is needed and hoped for is that a conversation with other traditions may, to some extent, be "mainlined" into all courses in a Christian curriculum, especially those courses traditionally identified as systematic or ethical. By this I mean that in teaching a standard course on evil or redemption or church or the question of God, professors will inject into the discussions what other religious perspectives hold, how they sometimes radically differ, how they provoke Christian tradition to further reflection. Naturally, given the expertise and general background of most theological faculties, such dreams of mainlining an interreligious conversation into the general curriculum cannot be realized overnight. But they will never be realized at all unless the ideal is affirmed.

Although we cannot realistically expect either students or professors to be proficient in all the major religious traditions of the world, we can entertain more modest, yet nonetheless helpful, expectations. What can be expected—eventually of professors, more immediately of students—is that every Christian theologian have, as it were, a minor in one religious tradition other than Christianity. After taking a broad, introductory course in "comparative religions," seminary or divinity students should be encouraged (required?) to subspecialize in the history, beliefs, and spirituality of another non-Christian religious path. The goal would be for the student to become so "at home" in this other religious tradition that it would become a conversation partner for the student in the study of Christian theology. Thus a student who has subspecialized in Buddhism would not be able to interpret and evaluate Christian beliefs such as trinity or incarnation, or Christian practices such as baptism or eucharist, without hearing or feeling what a Buddhist might say to such a belief or practice, or what might be its Buddhist equivalent. Such a conversation partner can enhance, challenge, perhaps even invigorate the study of Christian theology.

In order to move toward this goal of providing conversational courses in other traditions and of including other religious perspectives in mainline courses, changes in the composition of a theological faculty are also required. No seminary or divinity school faculty should feel itself complete or properly balanced unless it includes one or more faculty persons specifically trained in one or more non-Christian traditions. This would require someone who knows the language(s) of the sacred texts and who has been steeped in the parent culture of the religion. Ideally, such persons should be able to represent the other tradition(s) not only academically but personally, not only with scholarly expertise but also with existential commitment. To have such a person or persons available for advice to the entire faculty, present at faculty meetings, in chapel, in the lounge, and at Christmas parties would contribute mightily to overcoming the mono-religious mentality of most theology programs and to "mainlining" an awareness of other religious perspectives into the school's courses and activities.

For the above practical suggestions to be properly assessed and possibly implemented, faculties and administrations of seminaries and divinity schools will first have to undergo a fundamental attitudinal shift (a conversion!). They will have to recognize intellectually and feel existentially that the theological enterprise must move from a mono-religious to a multi-religious structure. On such a conversion depends the future health of theological education—and of Christianity.

NOTES

1. Edward Farley, *The Fragility of Knowledge: Theological Education in the Church and the University* (Philadelphia: Fortress Press, 1988), 133.
2. Francis Schüssler Fiorenza, "Theological and Religious Studies: The Contest of the Faculties," in this volume, 17, chap. 4.
3. Farley, *The Fragility of Knowledge,* 128; see entire chap. 6.
4. Ibid., 148–62; David Tracy, *Blessed Rage for Order: The New Pluralism in Theology* (New York: Seabury Press, 1975), chap. 2; Schubert M. Ogden, *On Theology* (New York and San Francisco: Harper & Row, 1986).
5. Farley, *The Fragility of Knowledge,* 104.
6. Ibid., 125, emphasis mine.
7. Mark Kline Taylor, *Remembering Esperanza: A Cultural-Political Theology for North American Praxis* (Maryknoll, N.Y.: Orbis Books, 1990), chap. 1.
8. Francis Schüssler Fiorenza, *Foundational Theology: Jesus and the Church* (New York: Crossroad, 1984), 289; George Lindbeck, *The Nature of Doctrine: Religion and Theology in a Postliberal Age* (Philadelphia: Westminster Press, 1984); Richard Rorty, *Philosophy and the Mirror of Nature* (Princeton University Press, 1979); Richard J. Bernstein, *Beyond Objectivism and Relativism: Science, Hermeneutics, and Praxis* (Philadelphia: University of Pennsylvania Press, 1983).
9. See Rebecca S. Chopp, "Situating the Structure: Prophetic Feminism and Theological Education," in this volume, chap. 2, as well as her "Practical Theology and Liberation," in *Formation and Reflection: The Promise of Practical Theology* (Philadelphia: Fortress Press, 1987), 120–38.

10. See S. Mark Heim, *Is Christ the Only Way? Christian Faith in a Pluralistic World* (Valley Forge, Pa.: Judson Press, 1985), 33–38; Carl Braaten, "Christocentric Trinitarianism vs. Unitarian Theocentrism," *Journal of Ecumenical Studies* 24 (1987): 17–21.

11. Langdon Gilkey, "Plurality and Its Theological Implications," in *The Myth of Christian Uniqueness: Toward a Pluralistic Theology of Religions,* eds. John Hick and Paul F. Knitter (Maryknoll, N.Y.: Orbis Books, 1987), 39–40, 48.

12. Wilfred Cantwell Smith, *Faith of Other Men* (New York: Harper & Row, 1962), 132–33.

13. David Tracy, "On Crossing the Rubicon and Finding the Halys: Religious Pluralism and Christian Theology—Some Reflections" (Unpublished paper delivered at the Blaisdell Conference on Religion, Claremont, Calif., March, 1986), p. 22.

14. In what follows, I cannot go into the nature and requirements of authentic conversation. If space allowed, it would be an expansion on David Tracy's summary: "Conversation is a game with some hard rules: say only what you mean; say it as accurately as you can; listen to and respect what the other says, however different or other; be willing to correct or defend your opinions if challenged by the conversation partner; be willing to argue if necessary, to confront if demanded, to endure necessary conflict, to change your mind if the evidence suggests it." *Plurality and Ambiguity: Hermeneutics, Religion, Hope* (New York: Harper & Row, 1987), 19. See my own guidelines for dialogue in *No Other Name? A Critical Survey of Christian Attitudes Toward World Religions* (Maryknoll, N.Y.: Orbis Books, 1985), 207–13.

15. See W. C. Smith's case for a critical and corporate consciousness in *Towards a World Theology: Faith and the Comparative History of Religion* (Philadelphia: Westminster Press, 1981), 94ff; for Bernard Lonergan's transcendental principles, see his *Method in Theology* (New York: Herder & Herder, 1972), 3–25.

16. C. S. Peirce, quoted in Bernstein, *Beyond Objectivism and Relativism,* 224.

17. For an extensive treatment of the inherent corruptibility of knowledge from a theological perspective, see Farley, *The Fragility of Knowledge,* chap. 2.

18. Walter Benjamin, quoted in Tracy, *Plurality and Ambiguity,* 69.

19. Ibid., 73.

20. Fiorenza, "Theological and Religious Studies."

21. Paul Tillich, *The Future of Religions,* ed. Jerald C. Brauer (New York: Harper & Row, 1966), 31, 91.

22. Wilfred Cantwell Smith, "Theology and the World's Religious History," in *Toward a Universal Theology of Religion,* ed. Leonard Swidler (Maryknoll, N.Y.: Orbis Books, 1987), 55; see also Smith's "The World Church and the World History of Religion: The Theological Issue," *Proceedings of the Catholic Theological Society of America* 39 (1984): 52–68.

23. John B. Cobb, Jr., *Beyond Dialogue: Toward a Mutual Transformation of Christianity and Buddhism* (Philadelphia: Fortress Press, 1982).

24. Smith, *Towards a World Theology,* 101, 126.

25. Raimundo Panikkar, "*Rtatattva:* A Preface to a Hindu-Christian Theology," *Jeevadhara: A Journal of Christian Interpretations* 49 (1979): 13.

26. Fiorenza, "Theological and Religious Studies." For criticisms of Hick, Smith, and Knitter, see Cobb, *Beyond Dialogue,* 43–47; Gavin D'Costa, *Theology and Religious Pluralism: The Challenge of Other Religions* (London: Basil Blackwell, 1986), chap. 1; S. Mark Heim, "Thinking About Theocentric Christology," *Journal of Ecumenical Studies* 24 (1987): 1–16; William C. Placher, *Unapologetic Theology: A Christian Voice in a Pluralistic Conversation* (Louisville: Westminster/John Knox Press, 1989), 144–46, 152.

27. Placher, *Unapologetic Theology,* 13. Elsewhere, Placher states: "For the recently emerged *postliberal* theology, the theologian's task is more nearly simply to describe the Christian view of things. Postliberal theologians note ad hoc conjunctions and analogies with the questions and beliefs of non-Christians, but their primary concern is to preserve the Christian vision free of distortion" (p. 154). See esp. Placher's chaps. 7, 9–10. Lindbeck's *The Nature of Doctrine* remains the best-known statement of postliberal theology. For another statement, see William Werpehowski, "Ad Hoc Apologetics," *Journal of Religion* 66 (1986): 282–301.

28. See, for instance, James M. Gustafson, "The Sectarian Temptation: Reflections on Theology, the Church, and the University," *Proceedings of the Catholic Theological Society* 40 (1985): 83–94.

29. Placher, *Unapologetic Theology,* 112.

30. Mark Kline Taylor, "In Praise of Shaky Ground: The Liminal Christ and Cultural Pluralism," *Theology Today* 43 (1986): 36–51.

31. For a description of this process, see Tracy, *Plurality and Ambiguity,* 18–21, 90–93. See also John Dunne, *The Way of All the Earth* (New York: Macmillan, 1972), ix, 53.

32. Raimundo Panikkar holds that interreligious dialogue cannot be based on any theories or a world theology or common essence, but that what is needed is a "cosmic trust" in the process itself. See his "The Invisible Harmony: A Universal Theory of Religion or a Cosmic Confidence in Reality," in Smith, *Toward a World Theology of Religion,* 118–53.

33. Placher, *Unapologetic Theology,* 167–68. See Hans Frei, "Eberhard Busch's Biography of Karl Barth," in *Karl Barth in Re-View,* ed. H. Martin Rumscheidt (Pittsburgh: Pickwick Press, 1981), 114; and Werpehowski, "Ad Hoc Apologetics."

34. See the Introduction to this volume, pp. 7, 30.

35. Mark Kline Taylor, "Religion, Cultural Pluralism, and Liberating Praxis: In Conversation with the Work of Langdon Gilkey," *Journal of Religion* 71 (1991): 164. See also 157–59.

36. Karl Marx, "Contribution to the Critique of Hegel's Philosophy of Right: Introduction," in *Karl Marx's Early Writings,* ed. Quintin Hoare. (New York: Vintage Books, 1975), 245.

37. Tracy, *Plurality and Ambiguity,* p. 84.

38. Knitter, "Dialogue and Liberation," 26–32, and "Toward a Liberation Theology of Religions," in *The Myth of Christian Uniqueness,* 178–202.

39. I have tried to say more about how such a hermeneutical link functions in interreligious discourse in "Dialogue and Liberation," 22–26. See also John Hick, *An Interpretation of Religion: Human Responses to the Transcendent* (New Haven, Conn.: Yale University Press, 1989), 21–69; Fiorenza,

in this volume, chap. 4.

40. See Farley, *Fragility of Knowledge,* chap. 4.

6

Overcoming Alienation in Theological Education

Peter J. Paris

The purpose of this essay is to propose a possible solution to the problem of alienation that African American students continuously experience in predominantly white seminaries and divinity schools. Like many other institutions in our society, most theological schools continue to be in a state of transition from a racially exclusive past to a racially inclusive future. Unfortunately, these institutions have tended to view the entire civil rights struggle of the 1960s solely as an issue of African American access to white institutions. Accordingly, few have thought about the necessity of reforming themselves in order to meet the needs of African Americans, and virtually none have thought seriously about reciprocal benefits that would be derived from interracial association. Thus much energy has been exerted over the past decades in advocating the need for an academic ethos characterized by a heightened sensitivity and genuine responsiveness to the concerns of oppressed peoples in general and of African Americans in particular. How such an ethos might permeate all dimensions of theological education is the subject matter of this essay.

The moral claims of the civil rights movement of the late 1950s and early 1960s had a profound effect on numerous teachers, students, and administrators in theological education. Inspired by the persuasive oratory of Martin Luther King Jr. and by the immense courage of those who participated in the nonviolent resistance demonstrations, the moral sensibilities of many were transformed, and, similarly, their loyalty and commitment to the goals and strategies of the civil rights movement were increased. Such changes in moral attitudes, reinforced by various changes in the law, motivated many to respond positively to the various demands for racial justice both within and without their respective institutions. Thus it soon became a trend for seminaries and divinity schools to affirm the need for increased black student enrollment, and, accordingly, many special recruitment procedures, financial assistance programs, and other support systems were established.

Enlightened and motivated in varying ways by the wisdom implicit in the Black Consciousness Movement of the late 1960s, African American students soon issued demands for the inclusion of their religious experience in the educational curriculum, and that demand, in turn, implied the appointment of competent African American professors. Institutional responses to these demands tended to assume the form of either special programs in African American studies or the addition of elective courses in the subject area. In addition, academic enhancement programs were often provided, such as special conferences, lectures, and the like. Generally, however, theological institutions were slow to make full-time appointments of African Americans to their faculties, especially at the senior level. Some few institutions established special chairs in black studies, but most job profiles were designed to combine administrative and teaching functions so as to avoid the question of tenure. For varied reasons, many who did receive tenure-track appointments at the entrance level eventually failed to gain the coveted prize.

Although the admission of black students to many of

these schools was a novel event, to say nothing of the inclusion of black church studies in the curriculum, few anticipated any significant impact on theological education as such. In fact, many, then and now, looked upon the whole process as little more than an important institutional concession to the current trend of pluralizing the educational context with the addition of blacks, other minorities, and white women. Few could have predicted that the nascent black theology challenge was destined to become an academic movement effecting a profound influence on all subsequent research in African American religion.[1] The Society for the Study of Black Religion was founded in 1970 as a locus for black religious scholars to investigate critically the basic tenets of the Black Theology Movement in order to discern its implications for their own research and writing.[2] In short, a militant revisionist academic enterprise was soon underway challenging the most fundamental presuppositions of established Western theological scholarship. This movement soon gained dominance in all areas of black religious scholarship. Thus, for the first time in the history of religious academe, African Americans had a subject matter and a methodological perspective that was peculiarly their own and capable of rigorous academic defense. Ironically, all its major proponents had been well schooled in the content and methodologies of traditional Western scholarship.

Ambiguously related to the African American churches, the aim of this new theological scholarship was, on the one hand, to challenge those African American churches that had a history of political quietism and, on the other hand, to condemn the theology of the white churches that, it was claimed, had long reinforced societal structures of racial injustice. Hence it is not surprising that this new movement found open ears primarily among militant African American religious leaders in predominantly white denominational structures and among those whites in various "liberal" contexts who considered themselves to be progressive thinkers.

Similar alliances between African Americans and whites

in theological education have a long history. Hitherto, however, the relatively few African Americans trained in predominantly white theological institutions usually became pastors in African American congregations of predominantly white denominations or served in some other situation significantly linked to a white constituency. Similarly, those who received doctoral degrees were usually appointed to the faculties of African American colleges and universities. In every situation, they represented models of the white educational system, which, more often than not, they uncritically appropriated and passed on to their students.[3] Not surprisingly, these were often those who strongly opposed most of the tenets of the Black Consciousness Movement by resisting virtually all the demands militant black students were issuing for radical changes in the style and content of their education.

It is important to note, however, that from its genesis up to the present day, this nascent African American religious scholarship has had an ambiguous relationship with predominantly white theological institutions. The logic of the former implied rigorous criticism of the theological orientation of its white counterparts in both their teaching and writing. Ironically, most of these African American theologians were employed by the white institutions they were criticizing, doing their research and writing during sabbatical leave periods provided by the policies of those institutional adversaries and having their manuscripts published by publishing houses owned and controlled by white churches. Happily, none of this activity was deceptive, because all of it took place in the public spaces of classrooms, auditoriums, published journals, books, and the like. Like all prophets, these theologians also preferred to speak directly to those whom they sought to reform.

The moral significance of this situation is evidenced in two loci: (1) the values inherent in the prophetic aim of this newly emerging African American religious scholarship; and (2) the moral capacity of those predominantly white institutions that responded positively to student demands for the incorporation of the African American religious experience into their schools via faculty appointments and the teaching of specific courses. Thus, to a certain extent, several predominantly white theological schools facilitated the development and expansion of the Black Theology Movement. Yet for the most part, they have been reluctant to effect any major curricular changes. Rather, most programs in African American religion have tended to be addenda to the curricula and, thus, quite marginal to the central requirements of theological education. In other words, most institutions have been reluctant to think of African American studies as anything more than a special accommodation for African American students.

In terms of theological education, this ambiguous situation has led to a crisis of confidence among African American students. Inspired by the radical criticism of white theological scholarship explicitly argued by the Black Theology Movement, many African American students have a heightened attitude of suspicion toward the general curriculum of theological studies. Thus they have tended to register enthusiastically for all courses taught by African American teachers on the African American experience, although assiduously viewing most of the other academic requirements as necessary for matriculation but irrelevant for their ministry.[4] Thus African American theological scholarship has been a principal cause of the alienation of African American students from traditional theological studies by its convincing proof that over and against the "infidelity" of the Eurocentric churches, the African American churches have been "faithful" in their devotion to the authentic norm of Christianity. That is to say, the latter have sought the promotion of God's justice in the world, whereas the former have supported structures of racial injustice.

This crisis in confidence signals a fundamental problem that will increasingly threaten the viability of theological education for African Americans if not resolved in some deliberate way. It would be folly to underestimate the power of this threat. The problem we face is a possible contradiction in the theological curriculum itself. No theological school would permit the teaching of biblical fundamentalism and biblical historical criticism simultaneously because of the obvious contradiction such would imply. Similarly, we contend that the teaching of African American religion as a marginal addendum to the traditional curriculum of theological studies is also a contradiction because the former judges the latter as morally and theologically corrupt.

Although relatively few white students register for courses in African American studies, the brunt of the problem we describe is felt primarily by African American students who become increasingly alienated from the educational ethos of the institution. The marginalization of African American studies in the curriculum, along with the small number of African American faculty members, combine in keeping the threat constantly in check. Unfortunately, good personal relationships between African American and white students may often mask the problem itself. Similarly, the many and varied palliatives employed to keep the problem at management levels are all equally vulnerable each year to unpredictable explosive disruptions by frustrated, angry African American students. African American faculty members frequently find themselves in the difficult position of trying to mediate between the students and their white colleagues, both of whom look to them for understanding, support, and guidance.

In spite of the rhetorical style and emotional fervor of many of its most ardent proponents, African American theological studies, like the ecclesial tradition it seeks to explicate, is not a revolutionary movement in any strict sense; rather, it is a reform movement within a tradition in which both races can learn more from each other than is readily assumed by either. This perspective is rooted in the view that African American Christianity has always been a prophetic movement both explicitly and implicitly seeking to effect religious and moral changes in the thought and practice of white Christians both in their individual and associational lives.[5] It is the nature of all prophetic movements to call the unfaithful to turn away from their wrongdoing and to return in faithfulness to the tradition from which they have strayed. Thus prophets are watchdogs of the tradition and seek to reform those who stray from it.

The Two Functions and Two Theologies of the African American Churches

Although the African American churches have had a prophetic orientation toward the white churches, they have a long history of priestly and pastoral ministry among their own people. Long before they were able to express their prophetic character in any public way, the so-called invisible African American churches in the slave era nurtured in their people the discipline of religious and moral transcendence over their suffering as a means of maintaining their humanity while being treated in an inhuman way. Herein lies the story of how the African American churches gave rise to a survivalist theology that reflected the life-style of the people. Because survival is a necessary condition for social change, African American survival theology preceded African American liberation theology. In terms of biblical symbolism, slave Christianity tended to center more on the so-called theology of the wilderness (i.e., survival) than that of the promised land (i.e., salvific gift). Although the promise of the latter was an immense source of inspiration, the experience of freed slaves in northern cities, Canada, and elsewhere resulted in a destiny of dependency and deprivation rather than freedom and equality. Consequently, in that context, the promised land came to be viewed wholly in eschatological terms, whereas the pragmatic experience of coping with suffering preoccupied every dimension of the people's lives.

The meaning of life in the midst of the existential threat and actual experience of suffering is the subject matter of survival theology. In other words, how does one believe in God while suffering? How does God render help to suffering victims? This is the problem of theodicy that pervades the condition of oppressed peoples. It is the problem of Hagar who was betrayed by Abraham and Sarah and exiled from their care; the problem of Job; the problem of the Babylonian exile; the problem of the psalmist who felt forsaken by God; the problem of the passion and of the crucifixion of Christ.

Survival theology implies neither contentment with adversity nor the justification of social injustice. Rather, the maintenance, preservation, and enhancement of meaningful life comprise the primary concern of survival theology. "Making a way out of no way," "keeping body and soul together," "being alive and kicking," "remaining on this side of the grave" are all folk sayings that evidence the day-to-day practical defeat of suffering and social injustice.

Divine providence is a fundamental spiritual value for all oppressed peoples and particularly for African Americans. The ubiquitous possibility of death kept them humble before God. In fact, each day's survival was attributed to the protection of God, who was thanked continually for bestowing upon the people the capacity to transcend adversity. In their view, God's mercy and providence were manifested to them in the necessary conditions for survival: family life, a livable wage, good health, physical safety. Thus African Americans have always felt blessed by God when they had the necessary conditions for survival. Without them, they tended to pray trustingly, work diligently, and wait patiently for their restoration.

Thus maintaining one's humanity in the midst of oppression and suffering is a fundamental moral and religious problem. Yet African Americans have always recognized the insufficiency of a survivalist orientation to life, which they regularly sought to transcend by resisting unjust treatment in various ways. In general, however, their resistance was motivated by the desire not for revenge but, rather, for the restoration of racial justice. Such activities mark the presence of the prophetic tradition among African Americans—a tradition that the contemporary Black Theology Movement has sought to explicate.

African Americans and other minorities together with Third World students represent ecclesial traditions that have long wrestled with both survival- and protest-type problems, and they seek the necessary training that will enable them to relate new insights, knowledge, and skills to their inherited traditions of ministry. For effective ministry in their respective communities, African Americans and other minorities need training that is relevant to sociopolitical contexts that are characterized by structures of racial and economic injustice. They need to learn how to enable their people to sustain themselves psychologically and become empowered politically, economically, and culturally. They need to draw on the resources of the social sciences in their quest for relevant knowledge. The needs of these students require a learning context in which such concerns are pervasive in the curriculum and not merely the preserve of a few elective courses. They need an academic ethos quite different from that which presently dominates our theological schools—one that Gayraud Wilmore accurately describes in the following:

> It is, nevertheless, true that today Roman Catholic and Protestant theological seminaries (it is a somewhat different case for Orthodox institutions), for the most part, determine their curricula and institutional priorities according to the needs of churches that are composed primarily of the middle-aged, middle-class, white descendents of Western European people who live, for the most part, in predominantly white, nuclear family-centered, city-residential, suburban or small-town communities.
>
> There are, to be sure, diversities of various kinds in these communities. . . . But the salient fact is that they are more or less integrated by an ethos and worldview grounded in a common religious and cultural perspective, i.e., one containing common elements found in the

> national cultures of the North Atlantic Community—the U.S., Canada, Great Britain, Germany, the Netherlands, France and Spain (with later and lesser infusions from Italy, the Balkans and Eastern Europe). The understanding of the faith, and consequently of theological education, that is fostered by this majority population group is characteristically (though not exclusively) evangelical (i.e., Bible-centered, proclamatory, and oriented to renewal and revivalistic enlistment strategies). It is also mainly middle-class, mainly politically conservative, and accommodated to a private property, profit-motivated, free enterprise economy that is charged with the welfare and preservation of a burgeoning white, urban middle class—often suffused with an inordinate fear of differentness and given to the deliberate exclusion of the poor and non-white.[6]

I have quoted the above because it describes both accurately and succinctly the reigning contextual paradigm of theological education in predominantly white seminaries and divinity schools. All racial and ethnic diversity in their schools is brought under the control of this paradigm administratively and educationally. Any resolution of the problem we confront must aim at some effective change in this ethos such that both students and faculty, black and white alike, will welcome the constructive change as both theologically sound and educationally helpful. In other words, we seek a solution not for African Americans and minorities alone, but for all who seek a meaningful education for contemporary ministry. The problem affects the whole of theological education. The solution must do no less. In other words, seminaries should make every effort to model the type of world the gospel proclaims as God's will. Hence, all seminarians should be exposed to a curriculum wherein respect for and commitment to racial justice is not only implicitly affirmed but explicitly evidenced at its center. All seminarians should expect to receive adequate training in the requisite skills and thought needed to promote racial justice in their respective ministries.

A Dialogical Paradigm for Theological Education

The conditions of survival and liberation comprise the most fundamental requirements of human existence. Apart from these basic conditions there can be no freedom and, hence, no possibility of exercising any distinctively human activity. For the most part, the history of African Americans from slavery to the present time has been characterized by perpetual struggles for the realization of these conditions. The ministry of the African American churches has always striven to relate itself closely to the communal vision of freedom and the more proximate conditions of survival and liberation. Accordingly, the pastoral function of the churches correlated well with the many and varied survivalist endeavors of their people, whereas the prophetic function was naturally allied with liberationist activities. As conflicts have arisen from time to time between survivalist and liberationist activities, so also has conflict occurred between the pastoral and prophetic ministries of the churches. The tolerance of the latter for diverse ministries and theologies has aided in minimizing the conflict within the churches. Yet, in the community at large, conflicting styles of life have resulted from a habitual orientation to either survivalist or liberationist activities.

The Black Theology Movement of the past two decades has focused almost exclusively on the prophetic dimension of the African American church tradition, and this has been its great strength and novel contribution. As stated above, such a focus clearly highlights the discontinuities between the black and white religious traditions, with the one constantly calling the other to repentance and the latter doing little more than tolerating the presence of the former. This constitutes a divided household where the parts struggle against one another rather than seek the means of mutual support and enhancement.

The problem that confronts us is how a marginalized prophetic movement can become an integral part of a theological curriculum. Now if this be construed to imply a search for a way of effecting a compromise between prophets and nonprophets in order to achieve a more coherent context, then our efforts will be in vain. This is so because it is the nature of prophetic movements to speak the Word of God unambiguously and to call uncompromisingly for full obedience to God's love and justice.

In contemporary theological education, the prophetic challenge from African American religious scholars calls for fundamental reform in the content of the teaching, the principles of interpretation, the socio-religious formation of the instructors, to mention only a few. As with all prophets, the problem addressed is decidedly political, theological, and ethical. Hence, a radically new approach to theological education is needed in order to overcome the alienating process experienced by blacks and other minorities who come to theological education from outside the dominant mainstream of white American Protestantism. Apart from such a change, African American and other minority clergy will need to resist much of what they are presently taught lest they be trained for dysfunctional ministries in their respective communities. A major danger implicit in the present situation is that of African Americans and other minorities leaving seminary with a good foundation in the black prophetic tradition and little preparation in other areas of ministry that they will surely need. Without appropriate guidelines and relevant knowledge, they will be destined to adapt themselves uncritically to some "traditional" style of ministry in which they will be restrained from rendering much needed constructive leadership.

The structural answer to the problem we have been describing is not an easy one to discover, because any solution must serve the good of the whole as well as its diverse parts. Let me hasten to add, however, that many have tended to view the problem outlined in this essay as little more than an interest group concern that, if left unchecked in its demands, would assume an imperial orientation toward everyone else. Usually such a judgment issues out of a deep concern for power relationships and the desire on the part of those in power to resist significant change in the status quo. In my judgment, James Gustafson illustrates this problem:

> If there is a lesson in this history for the future, it is this: theological educators ought to be careful about their judgments about the scope and depth of social change, and careful about the weight those judgments carry in their proposals for reform of their enterprise.[7]

I agree that an institution should be careful about policy changes of every sort and that careful reasoning relative to the issues at stake should be the rule. But the caution Gustafson mentions is often understood to imply rigorous resistance to institutional change; in fact, his own contextual ethic exercises great care in assessing all relevant data while carefully avoiding prescriptive judgments and policies on many important issues of the day.

Given the presence of racial and ethnic minorities in predominantly white theological institutions and given the desire on the part of the latter to continue to encourage their presence, how can the educational process become less alienating and more enriching for all concerned? Clearly, theological education must be adequate in preparing ministers to meet the real needs of the people they serve. This requires training not only in the historical thought and practice of the Christian churches, as is presently the case, but also relevant study in the human sciences and the arts. In fact, this is presupposed by the prerequisite of an undergraduate degree prior to pursuing training for the ministry. Unfortunately, however, the undergraduate study is undertaken, more often than not, in isolation from one's vocational focus and hence is not preparatory for it in any elaborate sense. Inadequate vocational counseling of undergraduates leads most to assume that a major in religious studies is the best preparation for theological studies. This causes them to view everything else as necessary for the degree but irrelevant for ministry. Consequently, their lack of study in the human sciences and racial and ethnic studies constitutes a serious deficit in pursuing various types of ministry. Unfortunately, this deficiency cannot be overcome within the present structural arrangement for pursuing a master of divinity degree. Thus I propose a new approach to theological study based on a dialogical model that would enable significant ongoing relation with the human sciences and the arts while pursuing professional study for the ministry.

In other words, the gist of my proposal is that theological education be undertaken either within or in collaboration with a university. This proposal implies a reconceptualization of theological education that would result in a core program of study within the seminary or divinity school and as much as a year's study in university disciplines or programs considered relevant to the professional needs of the students. Obviously, the implementation of such a proposal would require an enhanced advisory system and, in many cases, special contractual arrangements between the seminary and the university.

Greater access to various disciplines and programs within the university is a necessary condition for overcoming the problem of alienation that African Americans presently encounter in theological education. They desire knowledge and skills that theological schools cannot offer due to their lack of the necessary learning resources. African American studies, urban studies, programs in criminal justice, public services, drug abuse, health and education, to mention only a few, must become more accessible to theological students, because therein lies the knowledge of the social realities that form the context for African American ministry. In fact, this process has already begun, as evidenced in the increasing number of African American ministers pursuing degrees in social work, education, law, criminal justice, public administration, and so forth, as supplementary expressions of their ministry. Civil rights activity, community organizational work, and electoral politics have long been other avenues of ministry for African Americans who gained the relevant knowledge for such activities via experience acquired outside the parameters of theological education. How much better it would be for African Americans and others to gain some of the relevant knowledge they need for ministry while in seminary, because it would give theological legitimation to their quest for relevant training. Further, it would enable theological education to view a variety of courses in university departments as integral to a theological education rather than tangential to it, as is currently the case.[8]

Such a dialogical relation between the seminary and the university would enable students to focus their entire program on study in specific directions. For example, those desirous of preparing themselves to serve oppressed communities would be helped to develop appropriate programs of study from a wide breadth of resources both within and without the theological schools themselves.

Developing an integral relation with various disciplines within the university is no novel venture for theological education. The disciplines of social ethics, pastoral care, Christian education, and history of religions are necessarily related dialogically with specific university disciplines. In fact, the biblical, historical, and theological disciplines are related respectively to archaeology, history, and philosophy. My proposal builds on that tradition in a different way. Instead of "domesticating" those university disciplines by subordinating them to the purposes of theological education, I propose a dialogical relation with them that makes no attempt to reshape them. Rather, I suggest a relation similar to that operative in the several joint degree programs between theology and law, between theology and social work, to mention only two. In brief, the relation is strictly dialogical, each discipline exhibiting mutual respect for the other.

The present need is for theological education to permit African Americans and other students as well who are concerned with specialized social ministries to draw more widely from various university disciplines and programs in order to gain the knowledge they need for their respective ministries.

Clearly, one of the chief functions of theological schools in this dialogical relationship would be that of raising normative questions and various other issues relative to the practice of ministry. This dialogical paradigm would enable academic faculties to raise to the center of their teaching and research the three major issues that have long preoccupied the World Council of Churches: justice, peace, and the integrity of creation. These constitute the most crucial theological, biblical, historical, ethical, and practical problems facing the world today and merit the sustained study of all who train for ministry. All the tools and resources of each relevant discipline would be brought to bear on these fundamental problems. The theological justification for such a focus would be grounded in an understanding of God as primarily a God of love and justice whose relationship to history and nature has been thwarted by the unloving and unjust desires and designs of human beings. Openness to such a focus would enable theological curricula to be arranged thematically; for example, the history of the church's relation to the problems of justice, peace, and the integrity of creation. Similarly, biblical studies, theology, ethics, and the various so-called practical disciplines would orient themselves more deliberately to these and related problems threatening the well-being of humanity.

The result, one hopes, would be the creation of a new ethos in theological education—an academic community of students and faculty concerned with the issues of suffering and oppressed peoples. Further, those who come to the theological schools from oppressed communities would find a relevant environment for sharing and learning. Further still, such an orientation would also provide the conditions that would enable both students and faculty to become aware of their many prejudices and other divisive attitudes bequeathed to them by their varied sociocultural backgrounds. Clearly, the special needs of those who choose to minister to suffering peoples, as well as the needs of others who desire to be advocates for social justice, could be met in such a program. Similarly, those who seek ways of leading middle-class congregations into various types of rescue activities, support programs, educational and advocacy projects could have their needs met as well.

In other words, a common ethos concerned with the

relation of Christianity to the preservation of and quest for justice, peace, and the integrity of creation does not imply that all the students would be in training for one type of ministry. Rather, diverse forms of ministry would not in any way be threatened by such an approach, because pastoral and prophetic functions have always been integral to Christian ministry. It is hoped that the dialogical paradigm would keep the pastoral and prophetic functions united by demonstrating their complementarity. That is to say, the conflicts between the pastoral and prophetic functions would no longer be characterized by the type of polarized anger that so often attends them. Rather, such conflicts would take place in a larger context where the entire theological community would have an interest in the issues involved as well as contributions to make to their resolution by virtue of the educational focus permeating their various programs of study. Such a dialogical approach would greatly help those who are the bearers of the prophetic mission by bringing academic criticism to bear on their mission itself. In that way, these ministers could help preserve the prophetic knowledge from becoming corrupted by failing to discern its limitations;[9] that is, those limitations implied by the criticisms that issue from feminist, womanist, and other social critiques as well as various imperial claims implicit in the dogmatic nature of the black theology project. And, make no mistake, black theology is dogmatic theology.

> Liberation theology is dogmatic theology, and black theology is no exception. That is to say, both possess a fixed, uncritical understanding of the substance and meaning of the Christian faith. Both have formulated their respective understandings in definitive ways. By conjoining the essence of Christianity with the liberation struggle of the oppressed, liberation theology has become a school of thought that aims at systematization. In claiming possession of the truth it claims to be the authority for all normative thought and practice. In other words, as with every dogmatic theology, discipleship is the only appropriate response black theology seeks.[10]

Thus adequate theological preparation for the contemporary ministry of African Americans in particular and all others in general requires significant relationships with the human sciences and the arts. Various specialized ministries in law, social work, education, and government have already seen the value of such a dialogical approach. Clearly, no school can do everything in this respect, and no one person can become proficient in every field. The viability of such a program would depend a great deal on its advisory apparatus.

The above dialogical proposal implies a new relationship between the seminary and the university, drawing upon the resources of both in preparing men and women for relevant ministries of pastoral care and prophetic witness in our contemporary world. We have set forth the threefold themes of the World Council of Churches—namely, justice, peace, and the integrity of creation—as principles of unity for the theological curriculum as a whole. Our proposal implies that the openness of the seminary to the university could liberate it from its present state of narrow professionalism, which is not only alienating to African Americans and other minorities, but is inadequate for training *anyone* for ministry in our day. Similarly, the adoption of the World Council of Churches thematic program as a guiding principle could liberate seminaries from a narrow denominationalism that characterizes so many of our schools. Finally, a focus on peace, justice, and the integrity of creation necessitates respectful dialogue with the many and varied theological voices of the world community. Such a process would militate against the domination of any one voice, thus alleviating the primary cause of alienation in theological education.

NOTES

1. An excellent discussion of the origin of the Black Theology Movement is contained in various chapters in James H. Cone, *For My People: Black Theology and the Black Church* (New York: Orbis Books, 1984).

2. The Society for the Study of Black Religion was founded in 1970. All blacks teaching in seminaries either full-time or part-time were invited to become members. The initial membership list was less than fifty. Major leaders in its formation were Charles Shelby Rooks, James H. Cone, Charles H. Long, and Gayraud S. Wilmore. A brief history of the society's founding is contained in Charles Shelby Rooks, *Revolution in Zion: Reshaping African American Ministry, 1960–1974* (New York: The Pilgrim Press, 1990).

3. One of the most important analyses of this phenomenon is found in Harold Cruse, *The Crisis of the Negro Intellectual* (New York: William Morrow, 1967).

4. Unhappily, black students often avoid taking more traditional courses taught by black instructors and, hence, unwittingly, fail to see how black scholars attend to classical texts and traditional scholarship.

5. This argument is fully demonstrated in the author's *The Social Teaching of the Black Churches* (Philadelphia: Fortress Press, 1986). It is an argument that is contrary to various attempts of others to ground the primary Christian sources in a normative black nationalist perspective, as Albert Cleage sought to demonstrate in his writings. See Albert Cleage, *The Black Messiah* (New York: Sheed & Ward, 1968), and *Black Christian Nationalism: New Directions for the Black Church* (New York: William Morrow, 1972).

6. Gayraud S. Wilmore, "Theological Education in a World of Religious and Other Diversities," suppl., *Theological Education* 23 (1987): 150–51.

7. James M. Gustafson, "Reflections on the Literature on Theological Education Published Between 1955–1985," suppl. 2, *Theological Education* 24 (1988): 19–20.

8. For example, the present joint program in Afro-American studies between Princeton University and Princeton Theological Seminary enabling a senior concentration in Afro-American Studies for Ministry is, in part, illustrative of this proposal. Its deficiency, however, is its limitation to the senior year, which makes it less than integral to the student's whole program.

9. Edward Farley, *The Fragility of Knowledge: Theological Education in the Church and the University* (Philadelphia: Fortress Press, 1988), 26.

10. Peter J. Paris, "The Task of Religious Social Ethics in Light of Black Theology," in *Liberation and Ethics: Essays in Religious Social Ethics in Honor of Gibson Winter,* eds. Charles Amjad-Ali and W. Alvin Pitcher (Chicago: Center for the Scientific Study of Religion, 1985), 135.

7

Christian Social Ethics as a Theological Discipline

Thomas W. Ogletree

Edward Farley has heightened our consciousness of the difficulties contemporary theological faculties have in providing a credible rationale for their enterprise.[1] These difficulties have two principal sources. To begin with, there has been a proliferation of specialized subdisciplines within theological studies. These subdisciplines have, quite rightly, made systematic use of various companion disciplines in the academy in pursuing their inquiries. Inevitably, they bear the stamp of the materials and methods they use. In the midst of such a multiplicity of approaches, however, it is no longer clear that work within the theological specialties amounts to the critical investigation of a common subject matter.

At the same time, there is growing awareness in the university of the plurality of religious communities and subcommunities within the contemporary world. Not infrequently, these communities have significantly differing sensibilities about what constitutes authentic religious existence. As a result, they do not easily converse with one another about shared or overlapping concerns. Given this state of affairs, theology appears by its nature to be tradition specific and hence incapable of encompassing within a single academic enterprise a constructive interest in the beliefs and practices of multiple religious traditions.

Because of multiple critical investigations and multiple views of religious existence, theology is on the verge of disintegrating as an identifiable field of knowledge. Not surprisingly, religious studies, which are largely forms of social and cultural studies, increasingly replace theological studies in the university.

The Place of Specialization in Theological Studies

In this essay I will not attempt to resolve the problems of the unity and integrity of theology, still less to meet the challenge of establishing critical theological inquiries that cut across diverse religious perspectives. My interest is more restricted. I wish to offer a way of thinking about specialization within theological studies that might simultaneously advance our insight into theology as a proper subject matter for the contemporary university. More specifically, I will provide an account of Christian social ethics as a theological discipline and suggest how work in this subspecialty might contribute to theological studies as a whole.

In effect, I will be affirming the importance of specialization within theological studies and also insisting upon the necessity of linking such studies to identifiable religious traditions. Although these developments may have complicated our attempts to conceive of theology as a genuine field of knowledge appropriate for the university, they are not, I would contend, the root causes of our problems. Rather, those causes have to do with the difficulty of sustaining credible public understandings of religion in secular and religiously plural societies.

Christian Social Ethics as a Vantage Point on Theology

My basic thesis is that the various theological specialties are not components or subdivisions of theological study, but rather distinctive vantage points on the subject matter of theology envisioned as a whole. On the one hand, none of the several vantage points has privileged standing in relation to the others, for none can finally grasp conceptually what constitutes the whole. In this respect, the whole is more apprehended than comprehended. On the other hand, some sense of the whole is presupposed if not explicitly stated in any adequate articulation of the subdisciplines of theology. Consequently, focused attention on any one of the subspecialties has the potential of significantly enriching, modifying, or perhaps qualifying all facets of theological study.

As far as I can see, moreover, there is no fixed number of subspecialties that might complete the spectrum of theological studies. Rather, there are as many or as few subspecialties as may prove practically illuminating in the quest for theological understanding. For that matter, there are no clear and fixed boundaries that properly separate the subspecialties within theology, nor can any subgroup of scholars legitimately claim exclusive rights to the critical study of particular materials. Students of theology continually cross existing boundaries among theological subfields when such a move serves a particular investigation. They do so quite properly, provided they exercise due regard for prior critical accomplishments within the subfields they enter. Thus limitations on the number of theological subspecialties and delineations of their proper boundaries are more practical than theoretical.[2]

For this view of specialization, the twin problems of the unity and integrity of theological studies reside not simply in the interfaces of the several subspecialties within theology. They are already present within the subspecialties themselves. Each of the subspecialties requires for its own critical investigations a conception of the distinctive subject matter of theology. Without such a conception, it cannot establish itself as a form of theological study. But once the subspecialties are adequately grasped as forms of theological study, then their relations to one another need not be so problematic. Moreover, insofar as we can successfully identify the distinctive subject matter of theology, we will be in a better position to construct manageable frames of reference for attending critically to multiple patterns of religious existence in the contemporary world.

What then is the subject matter of theology? How shall we identify and explicate it? Farley's proposals are promising. In the most general terms, he suggests, theology has to do with the divine mysteries that undergird and suffuse the universe. We can attend to these mysteries, however, only as they are manifest to human awareness and as human beings are responsive to them in concrete forms of religious life. In Christian contexts, this responsiveness is called "faith," conceived as an all-encompassing way of existing in the world. Theology, then, is the "wisdom and critical reflection attending faith."[3]

Because of its orientation to the elemental mysteries of the universe, Farley rightly observes, the subject matter of theology cannot be conceived as a specifiable segment of reality. Unlike the sciences, for example, theology cannot be located on a "world territorial map" of scholarly disciplines, each of which occupies itself with some portion of reality. It is more akin to philosophy, because it concerns itself with matters that bear upon all aspects of existence.[4] In effect, theology is for Farley a vantage point on the whole of reality. My intention here is to extend his claim to the subspecialties of theology as well. The subspecialties themselves are not segments of theology, but rather particular ways of articulating the mysteries with which theology is occupied. They seek to relate those mysteries to certain facets of experience or patterns of acting or lines of thinking or modes of creativity within the worldly existence of concrete communities of faith.

If Christian ethics is to be grasped as a theological subspecialty, then we must specify its distinctive ways of attending to the divine mysteries that awaken and sustain faith existence. Christian ethical inquiries, I would contend, focus on human accountabilities for the well-being of the creaturely realm. Historically, these inquiries have highlighted human well-being within a context of accountability to God. In a twentieth-century context, however, we can no longer take for granted the viability of the natural environment. Our collective activities profoundly impact the earth's capacities to sustain life of all sorts, not human life alone. Consequently, our ethical reflections embrace our accountabilities for the earth's ecosystem as well.

The theological substance of Christian ethics stems from the fact that we interpret and assess our human accountabilities in terms of the divine mysteries manifest to faith. Indeed, for a Christian perspective, such accountabilities are integral features of our responsiveness to those mysteries. To apprehend aright the divine mysteries is not to become preoccupied with God or caught up in the contemplation of God in isolation from our ongoing involvements with the world; rather, it is to discover ourselves both empowered and summoned by God in accountability for the world and its well-being. It is to take delight in our fellow human beings in the context of the divine life; it is to enter with them into covenants of mutual regard and care in terms of our covenant with God. Likewise, it is to relish the earth and its beauty as the creation of God even as we use its resources for our subsistence, all the while honoring the earth's limits and protecting the conditions for its continual renewal.[5]

The ethical interest in human accountabilities before God and our fellow creatures, then, is of a piece with our recognition of God's beauty, trustworthiness, and compassion. It conveys our sense of being drawn toward the mysteries of God in faith existence as we strive to live up to the moral claims that rest upon us as creatures of God.

Unfolding the Structure of Theology in Christian Ethics

In concert with Farley, I have portrayed theology as critical reflection on the wisdom and understanding accompanying faith existence. I have argued that Christian ethics is not a subsection of such reflection, but rather a distinctive vantage point on the mysteries that establish faith existence. This vantage point concerns the totality of those mysteries and also the totality of faith existence, but in terms of their bearing on human accountabilities for creaturely well-being. Consequently, there is no aspect of theological study that does not play a role in Christian ethics insofar as it bears upon those accountabilities. In turn, attention to these accountabilities has implications for vantage points represented in the other theological subspecialties.

How then are we to unpack the various aspects of human accountabilities that belong to the faith existence of Christians? Like Farley, I would note that faith's ways of existing are borne by religious traditions that shape the life and thought of communities of faith enduring over time. These traditions govern our manner of being in the world as persons of faith. In turn, our appropriation of formative religious traditions is conditioned by our social and cultural involvements, both within the communities of faith to which we belong, but also in the larger societies of which we are a part. In more concrete terms, therefore, the task of theology is to interpret and mediate authentic traditions of faith existence in their bearing on the communal practice of concrete communities of faith in contemporary social worlds.

With this set of understandings, theological inquiries consist essentially in interpretative activities of various sorts. This insight has led Farley to suggest that the structure of theology can best be displayed by describing its constituent modes of interpreting. He attempts to unfold that structure by identifying the modalities of interpretation that encompass the primary facets of faith existence. Actually, these modalities belong to life situations as such. As Farley puts it, "faith is not a discrete life situation but a way of being in life situations."[6] Farley's proposal is that the modalities of interpretation might outline the basic structures of theological inquiry.[7]

In structuring work in Christian social ethics, I will follow Farley's attempt to identify modalities of interpretation that compose faith existence, though I am not at all points in full agreement with his specific account of those modes. There is, however, one basic difference in my approach. Farley appears to view the modes of interpretation as possible ways of delineating the subspecialties within theology. Because I consider the subspecialties as vantage points on the whole of theology, I view these modes of interpretation as operative within each of the subspecialties. Thus, instead of ordering relations among the subspecialties, they guide critical investigations within them.

In principle, the same modes of interpretation should be manifest within all subspecialties, though perhaps with different weightings depending upon the controlling cognitive interests. In practice, we do not need to establish a definitive account of the relevant modes of interpretation before using Farley's fruitful suggestion. My attempt here will be to elaborate the modes of interpretation most pertinent to studies in Christian social ethics and to show how they might structure those studies. Further inquiries will disclose the value of this effort for the other subspecialties.

When we begin to unfold the structures that order ethical inquiries, two modalities of interpretation stand out, one relating to the practical activity of human beings and the other to social situations. These two modalities are intimately interconnected. On the one hand, practical human activity always occurs in concrete social and cultural situations, which means that it is ordered by institutions, social movements, their organizational expressions, and by the offices and roles we fill within these various processes. On the other hand, our interest in situations is governed by our accountabilities. We seek faithful yet realistic ways of acting in concrete social situations that will promote creaturely well-being in accordance with the divine promises.

In what follows, I will outline the interests that govern these two modalities of interpretation in Christian social ethics. I will also indicate how other modalities of interpretation crucial to theology come into play. The interest is to establish Christian social ethics as theological inquiry and to show its import for all aspects of theological study.

Practical Human Activity: The Structures of Moral Accountability in Faith Existence

The accent on accountability in Christian ethics presupposes that we are capable of more or less independent action, that for better or worse our actions have consequences for the creaturely realm, and finally, that our actions are subject to a valuative assessment, as congruent with or contrary to the promises accorded faith existence.

In my previous work, I have drawn upon phenomenological studies to formulate a theory of action that displays the moral significance of action. I used this theory as an interpretative guide for the critical appropriation of moral understandings contained in classic Christian traditions.[8] If sound, however, the theory should have relevance for any critical study of ethics, whether it be philosophical or theological, whether it be Christian or Jewish or Buddhist or perhaps comparative in its religious orientation. Here my intent is to develop the interest in practice in closer connection with the concrete social situations that organize human activity, and to do so in terms of the ethical vantage point on faith existence.

The terms *practice* and *action* are somewhat interchangeable. Practice suggests the repetition, even routinization, of particular patterns of acting, perhaps until they are virtually "second nature." Action may refer to a unique response or initiative within a particular situation. Action in this latter sense requires fresh deliberation and judgment about what is to be done. Specialists in ethics have tended to give the greatest attention to unique and conflict-laden situations of choice. After all, such situations present the most interesting problems for reflection. In most actual life situations, however, ongoing patterns of practice have by far the most importance for creaturely well-being precisely because they furnish order to everyday social interactions. However, the term *action* may also be used in reference to the basic structure of human activity, for example, in discussions of theories of action. In the latter case, it embraces both unique actions and routinized patterns of social practice.

In the structural sense just noted, Christian ethics centers in critical reflection on the moral dimensions of action. More specifically, it investigates the normative standards that regulate and guide action within the larger horizon of faith existence. Social ethics is a subdivision of Christian ethics that highlights the social contexts and forms of human action.

Action is, of course, more than its moral dimensions. Indeed, in the greater part of our day-to-day activity, the moral interest is by no means paramount. We work. We maintain the spaces where we live and work. We provide for our daily sustenance. We take part in ritual acts that maintain our relations with fellow human beings and renew a common world. We play and relax. We visit with friends. We spend time with those we love. Even actions that are central to communities of faith are not primarily moral in their import. There are liturgical acts, acts of instruction, acts of pastoral care, acts of collective deliberation about communal goals and objectives. At the same time, action of all sorts invariably has its moral dimensions, so that it is always possible to adopt a moral point of view on action.

Ethical discourse about human accountability has characteristically revolved around three sets of categories: obligations (or duties) and prohibitions, values and disvalues, and virtues and vices. These categories structure the ethical interest in human activity.

Obligations and the Conditions of Existence

Obligations and prohibitions have to do with the basic conditions of existence insofar as their effective operation is in our power. Obligations specify our responsibilities for sustaining basic life conditions. Prohibitions forbid overt actions that violate them. Obligations and prohibitions regulate human action. They define binding requirements for action that we must satisfy whatever else we might also choose to do, and they set limits to morally acceptable actions that we must honor in pursuing our various objectives. Their moral function is to sustain space for creaturely well-being insofar as the maintenance of such space is contingent on human activity. Normally, obligations and prohibitions cannot be overridden except where it can be shown that setting aside or violating a particular requirement promises in a contingent set of circumstances to further or protect the good they are designed to maintain.

For Christians, moral obligations and prohibitions enter into faith existence as divine commands or imperatives. They are integral features of a covenant of grace first offered by God to Israel. This same covenant was subsequently renewed in Jesus Christ in the face of persistent human failures and violations. In its renewal, the promises of the covenant were extended to all humankind. In that extension, they assumed diverse forms in multiple social and cultural settings. Christians hope for the ultimate completion of an all-encompassing covenantal communion, when God becomes "all and in all."

Theological themes do not simply provide divine sanction for obligations and prohibitions to which human beings are already subject, as though their function were simply to undergird human motivation to moral responsibility. By firmly placing the moral life within an environment of grace, these themes profoundly impact the character, scope, and even the content of the moral life. They transform the anxious delineation of rights and obligations into generosity and trust, the giving and receiving of life in the unfolding rhythms of grace. They point to the fulfillment of moral obligation in enjoyment —the enjoyment of all creatures of the earth in the context of our enjoyment of God.

Because their function is essentially regulative, obligations and prohibitions cannot exhaust the substance of the moral life. Their role is to protect the fundamental moral conditions of creaturely existence. They are, as it were, guardians of the boundaries of such existence: what must be done, what may not be done. Our everyday discourse discloses limitations in the simple two-value logic of these basic categories. To convey our moral sensibilities about various sorts of actions, we frequently turn to a range of intermediate expressions poised somewhere between the straightforward obligation and the unequivocal prohibition. These intermediate expressions furnish imprecise yet finely nuanced gradations of judgment for the moral assessment of action.

On the positive side, there is a scale of actions that are urged, praised, commended, desired, normally expected, approved, though not, strictly speaking, commanded or required. On the negative side, there is a contrasting scale of actions that are fully accepted (almost as though they were morally indifferent), permitted (though hardly praised), tolerated (usually with some discomfort), disapproved, and finally, actively discouraged, though not yet altogether prohibited. These gradations point to the second set of moral categories, those articulating values and disvalues. It is the latter that fill in the moral substance of these intermediary terms in guiding human activity.

Values and the Substantive Goals of Action

The second set of moral considerations is directed to the telos of existence. It conveys our aspiration after the fullness of creaturely well-being, again, insofar as it can be affected by our actions. It facilitates our reflections on the total meaning of action, embracing yet surpassing the more precisely defined regulative principles. Indeed, it identifies the ends that the regulative principles ultimately serve. These latter considerations are expressed as values and disvalues.

Values are notions that display, both for ourselves and others, what we conceive to be good about various realities, processes, or states of affairs in our world. Values are essentially ideas, not concrete realities. They express the purposes served by human action. In so doing, they furnish action its motivating ground. It is in reference to our value priorities that we justify particular action choices. In situations of choice, we adopt courses of action likely to result in outcomes that favor the values we prize. Disvalues in contrast convey what we judge to be bad about various realities in our world. The latter we seek to avoid or diminish. (The term *evil* is probably better seen as the negation or perversion of basic obligations and prohibitions because it does not so readily admit of gradations, despite our talk of "lesser evils.")

Value is not exclusively a moral term.[9] Indeed, there are as many sorts of values as there are regions of experience where we distinguish good or bad, better or worse. Values have to do with qualitative comparisons among various kinds of realities. As one identifiable value-type among others, moral values are associated with the integrity of persons, groups, communities, whole societies, and finally, a comprehensive world order.

A moral perspective on values concerns a comprehensive ordering of values. It involves discriminating judgments about value relationships. Through critical reflection, we strive for value harmonies—values that mutually enrich one another and that resist polluting disvalues. We also face up to value conflicts with difficult trade-offs, for example, a long, healthy life on an even keel versus a shorter life full of uncertainties but with highly pleasurable gratifications. Many values that offer attractive life possibilities are, of course, essentially incompatible. We then have to decide what matters most, thereby rejecting arrangements that jeopardize our more encompassing sense of the good.

A moral ordering of values specifies a pattern of life that promises fulfillment to human beings in their personal and communal existence. In Christian ethics, such an encompassing vision is characteristically conveyed in primal images—the coming realm of God, the beloved community, the realization of God's shalom—or perhaps by way of abstract concepts such as justice, freedom, peace. Constructive work in Christian ethics, therefore, consists of critical interpretations of such notions in their bearing on a normative ordering of values.

Unlike obligations and prohibitions, which refer directly

to specific kinds of actions, values concern situations, processes, or states of affairs that are the likely consequences of human actions. In this respect, they are related to action only indirectly, by way of the anticipated ends of action. This indirection is a reminder that the substantive goods we seek are not altogether in our control. We can state the point more strongly: no matter how carefully we plan and calculate, we cannot fully predict the outcome of our actions, especially in complex social situations. Indeed, the more complex the situation, the less we are able to predict or control what will follow from what we do. And when it comes to our grand, encompassing visions of creaturely well-being, we are often unable to devise any practical courses of action likely to promote the good we seek.

In practical planning, values have the greater moral import when we can translate them into measurable objectives likely to be furthered by identifiable courses of action. Even in this context, the better part of wisdom is to act in ways that themselves already embody the ends we seek; for although the ends may justify the means, it is equally the case that the means tend to determine the ends. The Christian sense of hope bestows moral significance on patient waiting and faithful enduring when no realistic ways are open for furthering God's encompassing vision for creation.

Ethical reflection on action discloses the fact that a broad interest in values is more elemental than a cognitive interest in truth, that is, simply knowing what is the case about some aspect of reality. Indeed, our value-laden involvements with the world are what generate specifically cognitive interests. It is because our valuative attachments have high importance in the economy of our lives that we urgently want to know whether and to what degree they have a basis in reality! As a cognitive notion, truth appears as one value among others in the total field of values. Universities recognize this fact when they include in their programs of study critical reflection on values and value harmonies.[10]

Morally speaking, truth is not in the first instance a

cognitive matter at all. It has to do with the requisites of human discourse: the obligation to tell the truth and the prohibition against deceit or lying. The values served are authentic human communication, mutual understanding, openness, trust, community. The accompanying virtue is, of course, truthfulness, a deep-seated disposition to tell the truth.

To sum up, obligations and duties are related to the basic conditions of creaturely well-being; values and value harmonies, to the total creaturely good. As expressions of faith existence, both of these interests are directed to the goodness, beauty, and majesty of God. We should not overstate the distinction between obligations and values. The life conditions we are obliged to sustain have moral significance because they foster values we honor. Likewise, we promote certain values because we sense that we are obligated to do so. These two modes of discourse flow into each other at every point, even though they represent contrasting styles of reasoning.[11]

Virtues and the Excellencies of Moral Actors

There is a third set of moral considerations that is also crucial to practice. This set has to do with the identity and integrity of the moral actor. It specifies strengths, cultivated through processes of maturation, that give a person the capacity for moral judgment and action. The relevant moral strengths consist of basic dispositions and attitudes that orient moral actors to concrete life situations in appropriate ways. They include skills in deliberation that reflect accumulated moral wisdom. Of special importance, however, are our developed capacities to handle our passions and feelings—our desires, our ambition, our greed, our anger, our fear—so that these drives and emotions become resources that energize morally good actions, not forces that overwhelm or thwart a moral response to the world.

In classical thought, moral considerations of this sort were articulated in a theory of virtues, that is, excellencies of character that are prerequisite to moral action.[12] In the Reformation traditions, moral strengths were interpreted as fruits of the pivotal relationships that constitute our existence as persons of faith, especially the relation with God, reflected in the transforming presence of God's Spirit in human life. In this context, virtues are not habits that an individual actor has cultivated, but rather stable accompaniments of significant relationships to which an actor is bound. In this respect, the Reformation traditions press us toward a relational theory of virtues. A major challenge to constructive thought in Christian ethics is to work out in a coherent conception the role that relationships, passions, feelings, and ongoing life disciplines have in the economy of the self's moral existence.

A theory of virtues moves us beyond the sphere of action as such to an account of human beings as moral actors. In Christian ethics, this account draws upon a broad range of theological themes, from anthropology to classical doctrines of sin, grace, forgiveness, and redemption, to ecclesiology. It uses as well contributions from developmental psychology and social psychology. Its normative content is provided by accounts of moral excellence: the self's settled dispositions to act courageously, temperately, justly, prudently; or the self's capacity to fulfill the two great commandments, the love of God and neighbor. The crucial point here is that a theory of virtues also has direct bearing on practice.[13] It concerns our accountability not just for our actions, but more fundamentally, for our character, for the kinds of persons we have become and are becoming.

Action presupposes concrete actors who are capable of determining their purposes and acting to achieve them. It is only as concrete actors occupying particular positions within a social system that we recognize our obligations and rank the values we prize. Commandments, laws, principles, rules, values—these notions are impotent unless concrete human beings use them as guides in responding to specific life situations. Indeed, our capacity to comprehend moral norms itself presupposes the achievement of a certain level of moral strength. We cannot grasp moral obligations that we are unable to honor in our actions; and the greater our capacities for moral action, the deeper and richer is our discernment of the moral meaning of the situations in which we find ourselves. It is as total selves that we deliberate, decide, and act. Similar points could be made about values and their promotion in human life. Thus a theory of virtues is, like theories of values and obligations, an integral part of a hermeneutic of action.

The Critical Study of Social Situations: The Concrete Context of Christian Practice

Action occurs in particular social and cultural settings. Consequently, attention to practical human activity leads to an examination of social situations. For Christian social ethics, the interest in social situations is governed by the accountabilities of faith existence. Faith existence is sustained by concrete communities that mediate authentic traditions of faith over time. It is through participation in such communities that Christians orient themselves to the wider social world. Thus Christian social thought is a fruit of the social practice of Christian churches and their affiliated associations and organizations.

The churches already belong to a social world whose composition has profoundly influenced their character. The experiences they have gained through their interactions with the larger society inform their witness to the social order and their contributions to its development. At varying levels of awareness, Christian thinkers have normally taken account of the church's social location in formulating their social thought. The critical development of Christian social ethics requires self-conscious attention to this context.[14]

The task of Christian social ethics is twofold: it is to help Christian people reflect on their social roles and their realistic possibilities for influencing the direction of social evolution; and it is to discover ways in which Christians can collaborate with persons of different religious and moral orientations in working toward a shared vision of a common good. In both instances, a critical grasp of social realities is essential to studies in Christian social ethics.

Societies are historical phenomena. They have beginnings in time and unfold in particular ways in the course of their development, perhaps renewing themselves and even undergoing remarkable transformations without losing a sense of their continuity with the past. As historical phenomena, they can also grow old, lapse into decline, and eventually collapse, perhaps giving way to new social formations through interactions with more dynamic neighboring societies. Despite the broad ranges of social variation, however, societies have certain requisites that bestow common characteristics upon them. The study of society takes account of both the functional requisites of social order and their distinctive patterns of evolution over time. Christian social ethics involves, therefore, a combination of historical thinking and social analysis.

Social Analysis: the Human Sciences and Critical-Ethical Reflection

The systematic interest in the structural-functional aspects of situations stems from the fact that human societies cannot exist at all unless they are able to accomplish certain essential things in the ordering of human relationships. Societies must, for example, guarantee their members a measure of physical security, maintain conditions for the production and distribution of the means of subsistence, nurture and educate the young, and build a sense of social cohesion capable of reinforcing social requirements. Although societies can provide for these functions in an amazing variety of ways, the variety is not endless. It revolves around a relatively limited set of possibilities. The social sciences furnish a substantial body of knowledge that sheds light on basic social structures and their primary social functions.

The social sciences have not been an unmixed blessing for Christian ethics. Paradigms of empirical research initially presumed the possibility of explaining the phenomena of experience on the basis of behavioral laws. This conception of explanation implied a deterministic view of social reality. It rendered naive the belief of moralists that human action flows from subjective resolve. Indeed, for the empirical sciences action ceased to be an intelligible concept at all. Behavior became the overriding category. The prospects of scientific explanation appeared to undermine the possibility of ethics.

In order to use the sciences in social analysis, students of ethics had to clarify the nature and limits of scientific explanation, especially as applied to human behavior. This problem did not prove to be so difficult. One simply had to display the abstractness of empirical scientific research, that is, its concentration on selected features of experience considered in isolation from their concrete occurrence. One could then show that the moral point of view dealt with aspects of experience that escaped the net of scientific abstraction. As is well known, Immanuel Kant's critical philosophy provided the decisive model for this delimitation of the empirical sciences. The more difficult problem was to conceptualize within a moral point of view the contribution of the social sciences to an understanding of social reality. This latter task continues to challenge social-ethical inquiry.[15]

In general, the social sciences enable us to isolate dynamics in social existence that condition and regulate human activity. These factors constrain, channel, and even enhance action possibilities, but they do not finally determine action. In Paul Ricoeur's happy phrase, "they incline, but without necessity."[16] Consequently, although knowledge of these factors can vastly expand our comprehension of human behavior, it does not equip us, not even in principle, to give full explanations of what human beings might say and do.

We may be tempted to suggest that the sciences deal with human behavior insofar as it is shaped by antecedent causes, whereas ethics deals with human action insofar as it is subject to direction by human volition. However, such a view falsely bifurcates the self into separate compartments, the determined and the free. It fails to recognize that both scientific and ethical vantage points on action are abstractions when taken in isolation. In concrete experience, the various facets of social existence are organically interrelated, intermingling with and suffusing one another. Thus the conditioning and regulating factors that play upon action enter substantively into its actual occurrence. They affect judgment, motivation, decision making and action. In turn, our choices interact back upon these same factors, shaping their operation.

Indeed, the more we grasp how these conditioning factors function in social life, the more we are able to use them in promoting our own purposes. We take them into account in anticipating the probable actions of others, and we adapt our own projects to their operation so that they work for us rather than against us. When they seem likely to frustrate our goals, we devise strategies for minimizing their impact. Comprehension of the dynamics of human behavior enables us to expand the reach of our purposive activity, whereas naïveté and ignorance leave us subject to processes that consistently overwhelm us. As our powers increase, so does the scope of our accountability.

In the American context, the most influential social theories have been functional in orientation. They have focused on the identification and explication of the basic functions of society. They have used a systems model to display the interrelations of processes that provide for these functions.[17] For functional theories, social order is a phenomenon to be explained, not a taken-for-granted reality. The presumption is that social order can be maintained only if a society is reasonably successful in providing for basic social functions. Social disorganization, social disintegration, and in the worst cases, social chaos, are indications of functional failures. Such failures are taken to be the most dangerous threats to social well-being.

More recently, critical theories of society have gained prominence in the American context.[18] These theories focus on the systematic ways in which societies disadvantage or oppress certain segments of the population. Race, class, and gender have received special attention. For critical theories, order as such is not the primary interest, but an order that in freedom nourishes the full development of the capacities of the people. In this respect, a moral perspective drives critical theory to a degree that is not so obvious in functional theories. The presumption of critical theory is that societies have an extraordinary array of devices for maintaining themselves even in the face of severe functional shortcomings. The task is to discover the possibilities of humanizing social change. Such possibilities are linked to points of stress or conflict in the functional interconnections of ongoing social processes. Points of stress disclose weaknesses in the existing order that social movements might exploit in seeking a more just social order.[19]

These two types of social theory have counterparts in Christian social ethics. Classical Christian thinkers in both Catholic and Reformed traditions have tended to conceive basic institutional forms as largely given. Order has been a paramount value. The central theological and ethical issues have concerned the role Christians might properly play within established institutional structures. Social gospel and liberation traditions have been preoccupied with the injustices of human societies. They have directed their energies toward movements for social justice and liberation.

Both of these perspectives have bases in the eschatological orientation of the early Christian movement. This orientation called for a provisional acceptance of existing forms of social order despite their distortion of God's ultimate purposes. Existing social structures furnished a God-given context for the proclamation of the gospel. The eschatological orientation also constituted a summons to the faithful to enter into an alternative community over against the dominant society. This community afforded new ways of being together in the world in recognition of the nearness of God's coming realm.[20] The dialectical interplay of the old age that is passing away and the new age coming into being, Troeltsch observes, nurtured both socially conservative and socially radical tendencies. Both have persisted throughout history and continue to figure in ecumenical discussions.[21] Consequently, both functional and critical theories contribute to Christian ethical reflection on social reality.

Social Analysis: The Critical Study of Institutions and Social Movements

Structural-functional treatments of society deal with social institutions and social movements. Both belong to the realities of social existence. Institutions furnish a stable framework for human interactions; social movements are instances of collective initiative to achieve shared goals. In general, institutions provide stability, whereas social movements make up the dynamic aspects of human societies. Yet dramatic changes can be produced within stable institutional contexts, for example, changes brought about by capitalist development. Basic value systems and patterns of economic behavior may remain more or less intact through fundamental social transformations. Similarly, social movements frequently emerge that are directed toward preventing particular kinds of changes, for example, movements to protect the ecology, or, to take a quite different example, groups mobilized to oppose open occupancy in suburban neighborhoods.

Social institutions are composed of deep, shared expectations regarding patterns of human interaction and structures of human relationships. These expectations are internalized in the elemental attitudes, beliefs, and dispositions of persons in the society. Through ongoing processes of socialization, they enjoy a high degree of self-evidence among members of a society. We take them for granted as "the way things are." In their self-evidence, they function as mechanisms for social control, assuring relative stability in human societies.[22] Institutional structures and processes order the principal regions of human association: economic, political, cultural, and familial. They provide the context of virtually all human action.

According to this schema, religious institutions function chiefly as culture-bearing structures.

Organizations articulate basic institutional forms in more or less explicit arrangements of offices and functions, so that continuity and effectiveness are assured in activities crucial to social existence.[23] At various levels of activity, members of an organization generate policies aimed at meeting organizational objectives. In most cases, these policies emerge through well-established procedures that reflect the distribution of authority and the division of labor within an organization. Thus they are products of deliberation, judgment, and decision making. However, to gain support, both within particular organizations and in the larger society, these policies must accord with institutionalized social expectations.

Social movements reflect collective investments of human energy in the promotion of shared goals that go beyond institutionalized patterns of human activity. The goals in question may be fully compatible with primary social values. In this respect, social movements do not necessarily represent a challenge to basic social institutions. They may reinforce those institutions, for example, popular demonstrations in support of a national war effort. More broadly, social movements may express central characteristics of particular social institutions. In the American context, voluntarism has been a prominent value, reflecting fundamental ideals of liberal democracy. When American people organize themselves to address certain problems or to promote certain goals, they are acting in accord with the voluntary principle of American democracy. Social movements may, however, be directed against established social practices, even in violation of public law. Their intent could be to protest oppressive social patterns and to open the way for substantive social changes, at least at the level of policy, perhaps at a structural level as well. Examples include the abolition movement, the women's suffrage movement, the labor movement, the civil rights movement, or the current right-to-life movement.

Movements committed to social change are not necessarily radical so long as they do not call into question the organizational principles of a society.[24] American democracy has been highly stable over a long period of time precisely because it provides spaces for collective initiatives aimed at shaping specific social arrangements. The constraint on such initiatives is that their goals and methods of protest prove themselves compatible with the requirements of basic social institutions.

In some societies, normally those that fail adequately to provide the requisites of social order, social movements may become radical and then revolutionary, seeking nothing less than the overthrow of an existing social order. To be effective, social movements must themselves achieve satisfactory levels of organization, and in that organization they must draw upon the internalized expectations and shared values of participants in the movements. In this respect, such movements invariably display a measure of continuity with existing institutional arrangements.

Attention to the structural-functional aspects of situations entails examining the institutional and organizational forms at work in those situations. It includes assessments of the effectiveness of both in providing the requisites of a well-ordered society. Social movements continually play among the basic institutions of human societies, articulating their possibilities, expanding their reach, frustrating their smooth operation, reordering their priorities, perhaps transforming their fundamental values.

In social ethics, we have special interest in the consensual features of social institutions and movements. In this context, consent means that people act in accord with societal norms, not simply in response to coercive measures or out of presumptions of personal advantage, but on the basis of respect for the moral worth of those norms. Coercive force and perceptions of mutual interest are undoubtedly crucial components of social order. Yet societies require moral authority for their regulative principles if they are to achieve functional effectiveness and maintain stability over time. They gain this authority from ideas widely shared in the society. Such ideas are integral features of social order.[25]

Peter Berger discusses how religious and moral ideas serve to explain and justify apparent social evils. Such ideas constitute a social theodicy; that is, they furnish an account of the social world that shows that it merits allegiance despite its manifest shortcomings. This theodicy displays the essential validity of basic social institutions; it reinforces the people's obligation to honor those in authority and to obey the rules of society; and it renders intelligible any seeming unfairness in the distribution of social benefits and burdens.[26] To be persuasive, a social theodicy must have a substantial basis in cultural materials esteemed within the society as a whole. It cannot simply be invented *ad hoc,* certainly not by those whose interest it most immediately favors. It requires roots in a rich tradition, preferably with a revered history of interpretation. The more a social theodicy participates in the central themes of a culture, the more the essential rightness of the social arrangements it sanctions enjoys self-evidence among the people.

Critical social theories proceed from the fact that the dominant religious and moral ideas of a society often sanction unjust and oppressive social systems. Then the social theodicy functions as an ideology; that is, it is composed of ideas without authentic social grounding. Such ideas conceal and distort the true realities of social existence. Their role is to protect the special interests of those who illegitimately benefit from the established order. Yet movements for social change also require moral if not religious legitimation—I would say both. Attempts to disrupt social order and to reorder social relations along different lines themselves demand justification. One must show their essential rightness and demonstrate that the suffering they cause is necessary or unavoidable or perhaps preferable to that which already exists.[27]

Building upon the insights of Karl Marx, critical social

theory shows how our social locations predetermine our judgments about social reality and its normative values. For both functional and critical approaches, however, moral and religious ideas are integral to social order. The challenge is to test the alleged grounding of such ideas in social reality. It is to discern whose interests they favor and whose interests they override.

In structural-functional terms, churches in modern, secular societies are voluntary associations. Their organizational expressions are complex, embracing local congregations, several levels of regional organizations, associations of congregational representatives, and general legislative and administrative bodies of the denominations. There are also program agencies and affiliated educational and welfare organizations within denominations, often with parallel structures in ecumenical bodies. Reflections on a Christian social witness are appropriate within each of these organizational components.

In addition to the formal arrangements that provide legitimate channels for official church pronouncements, there are innumerable subgroups, intimately linked to the churches, that offer their own distinctive social witness: caucuses, special interest groups, and issue-oriented associations. Examples include the Women's Christian Temperance Union, the Methodist Federation for Social Action, the Southern Christian Leadership Council, or Clergy and Laity Concerned About Vietnam. Such groups attest the shared convictions of individual Christians. They may function within particular congregations and denominations; they may be ecumenical and even interfaith in their reach; and they may draw people together in a common social vision without regard to explicit religious attachments. Organizations of this sort are able to take considerably stronger critical positions than are possible within representative denominational assemblies. They may attempt to enter directly into a public discourse, but they also interact back upon official church bodies, influencing their social practice. In short, both issue-oriented associations and representative church bodies play a role in the social teaching of the churches. Individual leaders in any of these contexts have special opportunities to shape conversations in Christian social ethics.

As voluntary associations, the churches have considerable freedom in activities that involve the individual choices of adherents. This freedom gives them ready access to families and neighborhoods; it permits them to sponsor and interact with other culture-bearing and human welfare institutions, such as universities and hospitals. The churches may also seek to influence economic patterns and to participate in the public life of basic political institutions. However, their access to these latter processes is more qualified. The limitations stem in part from the fact that there is a plurality of diverse religious communities whose freedom of expression must be protected. In part, however, they reflect the fact that economic and political institutions perform essential social functions that are not readily amenable to religious sensibilities.

In secular, pluralistic societies, the church's social teachings are normally able to make their way into the public arena only in conjunction with religious and moral ideas that undergird a normative social order, that is, what Troeltsch called the "civilizational ethic."[28] In the United States, the civilizational ethic consists of principles of liberal democracy and human rights. It includes normative values associated with capitalism, such as individual enterprise, self-sufficiency, and competitive acquisitiveness.[29] The civilizational ethic, Troeltsch contends, is invariably distinguishable from peculiarly Christian teaching, even in allegedly Christian societies, because it is linked to institutional structures whose underlying functions are independent of the religious impulses of the Christian message. This independence holds especially for political, legal, and economic institutions. Consequently, he concludes, Christian social teachings that are capable of engaging basic social institutions on policy matters must be combined in some fashion with the reigning civilizational ethic of the society.

Any effective synthesis of Christian ideas and civilizational ethic constitutes a "compromise," that is, an adjustment of Christian teaching to the reigning norms of a society. However, such a compromise gives distinctively Christian social thought a share in the authority of the civilizational ethic. It is by way of its participation in a civilizational ethic, Troeltsch contends, that Christian teaching has been able to influence social processes and policies.

The civil rights movement of the 1960s is a case in point. When Martin Luther King Jr. lifted up the moral vision of the black churches, he spoke of the "beloved community." In making his public witness, he appealed to human rights guaranteed by the Constitution of the United States, even though these rights are characteristically interpreted in individualistic terms and hence are somewhat in tension with a Christian vision of community. King's social message was an effective compromise of Christian teaching and the American civilizational ethic. Troeltsch believed that the churches cannot continue to play a role in social evolution unless they can maintain and renew such compromises.[30] The same point holds, I would contend, for social movements, for example, revolutionary movements, in which Christians become conscientiously involved.

Studies in Christian ethics consist of the critical mediation of normative Christian traditions in concrete situations of practice. Such mediation gains pertinence and effectiveness with the aid of structural-functional analyses of social processes. Of special interest is the relation that prevailing normative ideas have to those processes. The truth question primarily concerns the degree to which reigning social ideas—Christian or otherwise—reflect awareness of the interconnections of thought and social processes. Effective reconstructions of Christian social thought contain well-founded appraisals of social realities that both facilitate and hinder a faithful Christian witness.

Historical Thinking: Uncovering the Historical Aspects of Situations

Structural-functional approaches to situations are not self-contained. They gain their significance in contexts of historical understanding. Functional necessities constrain historical developments, but it is the latter that constitute the concrete reality of the social world. Thus social situations occur as features in the ongoing movement of unique configurations of social and cultural phenomena. To grasp a situation is to know its historical trajectories.

Like structural-functional studies, historical treatments of situations in Christian social ethics are guided by the churches' own placements in larger streams of social existence. It is out of the context of the churches' involvements in struggles for justice that historical thinking gains significance in social-ethical reflection. The scholarly task is to help the churches respond to their social settings out of a critical appropriation of their normative traditions, with full awareness of their own social locations.

When we turn to the historical aspects of situations, we continue to be occupied with matters treated in structural-functional approaches. Now, however, we examine functional components of societies in terms of their development over time. We reconstruct the pivotal events that shaped their evolution. We take particular note of the traditions that sanction their activities within a social order.

The primary interest at this point is to uncover the formative meanings of situations, that is, the significations they have for human actors who are involved in them. It is by way of these significations that we have access to the concrete moral import of situations. The contention is that the interpretation of situations is in itself an activity in moral reasoning. It is an attempt to discern the pivotal moral issues that already reside in a social world. In this respect, a hermeneutic of situations must not be confused with pure empirical description, especially when the latter is carried out in abstraction from value considerations. The hermeneutical interest is to uncover the moral meanings that figure in concrete human interactions and relationships. A formal account of the moral dimensions of action furnishes guidelines for recognizing such meanings.

A perceptive grasp of the moral import of a situation does not in itself tell us how we are to respond. Virtually any situation offers a range of moral possibilities. We have to sort out and rank these possibilities in terms of our individual and collective commitments. Furthermore, many situations confront us with perplexing moral ambiguities that the most discerning reading cannot resolve. Any response we make will, consequently, reflect that ambiguity. The challenge is to find ways of reordering the relevant considerations so that moral ambiguity is reduced if not dispelled. The careful interpretation of situations does, however, orient us to the questions requiring our attention.[31] The presumption of this approach is that moral values and obligations are not purely transcendent norms residing in a realm of ideality that must somehow be imposed upon situations in order to provide moral direction to action. Although the moral norms we honor may have an ultimate religious grounding that surpasses concrete, historical realities, they belong as well to social situations as lived.

We get at the formative meanings of situations through the critical retrieval of normative traditions. We approach these traditions in terms of their role in the formation of existing situations, guided by the questions we confront in attempting to deal with those situations. In this frame of reference, tradition functions as both burden and resource, as hindrance and hope. We seek to exorcise what is destructive and to reclaim what releases and empowers.

Self-consciousness about the historicity of situations is not always highly pertinent to moral understanding. In familiar, routinized situations, historical thinking scarcely comes into play at all. The moral sense of the situation is already more or less clear, and in general we know what to do. To be sure, our moral sensibilities have gradations of urgency that shade into one another. At one pole are moral ideals recognized by most but fulfilled only by the heroic few. At the other pole are acts so reprehensible that they are unthinkable except for the emotionally disturbed, or perhaps those who belong to a criminal underclass. Ordinarily, we know what is desirable or morally urgent or obligatory; likewise, we know what is morally dubious or disapproved or strictly forbidden. We do not require a fully articulated historical self-consciousness to deal with such matters.

Historical thinking takes on urgency in periods of rapid change that weaken an established moral order. Familiar, taken-for-granted norms lose their self-evidence. Willing consent to social expectations declines; the maintenance of order depends increasingly on calculations of self-interest—what can we get out of "going along"?—and on the coercive measures of the state. In such circumstances, the meaning of a situation becomes problematic, a matter to be examined and clarified. It is then quite evident, as Niebuhr argued, that the prior question is "What is going on?"[32] We strive to reorient ourselves to our situation by recounting the history that has brought us to moral crisis. We seek to estimate the possibilities for renewal in our normative traditions.

Crisis does not simply have the negative connotation of danger. It also suggests kairos, the opening up of the moment of opportunity for new creation. A social order in difficulty may reveal itself as an order of repression. Its difficulties open the way to the recovery of repressed memories and to the retrieval of neglected, even forbidden, traditions.[33] These memories and traditions place in question the taken-for-granted understandings that have previously determined the meaning of social situations. A struggle for hegemony follows, perhaps with an uncertain outcome. The reigning civilizational ethic may undergo transformation to incorporate knowledge derived from repressed traditions, thereby resulting in a new moral consensus. At the other extreme, social fragmentation may occur, with proposals for national partition and the relocation of conflicting populations as a device for restoring social order (e.g., India-Pakistan, Cyprus, Lebanon). Then again, social revolution may occur, or the hegemonic culture may reestablish itself and successfully subdue the challenger. Similar dynamics may be set in motion by increased interactions among human communities representing multiple cultures, though without necessarily implying a history of oppression.

A historical vantage point on situations becomes essential when the situations in question are dynamic and conflict laden. Under those circumstances, the moral import of a situation can come into focus only through the clash of interpretations, through intense polemical exchanges, through patient negotiations aimed at building a new moral consensus. Disputes of this kind are never purely theoretical. They involve power struggles. They occur in the crosscurrents of social, economic, and political forces. Consequently, they cannot be resolved simply by the construction of stronger, more cogent arguments, nor by a more rigorous application of the rules of evidence. They require social accommodation and reconciliation.

In complex, modern societies, a genuine moral consensus almost invariably eludes us. Such a consensus is more a moral imperative and a hope than a practical project. Normally, we have to content ourselves with compromises and trade-offs, with mutual accommodations of one sort or another that might permit us to live together in a shared world. Dealing with conflicting interpretations of important life situations becomes our ongoing pattern of moral existence. Such irreducible multiplicity is the nature of a genuinely pluralistic social order. Indeed, a key moral requirement of life in such a society is to honor diversity and, if possible, to celebrate it. Where such mutual respect cannot be sustained, threats of violence and social fragmentation are ever present.

Christian social ethics finally centers in the critical development of the social witness of the churches in their particular social situations. The questions have to do with how the churches are to place themselves among the conflicting interpretations of the social world. What do their traditions lead them to see in that world? What moral possibilities are suggested by their efforts to mediate those traditions faithfully? The churches have their distinctive traditions of social thought and practice. These traditions reflect not only social ideas associated with the gospel message, but also moral conceptions that amount to "compromises" previously accomplished with the civilizational ethic of predecessor human societies.

In secular, religiously plural societies, Christians have to develop their social vision in at least two frames of reference. They must become clear about their own witness and its grounding in fundamental faith convictions, and they must find ways of articulating their distinctive witness that are suited to a public discourse. In general, formulations of the latter sort can best be worked out through critical engagement with the reigning civilizational ethic. The civilizational ethic furnishes the moral notions that make possible a public discourse about the common good.

The churches are deeply implicated in their social situations, so that the moral conflicts of the society are replicated within their own internal life. Within the churches themselves dominant traditions of Christian thought clash with neglected and forbidden traditions, and multiple traditions reflecting the diverse social locations of the churches work against a coherent and unified Christian witness. The struggle for a common mind that faithfully expresses the church's mission is, then, an ongoing task with its own perplexities and ambiguities.[34]

Conclusion

The subfields of theology, I have been contending, are particular vantage points on the divine mysteries that awaken and sustain faith existence. Christian ethics deals with faith existence in terms of our accountabilities for creaturely well-being. Critical reflection on these accountabilities focuses on the personal and communal practice of Christians in concrete social situations. Such practice includes Christian contributions to a public discourse about a well-ordered society. Assessing Christian practice embraces both the critical mediation of normative traditions that provide guidance for action and also the critical assessment of the moral significance of existing situations of action. The latter requires a productive combination of historical thinking and social analysis. The intent is to discover realistic possibilities for social action that accord with divine promises given to faith existence. Where fidelity is sustained within the social practice of the Christian churches, inquiries proper to Christian social ethics can make substantive contributions to the total theological enterprise.

NOTES

1. See Edward Farley's two major studies of this problem: *Theologia: The Fragmentation and Unity of Theological Education* (Philadelphia: Fortress Press, 1983), and *The Fragility of Knowledge: Theological Education in the Church and the University* (Philadelphia: Fortress Press, 1988).

2. This portrayal of theological knowledge and its subspecialties is informed by the concept of perspective in perceptual experience. In perception, we can intuit an object only from a particular, finite perspective. Though we may continually adopt new perspectives on the same object, allowing additional facets to appear to awareness, we can do so only by letting go those appearances that were available to previous perspectives. Each perspective allows some features of the object to show themselves while simultaneously obscuring or concealing others. Though some perspectives may be more illuminating than others, allowing an object to appear to its best advantage, no one perspective finally enjoys precedence over the others. Nor can any one perspective furnish the conditions of the others.

At the same time, each of the finite perspectives includes an apprehension of the whole that goes beyond what we actually perceive. We convey this sense of the whole by means of language, even though our linguistic utterances both surpass and fall short of what is, strictly speaking, given to perception. I have in mind language that describes the uses of an object or perhaps articulates our relations to it. Yet the whole is already present to each of the discrete perspectives, at least in the awareness of a receding horizon at the boundaries of the various perspectives. This horizon draws us toward future possible perceptions and enables us to hold in memory previous perceptions. It permits us to recognize the multiple perspectives as perspectives on one and the same reality. Finite perspective, infinite whole—these dimensions of awareness constitute an indissoluble dialectic of perception and understanding. It is this dialectic that guides my treatment of specialization within theological studies.

This account draws upon Paul Ricoeur's discussion of the fallibility of human knowing, embracing "finitude of perspective" and "the infinity of the verb" (the latter bearing the meaning of what is perceived). Imagination mediates between the two, Ricoeur suggests. However, imagination is fallible, ever subject to faultedness. Though it permits a holistic apprehension of what is given to awareness, it tempts us to confuse our finite perspectives with the infinite whole, or alternatively, to lose the whole in the finite perspectives, reducing the latter to discrete and unrelated phenomena. The former is the flaw of idealism; the latter, of radical empiricism.

Ricoeur's discussion has direct relevance to the problematic of this paper. In theology, finite perspective is confused with the whole when one of the theological subspecialties, most often systematic theology, presumes to grasp the whole and to lay the definitive foundation for all other subspecialties. The whole disintegrates into the multiplicity of perspectives when the latter are reduced to isolated and discrete inquiries. As an example of such disintegration, we might attempt a historical reconstruction of the origins of the Christian movement without any consideration of whether and how such a reconstruction might constitute theological inquiry.

See Paul Ricoeur, *Fallible Man: Philosophy of the Will,* pt. 2, trans. Charles Kelbley (Chicago: Henry Regnery, 1965), 26–71.

3. The phrase is Farley's. See *The Fragility of Knowledge,* 133.

4. Ibid., 118. I also concur with Farley that we can no longer

view theology as the systematic ordering of revealed truth, in the manner of pre-Enlightenment theologies. For Farley's critique of the "house of authority," see pp. 124–28.

5. John Wesley's portrayal of the relation of law and gospel expresses the intimate connection of the ethical interest in human accountabilities with the theological interest in faith's recognition of God and trust in God. There is no contrariety at all, Wesley argues, between law and gospel. The very same words, considered in different respects, belong both to law and gospel. Considered as commandments, they are law; considered as promises, they are gospel. Thus, the commands to love God, to love our neighbors, to be meek or holy are but "covered" promises of God, promises that God will enable and empower our love and holiness. By the same token, the promises of the gospel, promises of forgiveness, freedom, joy, and love, convey imperatives to live in accord with that which is offered. See John Wesley, "Upon Our Lord's Sermon on the Mount. Discourse the Fifth. Matthew 5:17–20," Sermon 25 in *The Works of John Wesley: Sermons I,* ed. Albert C. Outler (Nashville: Abingdon Press, 1984), 554–55.

6. Farley, *The Fragility of Knowledge,* 137.

7. Farley identifies five elemental modes of interpretation that articulate the meaning of faith (ibid., 138–42). The first three, I would suggest, make explicit the distinctive character of faith existence: (1) the critical mediation of formative traditions; (2) the constructive articulation of those traditions as disclosing something true; and (3) the appropriation of the traditions in concrete practice. The remaining modes highlight the situatedness of faith existence in the life of the world: (4) the interpretation of situations; and (5) the interpretation of vocations as primary determinants of social location.

Farley on occasion refers to the first three modes as elemental and the last three as synthetic. In my view, the latter modes do not so much synthesize elemental modes as articulate the concrete context of faith existence. Accounts of faith existence without that context are abstract.

8. See my *The Use of the Bible in Christian Ethics* (Philadelphia: Fortress Press, 1983), 15–28. See also chaps. 2 and 3 of my *Hospitality to the Stranger: Dimensions of Moral Understanding* (Philadelphia: Fortress Press, 1985), 35–96.

9. For my account of values and my proposal for a constructive value theory, cf. *Hospitality to the Stranger,* 66–92.

10. This is one of the points where I may differ with Farley's view of elemental interpretative modes. Farley lifts up three notions: tradition, truth, and practice. Truth is a crucial notion for theology. We cannot complete our theological work by attending only to the existentially meaningful, as was in vogue for an earlier generation of theologians. We need to be able to show that theology concerns reality, that it is a way of attending to dimensions of reality not accessible to, let us say, empirical methods of inquiry.

Yet for theology, truth is not the most elemental mode of interpretation. It is a derivative mode, dependent upon prior valuative engagements with the world. Even for systematic theology, the prior question is not, Are Christian convictions true? It is, What are the meaning and significance of our Christian convictions for the ways in which we live in the world?

In some respects, the truth question is the most radical question we can ask. It has the potential of undermining our convictions, showing us that reality is something other than what we have supposed. In a practical sense, however, the value issues are more radical, for they present us with basic choices about how we will live our lives. I would contend, therefore, that the more elemental questions are axiological, at least for an ethical vantage point on theology.

11. In recent philosophical ethics, these types of moral interest are often discussed as deontology and consequentialism (or utilitarianism). See, for example, William K. Frankena, *Ethics,* 2d ed. (Englewood Cliffs, N.J.: Prentice-Hall, 1973), esp. chaps. 2–4, pp. 12–78. Cf. my *The Use of the Bible in Christian Ethics,* 15–28.

12. Aristotle's *Nichomachaean Ethics* is, of course, the basis of this approach. It became central in Christian ethics through the thought of Thomas Aquinas. Cf. Thomas's *Summa Theologiae,* I–II, esp. questions 49–67. For a useful collection of Thomas's discussion of the virtues, see St. Thomas Aquinas, *Treatise on the Virtues,* trans. John A. Oesterle (Notre Dame: University of Notre Dame Press, 1966).

13. Stanley Hauerwas in particular has sought to show

how a theory of virtues reorders the post-Kantian discussion of deontology and consequentialism. See, for example, his *The Peaceable Kingdom: A Primer in Christian Ethics* (Notre Dame: University of Notre Dame Press, 1983), 17–34.

14. This point holds for university-based theological education as well as seminary training for clergy. To be sure, one can study writings on Christian social ethics in abstraction from the social locations that sustain the thought they contain. But such work is abstract! To pursue concrete critical and constructive work in Christian social ethics, one must examine the associations that sustain a Christian social vision, that is, Christian churches. One must also attend to the social location and composition of those associations, including their relations with basic social institutions.

15. In my judgment, Gibson Winter's study *Elements for a Social Ethic: Scientific and Ethical Perspectives on Social Process* (New York: Macmillan, 1966) still provides the most sustained and comprehensive treatment of this problem.

16. Paul Ricoeur, *Philosophie de la Volonte: Le Volontaire et L'Involontaire* (Paris: Éditions Montaigne, 1950), 85.

17. Talcott Parsons' work represents the most ambitious recent effort at theory construction of this sort. For an overview of his approach, see Talcott Parsons and Edward A. Shils, eds., *Toward a General Theory of Action: Theoretical Foundations for the Social Sciences*, pt. 2 (New York: Harper & Row, 1951), 47–243. Parsons and Shils are the coauthors of this section. They attempt to display the distinctions and relations of personality theory, culture theory, and social theory. For a convenient summary of Parsons' application of this model to social theory, see his *Politics and Social Structure* (New York: Free Press, 1969), 5–57.

18. Jürgen Habermas has become the most influential representative of critical theory among students of Christian social ethics. Habermas locates his work within the history of social theory in his two-volume study *The Theory of Communicative Action*, trans. Thomas McCarthy (Boston: Beacon Press, 1984). For his application of this theory to the critique of advanced capitalist societies, see Jürgen Habermas, *Legitimation Crisis*, trans. Thomas McCarthy (Boston: Beacon Press, 1975).

19. Habermas identifies the key crisis of advanced capitalism as a "legitimation crisis"; that is, the value orientations of the society do not justify the social distribution of burdens and benefits. As a result, existing forms of social order lack clear legitimacy. See Habermas, *Legitimation Crisis*, 68–74.

20. See my discussion of these themes in *The Use of the Bible in Christian Ethics*, the final chapter, 177–206.

21. See, e.g., Ernst Troeltsch, *The Social Teaching of the Christian Churches* (Chicago: The University of Chicago Press; 1976), 82–86.

22. For a strong presentation of the institutionalization of human interactions, see Peter L. Berger and Thomas Luckman, *The Social Construction of Reality: A Treatise in the Sociology of Knowledge* (Garden City, N.Y.: Doubleday, 1967).

23. For a theoretical treatment of organizations, in distinction from and in relation to institutions, see Amitai Etzioni, *A Comparative Analysis of Complex Organizations: On Power, Involvement, and their Correlates* (New York: Free Press, 1961). Etzioni builds upon Parsons' functional theory of society.

24. Organizational principles give specific identity to particular social formations. They consist of central social processes that regulate and limit the range of possibilities for change and development in a particular society. See Habermas, *Legitimation Crisis*, 9–10.

25. See Peter L. Berger, *The Sacred Canopy* (Garden City, N.Y.: Doubleday, 1969), 3–51.

26. Ibid., 55. See the whole of chap. 3, "The Problem of Theodicy."

27. Jon P. Gunnemann speaks of revolution as "change in theodicy." See his *The Moral Meaning of Revolution* (New Haven: Yale University Press, 1979), 232–46. He specifically criticizes Karl Marx's presumption that a proletarian revolution would overcome the need for a theodicy by bringing into being a realm of freedom and of human mastery over nature. See ibid., 167–68, and the whole of chap. 4.

28. See Troeltsch, *Social Teaching*, 1001–1002.

29. I have elaborated these points in my essay "Renewing Ecumenical Protestant Social Teaching," in *Justice and the Holy: Essays in Honor of Walter Harrelson*, eds. Douglas A. Knight and Peter J. Paris (Atlanta: Scholars Press, 1989).

30. These ideas inform Troeltsch's treatment of the entire span of Christian social thought in the West. They are succinctly pulled together in the concluding section of his *Social Teaching*, 999–1002.

31. See H. Richard Niebuhr, *The Responsible Self: An Essay in Christian Moral Philosophy* (New York: Harper & Row, 1963), 55–68. For my discussion of Niebuhr's proposal for an ethics of the "fitting," see *Hospitality to the Stranger*, 100–22. Niebuhr also explicates the ethics of the fitting in terms of "society" and "time and history," though with less attention to the methodological implications of attention to these phenomena.

32. See Niebuhr, *The Responsible Self*, 60.

33. Drawing upon the work of Michel Foucault, Sharon D. Welch has demonstrated the usefulness of these categories for contextual understandings of theology. See in particular her discussion of "the insurrection of subjugated knowledges" in *Communities of Resistance and Solidarity: A Feminist Theology of Liberation* (Maryknoll, N.Y.: Orbis Books, 1985), 44–47.

34. I have displayed some of these complexities in my essay "Renewing Ecumenical Protestant Social Teaching." In that essay, I lifted up the recent difficulties of ecumenical Protestant social teaching, specifying what would appear to be necessary to accomplish its renewal in contemporary American society.

8

Theology Against the Disciplines

John B. Cobb, Jr.

The Failure of University Response to Our Shared Crisis

It is trite but true to say that we live in a time of crisis. It has been trite but true throughout my lifetime. It has been said so often and so long that it arouses little interest. Nevertheless the crisis deepens. What is at stake is the future of life on the planet.

Humanity is not responding effectively to the crisis. One reason is sin. To respond well would be costly. It would be most costly to those who have the most power and wealth. It is easy to refuse to change or to change superficially so as to deflect the anger of those who are most eager for change.

But the problem is not simply that of entrenched interests willfully refusing to change in ways they know they should. There are also entrenched beliefs, sincerely held, that assert that the present directions are the right ones to hold to—that we should stay the course. And there is massive confusion about what alternative there might be were we willing to try one.

Although the situation calls for the moralist or prophet, his or her work by itself can add to the problem. To arouse guilt and anxiety without providing a convincing way to move ahead blocks future possibilities rather than opens them up. There is need for the intellectual and the visionary, for the best minds of the world, to direct their attention to the most critical problems.

Without pretending that there is any one list that identifies just what these problems are, I will mention a few that, I think, would appear on many lists:

1. How can we resolve international conflicts peacefully without the loss of freedom?
2. How can we prevent the spread of global famines without disrupting the economies of the peoples to whom aid is given?
3. How can we slow the destruction of the ozone layer and the greenhouse effect without destroying the capacity of human beings to meet their economic needs?
4. How can we stop and reverse the increasing alienation and dehumanization that modernity has carried around the planet?
5. How can we alleviate the worst oppressions and injustices inflicted upon masses of people, especially women, on every continent?

Other lists may be quite different from this one. My concern here is not to argue that this list is a particularly good one. It is only to make the obvious point that there are mammoth questions confronting the world, the answers to which we do not know.

When humanity faces overwhelming problems of this kind, it naturally looks to leadership to give guidance. Because it is not a problem of implementing known answers but of throwing light upon the problems and then debating proposed responses, humanity turns for help to thinkers rather than to politicians. It is vaguely supposed that highly educated people engaged throughout their lives in scholarship and teaching would provide the pool from which such leaders would come. A high percentage of such people are located in universities; so there is a natural expectation that in this time of humanity's direst need, its universities could be a source of major assistance.

This expectation is doomed to disappointment. There are, of course, persons located in universities who take the world's problems seriously and think and write intelligently about them. But this is more in spite of the university than because of it. They are mavericks rather than proper representatives of the university's self-understanding.

Edward Farley's account in *The Fragility of Knowledge* of the Enlightenment ideal and what has happened to it in the university throws light on why this is so.[1] Originally, the Enlightenment held everything open to criticism and rewarded those who asked penetrating questions about assumptions. In that context, the failure of scholars to deal with the urgent issues of their time would have been noticed and criticized. There would be some motivation to ask, Why? and to propose alternative assumptions that would lead to better results. But as the original ideal gave way through several steps to today's specialty fields, this kind of criticism disappeared. The specialty fields constitute self-contained communities of research whose selection of topics is little affected by any needs but their own.

As one who finds the decent survival of humanity in the context of a healthy biosphere a matter of almost ultimate importance, I am appalled. As a society, we have created an institution of "higher learning." We have provided it with resources that enable it to prepare leaders for the future in all fields including the intellectual ones and to capture many of its best graduates for a lifetime of work within its walls. We encourage it to devote much time and energy to research. We then ask that it offer us guidance as to how to respond to the urgent issues of the day, issues that threaten to make this very nearly the last day. And we are told, implicitly at least, that these are not matters of interest to the university, that it has organized its life to other ends. In short, we find that the university has channeled the energies of those who work within it in ways that have little relevance to the real world, and it educates leaders for the future to continue in these irrelevant directions.

If anything, the situation is even worse in those areas that have important effects on what happens in the real world. Economics is a major example. The work of economists certainly does influence both business practice and public policy. The question is how.

Economic issues pervade the list of problems above. The capitalization of agriculture has been a major factor in the desertification that is responsible for many famines. Industrial growth is the major factor causing the greenhouse effect. Industrialization is also the major factor shaping the modernization that has generated alienation and dehumanization almost everywhere. One might hope that economists, faced with these disasters, would be devoting their research to considering alternative ways in which the national and global economy could be organized, but this is not the case. Economics is organized as a self-contained discipline.[2] This discipline excludes both the social world and the physical world from its range of discourse. It studies how the circular flow of money can become greater.

Economists confronted by the question as to whether this growth in production and consumption is a good thing may reply that theirs is a value-free discipline. It tells people how to increase wealth. Should there be nations that want to become poorer, they can ignore the advice of economists. But the artificiality of such an answer is patent. The whole discipline is ordered to the end of economic growth. Those who give their lives to the discipline certainly believe this is a good thing. Their discourse is filled with value-laden language. They constitute a collective political pressure group pushing for growth in all sorts of subtle, and not so subtle, ways.

In the real world, there are enormous social and ecological consequences of growth. There is an obvious need to find some way to solve the world's economic problems other than growth in gross product. But to this need, the advice of economists is not merely irrelevant –

it is positively hostile. Yet, given the virtual monopoly of the discipline on the study of economies, who else knows enough to provide guidance?

My point is not that economists are on the whole less moral or less humanly sensitive than are other people. On the contrary, most of them are deeply committed to benefiting humanity. My point is certainly not that they are less intelligent than others. On the whole, economics has garnered more than its share of the best and the brightest. My point is that economics has succeeded better than any other social science in measuring up to the norms of the disciplinary organization of knowledge. It is its faithfulness to the university ideal that makes it today such an obstacle to the changes that are urgently needed. My anger, therefore, is directed against that ideal rather than against economists, or even economics as a discipline. It is that university ideal that canalizes the activities and thought of so many of the best minds in ways that either make their work irrelevant or lead them to propose solutions to today's problems that are insensitive to crucial dimensions of those problems.

What about theology? Many theologians have declared theology to be a discipline too. Has this made it either irrelevant or damaging? I recently came across a quotation on irrelevance from Cornel West, which I will share. It comes from the foreword to a book produced by the Departmento Ecumenico de Investigaciones, in San José, Costa Rica. "Shunning the narrow confines of the intellectual division of labor in academic institutions, DEI . . . rejects the compartmentalized disciplines of our bureaucratized seminaries and divinity schools. Instead DEI promotes and encourages theological reflection that traverses the fields of political economy, biblical studies, social theory, church history, and social ethics. In this way, DEI reveals the intellectual impoverishment of academic theologies that enact ostrich-like exercises in highly specialized sand—with little view to the pressing problems confronting ordinary people in our present period of crisis."[3]

My own view is that West exaggerates. Academic theology has interacted somewhat with church theology and ecumenical theology and thus has maintained some contact with events in the church. More important, it has opened its doors to people like Cornel West who have forced on it *some* consideration of urgent issues. Nevertheless, he is not wide of the mark. The choice to view theology as an academic discipline has led theologians to write chiefly for one another and to have their problems posed by the history of the discipline more than by the needs of the church or the world.

In comparison with economics, however, I think it must be said that academic theology has been more willing to be self-critical and to allow new voices and new responses to emerge. My argument is that this is because of its continuing contact with the church, and *in spite of* its attempt to constitute itself as an academic discipline. One fears that the idealization of the disciplinary organization of knowledge is already reasserting itself in religious studies in general and in theology in particular, so that tenure questions are judged by contributions to the discipline rather than by the originality and relevance to the urgent human need for new insights and perspectives. If this continues, the vitality of theological discussion that we have enjoyed in the past two decades may die away as disciplinary characteristics tighten their control over theology.

How the Disciplinary Organization of Knowledge Inhibits

It is time for me to say how I understand a discipline. I propose that the disciplinary organization of knowledge is the outcome of a metaphysics that may be variously described as atomistic, materialistic, or mechanistic. In any case, this metaphysics views the entities making up this world as self-contained, that is, as being what they are independent of their present relations to other things. Of course, they are acknowledged to be related, but these relations are thought not to affect what the entities are in themselves. The relations are in this sense external.

This notion is taken over from Greek atomists who held that the units of which the world is made are related to one another only spatially. All qualitative changes are a function of changing spatial relations of the material units. This modern vision superseded the dominantly organic one of the preceding epoch.

Any powerful vision not only highlights those features of the world that it affirms but also makes the world more like it is affirmed to be. We live in a much more mechanical world than people did during the time the vision was taking hold. In all kinds of ways, organisms have been replaced by machines. But more important, human beings have become more like machines.

The great economic attainment of this modern world is the factory. The factory first made human beings more machinelike and then replaced their machinelike work with machines. The result has been a vast increase in production. Consider how this was done.

Adam Smith gave the famous example of the making of pins. Instead of one person making pins, as artisans had done for centuries, the labor involved in making the pin was analyzed into numerous steps. Ten men each performing repeatedly a few mindless acts could turn out 48,000 pins in a day![4] Then also, as these steps are thoroughly routinized, machines could be invented to perform them.

This procedure of analyzing what is involved in productive work into its simplest units and then subdividing the labor into these simplest acts has gone further and further in the process of modernizing industrial production and all forms of business. Scientific Management developed it to a fine art. The goal was to make each act so simple that a minimum of skill or strength was involved. Highly paid employees were then not needed. Frederick Taylor, the founder of Scientific Management, strove systematically to remove from the worker any remaining initiative. Instead of assigning a general task and then allowing the worker to figure out how to accomplish it, all such decisions were to be made by management. The worker was to act by rote only.[5]

E. F. Schumacher begins his book *Good Work* with a

quotation from the *London Times:* "Dante, when composing his visions of hell might well have included the mindless, repetitive boredom of working on a factory assembly line. It destroys initiative and rots brains, yet millions of British workers are committed to it for most of their lives."[6] Schumacher continues: "The remarkable thing is that this statement, like countless similar ones made before it, aroused no interest: there were no hot denials or anguished agreements; no reactions at all." His point, of course, is that everyone knows it to be true and believes there is nothing to be done about it.

In economic theory, *Homo economicus* is the rational consumer. Labor is viewed simply as a cost. People work only in order to be able to consume. Or, put in another way, labor is a commodity that is exchanged in the market for goods. Marx was deeply troubled by what was happening and wrote movingly of the alienation of labor. But when the Soviets came to power, they adopted Scientific Management as the necessary process of efficient industrialization. As long as the goal was to increase production, there seemed no other choice. And if an individual factory attempted to humanize the work process, its "inefficiency" would be such that market forces would quickly bankrupt it.

The modern world has need of another product, one it calls knowledge. The term *knowledge* is midway between wisdom and information, and is somewhat misleading. The modern world recognizes no need for wisdom. It needs only information.

Wisdom is a way of seeing things in the complexity of their ever-changing relationships. It cannot be captured in a formula or embodied in a formalized method. It cannot even be distinguished from foolishness except through processes of discernment that themselves do not belong to machines. Wisdom is qualitative; it makes judgments of importance and desirability.

Information, on the other hand, is quantitative. It is value free. One bit of information is just as good as any other. Which can be used when is a secondary matter.

Whereas it is very difficult to devise means of generating wisdom, it is not so difficult to devise means of generating information. Indeed, this requires the application of principles very similar to those operative in the factory—first and foremost, specialization.

The world must be divided into segments or aspects that can be treated as if they were self-contained, as if their relationships to any other segments or aspects of the world were external. In other words, the subject matter of the discipline must be thought to be unaffected by its removal from its matrix in the real world. The atomistic vision makes this assumption acceptable. Within this initially broad field, subspecialties and sub-subspecialties repeat the process of division until a manageable area is established for each worker in the information industry.

The next question is that of method. One needs a method that can be used in the same way by any adequately trained person; that is, a method that does not depend on individual insight or idiosyncrasy. This method will determine which features of the subject matter are highlighted. Indeed, once it is adopted, all other features of the initial subject matter are eliminated from the discipline. It is assumed that any relations between what is retained and what is eliminated are irrelevant to what is retained. Once these steps are taken, the discipline is ready to produce information. Workers are recruited to gather and process the appropriate data, and the methods do the rest. The workers need not be exceptionally bright.

Of course, the disciplinary system in the university remains for the most part an unrealized ideal. There are many reasons for this. First, whereas the factory system has been in place for two hundred years, it is only since World War II that the disciplinary organization of knowledge has gained unquestioned dominance. Even now there are many holdouts, sometimes whole departments. There are still liberal arts colleges that maintain a different organization of knowledge and have not entirely given up on wisdom. Whereas workers who have resisted their dehumanization have either lost their jobs or put their factories out of business, institutions of higher education are still given considerable indulgence for their inefficiencies. But the trend is there, and it appears particularly strong at the point of granting tenure. *The goal is to turn the university into an information factory.* To whatever extent the decision as to what bits of information to gather is other than arbitrary, that decision will be determined by the development of the discipline itself or by market considerations.

Because I have described the essential structure of disciplines so harshly, it will come as no surprise that I want to dissociate theology as far as possible from the disciplinary organization of knowledge. This organization is not, in my view, something neutral that can be used for good or ill. On the contrary, it is based on a view of reality that I reject and that I believe Christian faith opposes. I do not mean that theologians should not make use of some of the information generated by the disciplines. Much of that *is* neutral. It certainly does not mean that they should blind themselves to the wisdom that some of the practitioners of the disciplines manage, against the ultimate goal of disciplinary thought, to express. But it does mean that theology should not itself aim to be a discipline and that it should discourage disciplinary tendencies elsewhere.

Three disclaimers are needed. First, the rejection of the disciplinary organization of knowledge does not entail the rejection of disciplined thinking. The disciplining of thinking is very different from the routinization of methods of amassing information. For example, it is better to learn to reflect in a disciplined fashion about what is involved in using various methods than to adopt any one method and practice it regularly.

Second, the rejection of the disciplinary organization does not involve the rejection of specialization. No one can do everything. That is not the issue. The issue is whether the division of responsibility should be according to separate subject matters abstracted from the world, or whether other divisions are more useful. I began by noting some critical issues facing all of us to which the university has very little to say. Any one of those questions provides a specialized focus of inquiry. But these foci of inquiry are perceived as interconnected with all other topics rather than as bounded and self-contained. Investigation of any of those areas would recognize itself as involved with all the others and with many other matters as well. Specializations of this sort do not presuppose, and would not encourage, the view that the segments of the world are separable one from the other. It would produce results that are relevant to what is really happening and, in many instances, that are genuinely helpful.

I am not, however, arguing for the creation of a new set of long-lasting departments, each focused on a particular problem. That kind of organization of the university expresses the assumption that canalized and routinized specialization is what is of importance. It is precisely that vision that works against wisdom. A far more fluid and flexible community of inquirers would express the nondisciplinary style ready to respond to real needs of real people in the real world.

Finally, I would not preclude some canalized research activities as long as these are justified on particular grounds rather than as the self-evidently correct way of organizing knowledge. It would be important that those taking part in these long-term programs were willing to talk about their assumptions with other members of the community so that the judgments of one generation do not become the axioms of the next. It would also be important that they understood that their subject matter is interrelated with other subject matters and that they could explain the reasons for provisional abstraction from these relations. If they maintained this kind of openness in a context in which all recognized a special need for continuity, they might make distinctive and important contributions. The wider conversation would check the tendency to mindlessness built into the academic disciplines.

Theology as the Thinking of the Church

If academic disciplines have the character I have described, it is clear that they are not appropriate for the church as it organizes its own reflection. They should not be allowed to dominate the education of the clergy as they too often do today. The question is how the church should order its intellectual life. My answer to this question reflects my view of the nature and history of Christian thinking.

I understand Christianity as a socio-historical movement. It is, of course, a socio-historical movement with extensive religious aspects; that is, it is one in which mystery plays a large role. But I would not describe it as "a religion." To do so gives too much prominence to one aspect of its life. I view it instead as that socio-historical movement that understands the events that took place in Israel around the figure of Jesus as of determinative importance for its life. Through those events it finds itself heir to Israel's antecedent history. It is this shared origin and history that the many segments of the movement have in common rather than any particular beliefs or practices, although, of course, that shared history gives rise to beliefs and practices. When the segments of the movement come together to discuss their unity, they compare these beliefs and practices that have developed through their separate histories and may try to formulate areas of agreement. But their unity as Christians does not depend on their success.

This socio-historical movement—or its various branches—like all socio-historical movements, goes through many changes for both internal and external reasons. As it faces new situations, it is forced to decide how to respond. This raises questions as to what is the appropriate response for a movement constituted by this history. There is no set of rules, no system, by which the decision can be made. Insofar as the church really makes a decision, rather than simply being shaped by changing forces, it requires wisdom. The wisdom will draw on selected aspects of the tradition, on insightful interpretation of the present situation, and on realistic projections of the future. Sometimes the church responds well, sometimes badly. Looking back, studying the past, we can make better judgments about these matters than were possible at the time. Our own judgments about new situations can be informed by what we learn, but still no timeless rules can be formulated to guide us now.

Some of the problems faced by the church change rather slowly. There are perennial questions about the proper organization of the church, the meaning of ordination, the proper pattern of worship, the life of discipleship, the relation of the church to the wider society, the significance of work, the place of sexuality in life, the right attitude toward money, the meaning of salvation, the hope for the future, the nature of those events and that person in whom the whole history centers, the reality and nature of the divine to which Jesus pointed, and so on. These perennial questions require ever-changing answers as the interior life of the church develops and also as its cultural and intellectual context changes. Also, some of these questions become critical in some generations and dormant in others. In any case, the effort to respond to these questions *as a Christian*—that is, as a committed member of the socio-historical movement—is an important part of theology.

There are other equally important questions that arise as the historical situation changes. The fall of Rome and the encounter with Islam posed new questions to Christian thinkers, as did the rise of science and historical criticism. Changing political structures, or even the imagined possibility of change, introduce whole new ranges of questions. The rise of the industrial system and the modern university require fresh thinking. The more intimate relation with people of other religious traditions raises questions for believers. One could go on and on. Reflection on these questions as a Christian is also part of theology.

Finally, there are issues that are pressing not so specifically for the Christian as for human beings or the living system generally. Christians in Third World countries have been concerned about development and liberation, not so much in terms of how they affect their lives as Christians, as in terms of how they affect the whole community. Similarly, Christians in the United States reflected about civil rights, not so much because it required specific responses from them, but because they wanted to see justice implemented for the whole community. Today this type of issue has become dominant. The five questions listed at the beginning of this essay are all of this sort. Bringing to bear the wisdom of the Christian faith on matters of this sort is also a part of theology. *In short, all reflection about important matters in which the Christian consciously intends to be faithful is theology.*

If this is the nature of theology, then what should be the character of theological education and, in particular, the course of study for clergy? Joseph Hough and I have proposed answers to these questions in *Christian Identity and Theological Education.*[7] We have proposed that the teaching of the sources and history of Christian faith be reconceived. It should not aim to introduce students to the disciplines of biblical scholarship and church history, but rather, to deepen, clarify, and expand the students' understanding of who they are as Christians. We have proposed that much of the remainder of the curriculum be devoted, not to introducing students to the disciplines of theology, ethics, sociology, and psychology, but rather to self-conscious Christian reflection on issues faced by the church and the world.

The disclaimers I have introduced after my critique of the disciplinary organization of knowledge in the university can be applied to these proposals as well. First, disciplined thinking is certainly not to be scorned. The determination of what to include in the identity-forming story is chiefly a matter of wisdom rather than information, but such wisdom cannot be attained or maintained apart from both information and disciplined thinking. Further, students need to learn to think critically and rigorously about their heritage. Honesty about collective Christian sins, for example, is of central importance in the formation of Christian identity today if Christians are not to continue to be a threat to the well-being of others! Learning our story as a sinful one requires both a disciplined refusal to indulge in defensive denials and the development of a habit of openness to the evidence, wherever it leads. Similarly, the effort to bring the Christian heritage to bear on current issues is also a matter of wisdom, but it cannot be done well without disciplined study both of the heritage and of the current problems.

Second is the question of specialization. There is no reason to oppose all forms of specialization on the part of faculty members. Although it is highly desirable that all faculty members understand as much as possible of the Christian heritage and be able to relate it reflectively to the current situation, this does not entail that all should be equally informed with regard to every period of history or every facet of the current situation. On the contrary, a community is enriched by diversity on both counts. One person may know the wisdom literature especially well, another Paul, another St. Thomas. One may be particularly informed about the effects of modernization in Africa, another about the effects of chemicals on the atmosphere, still another about what is happening in urban ghettoes. Specializations of this sort make it possible for the faculty collectively to make contributions no individual Christian thinker could make. The rejection of the disciplinary organization of knowledge must not mean that individuals cease making concentrated efforts to understand particular topics! It should mean, however, that reflection on these topics will be ordered to larger purposes and sensitive to their interrelatedness with many other topics.

But third, I acknowledged that the academic disciplines may still play a role. They *are* powerful ways of gaining information. My strong opposition is to their constituting the organizing principle of knowledge and of the university. I have proposed a theological curriculum that is *not* organized by disciplinary concerns. Once this is established, can there be a subordinate place for disciplines also in the theological faculty?

The answer is that, if the place is truly subordinate,

then there can. But for a discipline to accept a truly subordinate role is for it to change its character. The discipline of New Testament studies, for example, now sets the agenda for research largely out of its disciplinary history, with secondary regard to what is occurring in related disciplines. To accept a truly subordinate role would be to have the direction of its work deeply affected by the needs of theological education that, in turn, are defined by the needs of the church and the world.

I do not want to be understood to say that in this organization of the curriculum, all the traditional topics would disappear. In my opinion, there remains no more important question than whether one believes in God, and if so, how one understands that in which one believes. My own definition of theology arises from my understanding of God. My perception of what are the most important problems facing us arises from that belief. My motivation for wanting to deal with them has the same source. One major obstacle to getting helpful attention to such topics as I have listed is that so many secular people lack both a perspective broad enough for consideration of the most pressing issues and sufficient motivation to address them. In my opinion, addressing urgent questions of this sort quickly leads to the recognition of the importance of traditional doctrines. These doctrines take on an importance in that context that is not so manifest when they are taken as the subject matter of a discipline.

Consider, for example, traditional discussions of divine attributes such as impassibility. In their academic or disciplinary context, few students find them exciting or important. But in recent times, feminists have raised fundamental questions about the idealization in patriarchal society of being self-contained and unaffected by what others say and do. They point out how the idealization of these values has disparaged the gifts and sensitivities of women, and they argue that being vulnerable and open to others is at least as important a value as being impervious. In this context, the traditional doctrine of impassibility takes on keen interest and is worth examining. Is it simply the projection of patriarchal values onto

God? Or is there some biblical or existential or metaphysical reason for affirming it? If so, does this mean that Christianity *must* come down on the side of male values?

Such reflection leads to a new interest in biblical texts. They, too, come alive when examined with these concerns. Their interpretation becomes an important matter. One will seek help from any hermeneutical method one can find, but the urgency of understanding may lead to a fresh interpretation that does not follow from any pregiven method. One need not judge that this new interpretation is the best for all time. The question is whether, in the interaction between situation and text as perceived by the Christian, there arise directives for responding to current needs that will move the church in a positive direction.

Can people in church and seminary be taught to reflect intentionally as Christians about important matters? The answer is emphatically affirmative; indeed, theology understood in this way will be more inviting and more accessible than theology as hermeneutic. It is not hard to persuade people that it is worthwhile to think about important questions, and it is not hard to get people to say what some of the important questions for them are. Often they will not be global issues of the sort listed, but immediate ones: how to relate to adolescent children or how to deal with a messy personnel problem in the church. Well and good. If these are important to people and if people are serious about being Christian, then it is worthwhile to think together about how being a Christian affects our understanding of these situations and our decisions. That is where the going gets tough. We are so accustomed to turning matters over to the psychologist or management specialist. We are so accustomed to keeping our theology in a special compartment, where it deals with the problems that are posed through the history of theology. But surely Christian faith has something to say in these situations, if only that it is appropriate to turn to a secular expert for help! In fact, it has more to say than that. The secular expert has some assumptions that deserve theological attention. And as we see how such assumptions shape advice, we can articulate our own assumptions and find our own voice in areas where we generally have been silent. We gradually can become aware of the rich potential for illumination and guidance in our heritage, a potential we have neglected because theology has become one discipline alongside others, with its separate province and distinctive method.

NOTES

1. Edward Farley, *The Fragility of Knowledge: Theological Education in the Church and the University* (Philadelphia: Fortress Press, 1988), esp. chaps. 1–3.

2. Perhaps I should follow Farley in speaking of a specialty field, but I believe that the consequences that trouble me follow also when economics remains more fully a discipline. Measuring up to the university's norms for academic disciplines leads disciplines to become specialty fields in Farley's sense.

3. Franz J. Hinkelammert, *The Ideological Weapons of Death: A Theological Critique of Capitalism,* trans. Phillip Berryman (Maryknoll, N.Y.: Orbis Books, 1986), v.

4. Adam Smith, *The Wealth of Nations,* vol. 1 (New York: P. F. Collier and Son, 1901), 44–45.

5. Frederick Taylor's views are summarized by Harry Braverman, *Labor and Monopoly Capital* (New York: Monthly Review Press, 1974), 100: "Workers who are controlled only by general orders and discipline are not adequately controlled, because they retain their grip in the actual processes of labor. So long as they control the labor process itself, they will thwart efforts to realize to the full the potential inherent in their labor power. To change this situation, control over the labor process must pass into the hands of management, not only in a formal sense but the control and dictation of each step of the process, including its mode of performance."

6. E. F. Schumacher, *Good Work* (New York: Harper & Row, 1979), 1.

7. Joseph C. Hough, Jr., and John B. Cobb, Jr., *Christian Identity and Theological Education* (Chico, Calif.: Scholars Press, 1985).

9

Celebrating Difference, Resisting Domination: The Need for Synchronic Strategies in Theological Education

Mark K. Taylor

Raúl, a Cakchiquel pastor of several Presbyterian base-communities in the western highlands of Guatemala, was explaining to me and several other North Americans how his church reads the Bible.[1] "We read it freshly, through the lens of our Mayan heritage and through our village experiences of suffering." Raúl works in a village occasionally termed "the widows capital of the world." Many of its women lost sons, brothers, and husbands during the ruthless military oppression Guatemala experienced in the 1980s. The next morning I rode the bus back up to the highland community for a Sunday morning worship and Bible study session. The church is barely marked and keeps a low profile, because Christian house churches or base-communities are easily viewed as revolutionary in Guatemala and, hence, are heavily repressed.[2]

The passage for study was Genesis 15, focusing on the promise to Abram of descendants (as many as the stars), good old age, and land. I asked in my then novice Spanish, *"Quién es como Abram hoy?"* (Who is like Abram today?). A response was quick in coming: *"los pobres"* (the poor). This answer and the ensuing lively discussion displayed what Raúl had described as the people's mode of Bible reading—appropriating their own Mayan cultural heritage, often in contrast to *Ladino* (Guatemalan but non-Mayan) or North American interpretive rules, and appropriating insights born from their own often desperate political status. From this kind of reading they, the landless Cakchiquel, whose offspring are often lost to malnutrition and "being disappeared," find a salvific vision that is replete with land and descendants.

In this Guatemalan base-community, and in many other communities, systematically marginalized and oppressed groups are finding biblical and theological visions for the practice of what I will call here an emancipatory Christian faith that sustains them in struggle against oppression and in hope for new freedom. Our North Atlantic theological institutions at times welcome this vital Christian practice. The emergence of this Christian emancipatory practice, however, is not merely a matter of realizing old truths; nor is it a matter of simply addressing new situations or considering new topics. Rather, I maintain that the biblical and theological visions integral to such emancipatory practice involve strategies that challenge the prevailing structures of interpretation in North Atlantic theological study. It is my general purpose in this essay to indicate how this is so and to propose some important reorientations for theological study.

A Distinction: Diachronic and Synchronic Dimensions

Crucial to the proposals I suggest is an understanding of the complexity of the situations in which Christian faith and contemporary theologies must work. There are many features of the situation within which theologians now labor and which they must address. Two features, however, are constant themes, although they are not easy to address together: (1) the need to affirm and celebrate the plurality of cultural and religious differences, and (2) the need to resist various forms of political domination.

In my example from the Guatemalan Cakchiquel people, both themes appear. Intrinsic to the Cakchiquel biblical and theological vision is an affirmation of their cultural particularity as well as a resistance on their part to the oppression worked by the racism and class exploitation to which they are subjected as Amerindians in Guatemala. Their faith involves an affirmation, indeed a celebration, of their cultural difference within a plurality of cultural differences; yet they also have "a place to stand" from which they wage a vigilant and sometimes militant resistance to tyranny.

Both of these themes—celebrating difference and resisting domination—are features of the Cakchiquel's complex present situation. Cakchiquel biblical and theological interpretations are heavily influenced by these present concerns with varied cultural experience and political power. Their pattern of interpretation is a movement among these present complexities, and those complexities constitute what I will call the *synchronic* dimension of their situation—a dimension wherein current cultural and political dynamics are at work.

The interpretive approach of the Cakchiquel reminds us that the contemporary situations we address are not only the result of historical process, enduring legacy, and appropriation of past traditions. They are that, and this historical dimension is a necessary one that I will term a *diachronic* dimension. But contemporary situations are also always structured by present cultural and political practices. Adequate attending to contemporary situations, therefore, requires study of them as both historical developments of past events and processes (as diachronic), and also as exercises of contemporary cultural and political dynamics (as synchronic).

There are many examples of the unavoidable interplay between the diachronic and synchronic dimensions of contemporary situations. The very narrating of a situation's historical emergence may entail a use or abuse of power in the narrator's present, as, for example, in the crafting of a racist history textbook. Conversely, such a present abuse of power is itself a development of a perduring legacy, a whole history of white supremacy on North American soil.

The hermeneutical import of this observation concerning human situations is that our interpretive strategies need to address both diachronic and synchronic dimensions. A Christian faith and a theological study that is evoked by and responds to its situations does so best with interpretive strategies that attend to both diachronic and synchronic dimensions. Interpretive strategies must themselves become both diachronic and synchronic.

What I mean by an interpretive strategy is similar to Edward Farley's notion of an "interpretive mode." These name "abstractable kinds of interpretive acts" that are evoked by situations in which people of Christian faith find themselves.[3] Identifying these interpretive strategies is crucial, because they structure the aims of theological study and of the pedagogical areas and diverse curricula that, in turn, discipline the interpretive strategies.

Diachronic and synchronic strategies of interpretation are not limited to any one discipline of the university, divinity school, or theological seminary. They do not correspond to any pedagogical areas. Rather, these interpretive strategies are pervasive orienting postures for interpreting the situations in which Christian faith occurs and conceivably could be employed in any pedagogical area or course of study in theological institutions.

I have already distinguished the terms *diachronic* and *synchronic* as dimensions of the situations within which we theologians work. Diachronic and synchronic strategies of interpretation can be further distinguished as (1) a general movement of interpretation and (2) a basic understanding of normativity.

Diachronic strategies are characterized by a general movement between temporal horizons, past and present. Diachronic strategies may include attempts to take present practice "back" to originary, traditional forms, efforts to repristinate the tradition, or also the more progressive attempts to update, apply, or appropriate tradition. The results may be as different as fundamentalism and revisionism are from each other, but these are both diachronic in their preoccupation with a movement between horizons of past and present. Diachronic strategies may be wielded by the blind devotees of tradition as well as by the sophisticated proponents of historical consciousness.

Consonant with this movement in diachronic strategies is a basic understanding of normativity. Normative and criteriological issues are notoriously complex, and I do not claim to do them full justice here. It can be said, however, that the vision of normativity for diachronic strategies is one that involves bringing into relation statements, events, and practices in one temporal horizon with those in another. In theology, diachronic studies often privilege a tradition, and then normativity becomes a matter of bringing present developments into accord with that tradition. Here, normativity is a matter of faithfulness of commitment to a tradition unfolding through past horizons. Critical methods are employed to delineate the nature of tradition in order to adjudicate the appropriateness of present belief and practice. Even more "presentist" oriented approaches to normativity, those which stress that present interpreters' prejudices, prejudgments, or interests make the appropriating of tradition a complex task—even these approaches are functioning in a diachronic mode. Such approaches will typically stress a view of normativity as not just appropriateness to tradition, but also as "credible," "intelligible," or "adequate to human experience."[4] Critical reflection and methods are used here to study the dynamics of present situations, and then "correlations" are made between past and present horizons, between normativity as appropriateness and as intelligibility. The pervasive interpretive strategy operative in these approaches to normativity—whether traditionalist, historicist, or correlationist—is oriented in terms of exploring relations between past and present horizons.

Unavoidably interacting with these diachronic strategies are synchronic strategies of interpretation, which I maintain are often neglected and which require more explicit attention by theological study than they have received to date. Synchronic strategies also can be identified in terms of a basic movement of interpretation and a consonant notion of normativity.

Synchronic movement is not from past texts to present ones, or a movement that works between two temporal horizons. It is interpretive movement occurring between horizons and boundaries encounterable *primarily in the present period.* It requires navigating the interpretive complexities arising when a presently received text's meanings are refracted, in any given present, into particular cultural forms or into diverse strata of political power. Such synchronic complexities are evident in the ways the Cakchiquel allow the present biblical text, around which they gather, to be formed by their own Cakchiquel identities and by their experiences of political power. Interpretive movement here plays not primarily between temporal horizons but between horizons shaped by present cultural identities and political patterns. Accompanying this movement are not just the problematics of historical consciousness, with which the more sophisticated representatives of diachronic interpretation have wrestled, but also the problematics of a sociocultural or political consciousness.

Synchronic strategies of interpretation also feature a distinctive approach to normativity. Here it is not sufficient to judge beliefs and practices only by their appropriateness to, or their correlation with, tradition, or by any fusion of two temporal horizons. Nor is it sufficient to refer to a single feature of the contemporary horizon. Again, the criteria operative here are more complex than I can summarize, but the distinguishing feature of synchronic approaches to normativity is their search for "breadth" or "width" in interpretation. A "good" belief or practice is one consonant with affirmations of a wide plurality of language games and cultural identities. Reasoning attains its truth not on a foundation or in correspondence with tradition, but in present dialogical communities in which there interact a "diversity of judgments, principles and theories, each entailing different kinds of justification that come together to support or to criticize, to reinforce or to revise ('wide reflective equilibrium')."[5] Richard Bernstein cites an image that ably captures this approach to normativity. In philosophy, one ought, he writes,

> to trust to the multitude and variety of its arguments rather than to the conclusiveness of any one. Its reasoning should not form a chain which is no stronger than its weakest link, but a cable whose fibers may be ever so slender, provided they are sufficiently numerous and intimately connected.[6]

This does not rule out the possibility that some arguments or perspectives among the present diversity of viewpoints are privileged or more valuable than others. In fact, I will argue below that one can privilege certain positions of oppressed and marginalized groups. The point here, however, is that arguments for the greater value of one or the other are made within the width and breadth of present positions, not only by the habit of citing tradition or past heritages. Normativity for synchronic strategies is less a matter of *being appropriate to* a past, and more one of *being with* diverse others in a present. Synchronic strategies look for the normative amid the systematic rechanneling of our initial commitments in such a way that each act or belief is judged in relation to many others.[7]

The Problem: Hegemony of Diachronic Strategies

Again, I stress that although I am indeed distinguishing synchronic from diachronic dynamics and strategies of interpretation, I am not separating them. The situations in which Christian faith and theology are embedded are both diachronic and synchronic, and our interpretations of those situations will feature a complex interplay of both kinds of strategies.

The problem, however, is that diachronic strategies have achieved a hegemony by often ignoring synchronic strategies, and this hegemony has had deleterious consequences for theological education and Christian practice.

The hegemony of diachronic strategies is evident in

biblical studies and also in systematic or constructive theology. Those forms of biblical studies, which give primary emphasis to biblical interpretation as a study of biblical texts, without focusing disciplined attention on the present social locations of biblical interpreters, are working in the diachronic mode. The contemporary challenges of feminist and African American hermeneutics have forced this diachronic preoccupation out where it can be better seen.[8] Elisabeth Schüssler Fiorenza's arguments, for example, that a present "advocacy stance" is integral to readings of past texts is all too often dismissed in our seminaries' Bible departments as "eisegesis."[9] If the argument for an advocacy stance is not dismissed in this way, practitioners of biblical studies still rarely give themselves to disciplined study of their locations, preferring instead to produce ever-more refined writing about the historical matrix of the Bible, the "subject matter of the text," or the "text itself." These studies are not to be neglected, but sole preoccupation with them dodges the question of how present configurations of culture and power shape historical and textual studies.

Systematic or constructive theology, too, exhibits the domination of diachrony in one of its most pervasive and significant doctrinal themes, revelation. One might think that at least the experiential dimensions of this theme might lead theologians to stress more the present character of Christian experience so as to produce disciplined study of that experience as intrinsic to revelation. By and large, however, theology has remained highly suspicious of the experiential side of revelation, seeking to control it by reference to the church's scripture and tradition.[10] When moves are made to scripture and tradition, as moves away from present experiences of illumination and transformation, in order to find norms or criteria in those historical sources, then revelation and theology are working primarily in a diachronic structure.

What is problematic about these or any other forms of the diachronic hegemony?

First of all, a diachronic hegemony in theological interpretation (in Bible, constructive theology, or elsewhere) easily becomes part of an ideology of exclusion in contemporary theological education. It is true that diachronic and historical methods focusing on scripture and tradition can provide critique of dogmatisms of authoritarian structures in the present. Enlightenment currents leading to a historical consciousness, for example, can have an emancipative force against authoritarianism. Accordingly, representatives of marginalized groups have cited historical-critical studies of the scriptures as part of an emancipative process, thereby releasing them from other hegemonies.[11]

When there is neglect of the way *present* cultural and political experiences impact interpretation, however, then reigning forms of interpretation easily become forces for excluding those whose cultural or political experiences are different. Every community of theological education is, and needs to be, engaged in tradition building. But this constructive act of forming a shared legacy or heritage becomes exclusive and silencing of others *unless* that act also carefully attends to the present locations of those doing the constructing. Under the guise of constructing a shared tradition, groups with privileged access to power, or groups that share a relatively homogeneous cultural identity, often overlook the ways that tradition serves their particular interests and often actually works against the interests of others. Professor Jones, say, may be a competent historian of biblical texts—highly skilled in the methods of biblical criticism, with a thorough knowledge of the biblical text's subject matter. If, however, he never gives disciplined attention to how his "social location" (a distinct amalgam of factors such as his male gender, ethnic tradition, economic status, often sexual orientation and cultural heritage) affects his scholarship, then he risks putting in place patterns of interpretation that may be neither accessible nor valued by other interpreters who labor in different social locations.

Second, a diachronic hegemony that fails to grant disciplined attention to synchronic complexities of social location inhibits theological educators' ability to address a particular challenge of our present period—developing a "critical pluralism."[12] A critical pluralism is a posture of practice and theory that includes not only an affirmation of plurality and difference, but also a critique of political domination. I have already cited both features of this posture as characterizing Cakchiquel interpretation in a Guatemalan church group. But in North Atlantic thought, across the disciplines generally, celebrating difference and forming critical resistance to domination do not come together as readily. Instead, they are often experienced as forming a frustrating aporia, thus making an "irritable condition of postmodern discourse."[13] In Christian theology, Langdon Gilkey has identified this as a most demanding puzzle: "That puzzle revealed itself as the apparent contradiction between the requirement within political action for some fixed or absolute center and an equally unavoidable relativism."[14] The problematics of this critical pluralism cannot be addressed solely by exploring the complexities of historical consciousness. A diachronic hegemony, as a practiced preoccupation with diachronic movements and notions of normativity, is not sufficient. What is required is an exploration of the world of *present* differences that make up the complex settings out of which we interpret. Within this exploration of present differences, then, we can ask about the possiblity of a critical resistance to domination. To undertake these explorations requires interpretation that navigates present social locations in all their cultural and political complexity. In short, what are required are synchronic strategies of interpretation.

A Proposal: Two Synchronic Strategies

To redress the hegemony of diachronic strategies of interpretation, I propose that theological educators, throughout their curricula and diciplines, practice synchronic strategies of two major types. The first is an "intercultural hermeneutic" that I present by attending to the field of cultural anthropology; the second is a "cultural-political hermeneutic" that I will craft from several hermeneutical theorists. I will conclude my discussion of each with comments on the implications of integrating these two synchronic hermeneutical strategies into contemporary theological education.

Intercultural Hermeneutic

An intercultural hermeneutic is one kind of synchronic strategy of interpretation that all fields in theological education do well to appropriate. This appropriation is already partly underway among theological educators insofar as they attend to cross-cultural research and to issues of "globalization."[15] Here, my presentation of a needed intercultural hermeneutic will come mainly from the field of cultural anthropology.[16]

In order to be more precise, I will identify a dynamic structure of intercultural hermeneutic. This structure consists of two closely related processes: first, description of cultural differences; and second, critique of one's own and others' cultural life. It is this structure that theological education might appropriate as an important synchronic strategy.

Describing Cultural Difference. The task of describing cultural difference has marked anthropology from its beginnings. Often, as in some of the early British evolutionists, the task of cultural description was bound up with a romanticization of exotic others or used to highlight contrasts between "the civilized" and "the savage." In North American cultural anthropology, perhaps most notably initiated by Franz Boas, and in British social anthropology emerging from the fieldworking example of Bronislaw Malinowski, cultural description achieved more exacting forms and more rigorous ethnographic, textual presentation. As cultural description became freer from ethnocentric romanticization or devaluation of others, it developed at times into a positivistic social science, championing cultural anthropologists' descriptive exercises as objective, even value free. Within this positivistic milieu, assorted theories about what "culture" and "society" were, and what dynamics played within them, were proposed and debated with reference to diverse ethnographic materials. Among contemporary anthropologists, positivism's milieu with its grand theories lives on, but there is now a widespread dissatisfaction with the theories and a yet more exacting development of ethnographic presentation of the culturally other. As anthropologists George E. Marcus and Michael M. J. Fischer show at length, impulses for totalizing frameworks are waning, and increasingly "a jeweler's eye view of the world" is preferred in anthropology, all conspiring to produce finer-grained and richer ethnographic portraits of the culturally other.[17]

Among theologians and theological educators, the influence of cultural anthropology has meant occasionally appropriating certain anthropological theories of culture and religion.[18] These appropriations of anthropological theory, however, whether by biblical scholars and theologians or by missions-oriented translators, are not necessarily exposures to the full impact of cultural anthropology's process of cultural description. In particular, what can easily be missed is the confrontation with unsettling and threatening differences. Appropriating anthropological theories about "culture" (however one defines that notion), or using those theories to facilitate intercultural communication, does not in itself entail a confrontation with cultural difference. It is possible, for example, to develop theories about culture and cultural variety without really wrestling with cultural difference.

What then does make a genuine encounter with cultural difference? If recent developments in the history of ethnographic writings are any guide, the key mark is a "reflexivity" about one's own descriptions of the other.[19] In other words, in a genuine encounter with cultural difference, the observers of culturally different people and life-ways find it difficult to describe the salient features of "the other" without also giving serious analysis to their own cultures' salient features.[20] The one who describes the other, is also other. Until that realization dawns and then issues in "reflexive analysis" (a "turning back" to analyze complexities of one's own social location), the other's and one's own cultural differences have not really been appreciated. As long as it is thought that only the described other has specifiable social and cultural locations, and that the describer can approach the other without reflection on his or her own otherness, then usually the other is being domesticated or romanticized, forced to dwell in the describer's world.

The first reflective process in the structure of intercultural hermeneutic, then, is one of describing cultural difference, and this not just as a scientific study of "others" or other "cultures," but also as a study of one's own cultural matrix. It is in this latter reflexive move, especially, that description of cultural difference becomes a genuine encounter with difference.

Cultural Critique. Taking difference seriously, through an exposure to ethnographic writing that is reflexive, initiates the second process in the structure of intercultural hermeneutic as an interpretive strategy—cultural critique. How is it possible that critique can emerge from ethnographic study of cultural differences?

Again, attending to the intercultural interpretations of anthropologists can help us respond to this question. Analyses of cultural difference, featuring a reflexivity focusing the difference of the describer as well as of the described, will reveal not just an interplay of individuals, but an intersecting of cultural worlds between which there are often disparities of power. This is particularly evident in an observation made by Robert Scholte about ethnography and fieldwork:

> The dialogue between interpreter and interpreted—the dialectic between question and answer—is a mediated

> reality which is rarely if ever an exchange between equals (historically, not normatively speaking). Irrespective of the ethnographer's democratic or egalitarian intent, the dialogue is situated in a historical context of conquest and oppression.[21]

An awareness that the study of difference occurs often within a matrix of oppression can be found not only among cultural anthropologists, but also among almost all members of North Atlantic societies engaged in the study of difference. The encounter with difference entails not only an awareness of cultural *variation*, but also of the forces of *domination* existing between interpreters and the interpreted. Reflexivity, in the study of cultural difference, then, means thematizing both cultural variation and the inequities of power between those taken as different from one another. It is indeed true that different value judgments can be applied to these discerned inequities of power; nevertheless, the awareness prepares for critique.

It is not surprising, therefore, that although cultural anthropology has been used to buttress conservative positions in North Atlantic cultures,[22] throughout its history its study of difference has usually entailed a cultural critique of Western domination.[23] Today, ethnographies that portray cultural difference do so in ways that frequently intensify description of differences as critique. This intensification occurs because the portraying of difference is a strategy of "defamiliarization."[24] As such, cultural description does not just garner attention by exotic stories of the other, but defamiliarizes and then provokes a critical reflecting back on the social location of the readers and even of the writers of the ethnography.

Marcus and Fischer identify two basic techniques of defamiliarization. One involves epistemological critique, a going out into the worlds of the other, those peripheral to Westerners, in order to bring back insights gained there "to the center to raise havoc with our settled ways of thinking and conceptualization."[25] Another technique is "defamiliarization by cross-cultural juxtaposition," which offers correlations of ethnography abroad with ethnography at home. Marcus and Fischer themselves value both techniques but push for an intensification of this latter technique, one that results in ethnographic projects carried out in contexts in North America that from their inception have "a substantive relationship to some body of ethnography elsewhere."[26]

Intercultural hermeneutic, as I have developed it from anthropological writings, finds critique at the heart of an affirmation of difference. This is enormously important to grasp. It is in a defamiliarizing exposure to difference, through both the descriptive and reflexive activities I have cited, that critique is generated. That which facilitates the generation of critique from what otherwise might be only a nonchallenging display of cultural variety is the experience of defamiliarization—a partial shaking loose of inquirers from their own lifeways and expectations. Anthropologist Paul Rabinow has described this experience of defamiliarization as entry into a "liminal self-conscious world between cultures."[27] This world is not above, below, or apart from cultural practices, but it is more than a confinement to our accustomed ones. It is to dwell in a defamiliarizing, intercultural realm out of which come new perspectives that can generate critique of those cultural practices that are not exposed to defamiliarizing intercultural dwelling.

The synchronic strategy of intercultural hermeneutic has as its aim the delivering of its inquiries into this defamiliarizing, liminal world where difference and critique dwell together. This synchronic strategy of interpretation involves disciplined analyses of cultural differences and vigilant attentiveness to the ways dominative power often interlaces a culturally variant world.

Implications for Theological Education. The structures of intercultural hermeneutic, entailing description of cultural difference and the generation of critique, can be appropriated in almost all areas of theological studies. I will simply note here four implications of this appropriation for theological education.

First, insofar as it seeks to address human situations, *theological studies should conceptualize situations ethnographically.* This need not mean that theological educators become ethnographers, any more than the need for theologians to think philosophically has meant that they become philosophers. Their work does need, however, to take on the kind of specificity portrayed in ethnography. Theological study has been too long preoccupied with "the human situation" as generally constructed with the aid of philosophy. I am not calling for the replacement or jettisoning of philosophy from theology. I am suggesting, though, that philosophies be let loose to do their work in relation to the riches and challenges of cultural difference provided by ethnographies. These materials invite explicit attention, not only from ecumenists and missioners in theological education, but especially from biblical scholars and theologians (systematic, constructive, practical).

Second, *theological study needs to nurture a disciplined reflexivity.* The various ethnographic studies of others should not be appropriated by theological study solely to produce a grand theory or classification of society and culture. We North Atlantic theologians are "others" too, and ethnographic materials can enable us to focus our own social locations as culturally specific, involving various factors such as gender, class, and ethnicity. Biblical scholars and systematic theologians have often eschewed such a reflexive turn, supposing that authoritative scholarship needed freedom from such specificities. But there is no freedom from those specificities apart from the acknowledgment and disciplined study of them in order to expose both their enabling and also their limiting powers.

Third, *strategies of cultural critique need to become intrinsic to theological critique in theological education.* Indeed, if theological study is ethnographically informed in the ways I have suggested above, cultural critique will be forthcoming from the defamiliarizing power of ethnographies. Critique of human situations has always been intrinsic to theological study, holding as it has that God or the gospel offer critique or "judgment" as part of restoration of the human cultural condition. But theological study's critique, if informed by the interpretive strategy of intercultural hermeneutic, becomes a critique of culture *from within and by* other cultural forms. Theological critique becomes culturally immanent critique. Theological study is thereby challenged to nurture strategies of critique that come not from above, from below, or apart from intercultural dynamics of difference and domination, but rather through configurations of those dynamics. This need not mean that theological critique is "reduced to" cultural dynamics. It does mean that theological critique is not just a matter of thematizing a critique of culture by God, but is a critique of culture by God in and through culture. If theological critique is really to be restorative of human cultural conditions and not just an alien imposition of norms, then it needs to be interwoven with the kind of cultural critique that comes through strategies of ethnographic defamiliarization.

Finally, it is almost inconceivable that any of the first three suggestions can materialize apart from the emergence of institutions that *facilitate the presence of trained cultural anthropologists on their faculties and the presence of culturally diverse faculty and students in their midst*. Very few trained cultural anthropologists teach in theological institutions, in part, because of a legacy of rivalry between anthropological critique and theological authority.[28] Some evangelical institutions feature well-trained and experienced anthropologists on their faculties, but often their work is largely for serving the interests of Christian missions and, even in those institutions, is not fully integrated with the other areas of theological study. In the so-called more mainline Protestant seminaries, the presence of cultural anthropologists is lamentably even rarer. The price often paid for this absence is a lack of resources for disciplined reflection about the different and dominated peoples to whom we Christian educators often pledge our "solidarity" and with whom we share a common task.

Cultural-Political Hermeneutic

Theological study, if it were to appropriate the structure of an intercultural hermeneutic, would exist with things in relation that theological educators may not be accustomed to relating. For example, combining exercises that accent both difference and also critique can be experienced as an unbearable tension, and sometimes seems inconceivable to theological educators. Max Stackhouse's book *Apologia: Contextualization, Globalization, and Mission in Theological Education*[29] is an example of theological educators' discomfort with the structural tension I presented as intrinsic to an intercultural hermeneutic.

On the one hand, Stackhouse does live in this structural tension by affirming both cultural difference and the need to critique all forms of domination; on the other, he opts out of this tension by insisting that theology needs to have a "basis for knowing" or "foundations" for assessing human differences and for grounding its critique.[30] He even advocates a "cosmopolitan apologetics" and a set of "basic Christian doctrines" as "universally true."[31]

Stackhouse's approach, of invoking foundations as a fulcrum for gaining control over cultural variability, is not the strategy of all theological educators when dealing with contextualization issues. His approach, however, does exemplify the inability of many of us to think of critique in relation to a heightening of difference and contextuality. The typical strategy for developing critique is to resort to universals and foundations unsullied by cultural or political specificity. This approach is a form of what Richard Bernstein has called Western thought's "Cartesian anxiety."[32] This anxiety finds it hard to accept that the universal foundations of its own position, from which other positions are criticized, are also socially constructed beliefs amid a sea of other beliefs. In the context of this Cartesian anxiety, we need to ask how critique can occur without the resort to foundations. It is the role of a cultural-political hermeneutic to respond to this question.

As with intercultural hermeneutic, a cultural-political hermeneutic has a particular dynamic structure, and its features are what need appropriating in theological studies. The structure of a cultural-political hermeneutic involves five features of conversation occurring between different persons or groups. I begin with three features from Hans-Georg Gadamer's hermeneutical theories of conversation; I then move beyond Gadamer to bring out the element of critique that Gadamer implies but fails to develop.[33] This cultural-political hermeneutic thereby shows step-by-step how the ever-more deliberate focusing of difference can give rise to a critical stance of solidarity with the voices of politically dominated groups. At each step, I will refer briefly to the case of the North Americans' conversation with the Guatemalan Cakchiquel Christians. My aim here is to show how critique can be generated through the heightening of difference and particularity, rather than through a resort to foundations.

Features of Conversation. As a first feature, and in a most general sense, *conversation is a movement of question and answer between two or more different parties.* Gadamer ably presents this as essential to conversation. It is an exploration of disagreement and potential agreement between different persons and groups. For the fieldworker, ethnographer, or for Christians who dwell with others out of an ethnographic sensitivity to difference, these are the interchanges of first encounter, false starts, assumed agreements, and breakdowns. In the context signaled by my opening Guatemalan example, conversation in this general sense was a listening and speaking—the sheer, initial struggle on the part of North American and Cakchiquel Christians to understand one another and their contexts.

Second, *authentic conversation highlights the particularity of the other.* Gadamer is also adept in presenting this feature. Conversation partners are not really accepted, heard, or "included" if they are not released from their interlocutors' first impressions and freed from stereotypical and classifying approaches to one another. In authentic conversation, there is a seeking and a highlighting of the otherness of conversation partners. Ways are sought to allow them to come forth in all their rich specificities, as determined not only by special events of individual life history, but also different modes of contextuality: class, race/ethnicity, gender, sexual orientation, and the ways these combine in different cultural configurations. For the North Americans and Cakchiquel to take this feature of conversation seriously, their interchange would move beyond the intrigue and vicissitudes of general interaction into intentional focusing on one another's differences. Pertinent to their conversations would be the deliberate description of one another's heritages, cultural contexts, political power, language, and other differences. A genuine conversation heightens these differences in conversation and allows all partners to present their own and one another's uniqueness.

What is often called the "liberal project" often ends here, with this delighting in the ever-more refined presentation of these differences, celebrating diversity, working to preserve an enriching plurality. Critics of this liberal spirit rightly point out the tendency of delight in difference to issue in forms of repressive tolerance, and they note its toothlessness especially in the face of oppression. Also, the delight in difference can obscure how different parties in a given conversation do not possess equal resources of power.

Go back to my Guatemalan example. It is possible, for example, and it happens often, that North Americans delight in the difference of Guatemala's Mayan groups, but fail to note that Mayan groups' difference is not merely a matter of cultural variation from North American society's customs; it is also one of their domination by North American society's practices, in which "delighting" North American tourists are implicated. This liberal, often repressive, tourists' delight, I suggest, is not the necessary result of a hermeneutics of conversation; rather, it is a distorting and truncating of conversational dynamics. For an awareness of the domination of Mayan peoples to emerge, we need to play out other features of an authentic, conversational approach to difference.

A third feature of conversation must be noted, therefore, and full exploration of it brings out the potential of conversation not only to highlight difference but also to generate critique. It is a feature that again Gadamer identifies in relation to conversation, but which he did not fully develop. Against those who would assume that conversation is only irenic exchange of ideas and perspectives, Gadamer noted that *real conversation entails clash and conflict*. A conversation in which difference is indeed highlighted will lead to parties' hearing and marshaling claims that are against one another. In Gadamer's words, "openness to the other" demands not just liberal inclusion of the other, but "the acknowledgment that I must accept some things that are against myself."[34] Openness to others is not real openness if it does not mean vulnerability as a source of valuable and new insights coming through conversation. There is a "fundamental negativity that emerges between experience and insight."[35]

In the Guatemalan case, again, taking difference seriously between North Americans and the Cakchiquel would mean, for the North Americans at least, moving well beyond the liberal delight in difference—surely beyond the "tourists' delight" in cultural diversity. It would mean exposure to critique from those discerned to be different. Indeed, in the instance I have been citing, the Cakchiquel pastor, Raúl, did not spare his North American visitors that critique. He spoke directly not only of the sources of oppression in Guatemala, but also of the responsibility or complicity of North American business pressures, Christian missionaries, and political leaders for their suffering. Vulnerability to this kind of negative critique is intrinsic to active affirmation of difference in conversation. Not all the North American visitors were willing to accept it. It also needs to be said that really taking our Central American interlocutors seriously means generating our own critiques of them, instead of only passively receiving critique. Although North Americans may receive the heftier dose of criticism in this case, in principle "clash and conflict" in conversation emerges from both sides and is received by both.

Although Gadamer, with this feature of vulnerability, makes negativity intrinsic to conversation, he blunts the effect of this source for critique by remaining in a diachronic dimension. That is to say, the other who must be allowed to say something against the interpreter is largely, for Gadamer, "the tradition." A "past other" is what Gadamer generally posits as possessing creative negativity. He rarely thinks synchronically, reflecting on how interpreters in any given present need to allow other contemporaneous interpreters to be against them and on how this is part of the process of constructing and reconstructing a tradition. Gadamer does not bring sufficient disciplined attention to the conversation occurring between contemporary, different, and often rival, interpreters.

To clarify further the way critique is generated by conversation, therefore, it is necessary to consider carefully the world of rival claims in any given present. For such a consideration, we need to leave Gadamer and draw more from another area of hermeneutics, a more analytic one, though it too will need correction by another step in the logic of conversation's play between affirming difference and generating critique.

When representatives of North American pragmatism appropriate hermeneutics, then further insights are available. These representatives add a fourth feature of conversation—*the nurturing of breadth*. Revised pragmatism has given itself explicitly to reflection on how conversational play among different, and often seemingly incommensurable, perspectives or contexts can be navigated such that we can still speak of reason, truth, or intercontextual agreement.[36] To summarize this complex and large body of philosophical literature is risky, but we may say this: reasoning, in a conversational setting, attains its truths not by opting out of the heightening of difference by fixing on some fulcrum outside cultural differences, or on some foundation below them; rather, those truths are attained through the maximizing of the breadth of the conversation, so that insights in the conversation play between different perspectives emerging within the widest possible fields. The conversation in which difference is really valued, then, will not simply highlight difference, nor only value the vulnerability that goes with openness generally, but also will seek those experiences of difference and negativity had in encounters *with the most distant, widely arrayed "others."* This nurturing of breadth, by considering alternative positions and counterpositions, is a feature of the conversational valuation of difference generally; but it begins to privilege certain positions or parties—the often neglected ones or the "far-flung" ones who make for the breadth of a given conversation. Conversation attains its truth by striving for and maintaining what some of the analytical thinkers have termed a "wide reflective equilibrium."[37]

North American Christians' engagement with the Cakchiquel, then, might be viewed as one instance in the pursuit of wide-reflective equilibrium. Insofar as the Cakchiquel are often absent from North American conversations (ecclesial or theological), active orientation of our thought and practice toward them and their perspectives is necessary to North American reasoning. Their voices, coming from a community precariously poised under oppression (both racial and economic) at once challenge our North American perspectives and also constitute the far reaches of our conversation.[38] What is involved in this orientation toward these lives is not just travel or the garnering of new cultural exposure, but rather the constituting of a world within which there can be something like "truth" in North American reasoning and practice. In saying this, however, it should be noted that the Cakchiquel are not just being made servants of North American reasoning; rather, as the earlier features of conversation instruct us, it is critique of North Americans by Cakchiquel, and continuing mutual critique, that issues in communal conditions for North American experience of "truth."

Yet this insight concerning the necessity of breadth, or a "wide reflective equilibrium" between diverse perspectives, leaves unaddressed the question of precisely which positions and voices constitute the widest parameters of a conversation. Hence, I propose a fifth feature of conversation—*the acknowledgment of a privilege for those excluded or absent from the conversation.* Recognizing the voices of those absent from conversation—often voiceless because of death, persistent hunger, or by systematic distortion of social and political life—is the crucial way by which fullest breadth of conversation occurs, a breadth needed for the truth of reasoning to occur and be sustained.

I say that those who are excluded by systemic oppression have a privilege, not in the preposterous sense that *only* the excluded ones have the truth or that they *always* speak the truth, but in three other senses.

First, those marginalized and absent from a given conversation constitute the outer-reaches of conversational community, where the width or breadth of the conversation is intensified. Those excluded and marginalized from our conversations constitute and intensify the communal breadth that is necessary for experience of truth. They constitute and intensify this width in a way that those "expert in," long-accustomed to, or at the center of the conversation cannot do. They make possible the constitution of a community that features the kind of breadth necessary for a genuinely *wide* reflective equilibrium.

Second, this privilege lies in the oppressed's greater experiences of negativity. True, all parties to the conversation suffer, have negative experiences, and draw insight from them. But on top of the negativity and suffering borne by all people, other systemic distortions are imposed on some groups. The oppressed, then, not only occupy a privileged position that intensifies the breadth of a conversation; they also have a distinctive content of insight borne out of sustained, radical suffering. Many occasionally affirm the role of suffering in seasoning one's knowledge and in generating insight.[39] But the relationship of negativity to insight needs to be affirmed, such that those forced to cope with sustaining life and joy under the conditions of imposed, systemic injustice are affirmed as possessing unusual insight—possessing a "privilege" in the sense of an insight borne of radical negativity not experienced by more elite, centrist groups.[40]

Third, there is a certain privilege lying in the expanded vision of social and political life that marginalized, oppressed groups have that those at the center of social political systems usually do not have. As Janice E. Perlman's studies of the poor in the slums of Rio de Janeiro show, those marginalized and oppressed are not cut off from structures of power such that they lack familiarity with them. Rather, their marginality is a thoroughgoing integration into the world of the powerful, whereas their opportunities and benefits are unequally restrained.[41] Not only in Rio, but also in Washington, D.C., Houston, and Princeton, subordinated groups not only have learned how to survive in the powerless regions of a system; they also have learned about the culture of the powerful. They tend to know the dynamics not only of their own muted group, but also of many dynamics in the groups that dominate them.[42] They tend to be "bi-cultural" in this sense. With respect to African American women, for example, Bell Hooks has written:

> Living as we did—on the edge—we developed a particular way of seeing reality. We looked both from the outside in and from the inside out. We focused our attention on the center as well as on the margin. We understood both. This mode of seeing reminded us of the existence of a whole universe, a main body made up of both margin and center.[43]

In such greater wholeness of vision, there is another meaning of the privilege of marginalized and oppressed groups.

The North Americans' encounter with the Cakchiquel then takes on additional significance, from the perspective of such a privilege. The Cakchiquel are not just widely arrayed ones, constituting the breadth or outer regions of North American conversational practice. They are also privileged voices with indispensable insights about the nature of the whole within which North and Central American interaction occurs. Without making the Cakchiquel themselves immune from criticism, their words and critique have all the force that I have suggested is displayed by the privileged, excluded, and oppressed ones.

A cultural-political hermeneutic is, therefore, far from conversation in the sense of an urbane talking or exchange of ideas. Through its heightening of difference, it highlights particularities in all their cultural specificity and involves exposure to the radical critique emerging from politically subjugated groups who systematically are made absent from conversation. The logic of this cultural-political hermeneutic, moving through the five features I have discussed above, provides the structure for a basic interpretive strategy needed by theological study if it is indeed to appropriate the structure of intercultural hermeneutic, with its dwelling between an ethnographic heightening of difference, on the one hand, and the generation of critique, on the other.

Implications for Theological Education. If this cultural-political hermeneutic were to be appropriated, again by scholars working in any of the areas of theological education, some further implications for theological study result in addition to those I have already enumerated as implied by the interpretive strategy of intercultural hermeneutic.

First, and above all, *theological study needs to reorient its understandings of authority, norms, and criteria.* Within the interpretive structure of a cultural-political hermeneutic, our norms and criteria must be sought less through the finding of "bases" and "foundations" (whether these be philosophical "depths," biblical "grounds," or theological "foundations") and more by intensifying the *breadth* of perspectives and contexts in which our conversations and criticisms are practiced and tested. Biblical interpretation's authority, for example, rests not primarily on kinds of expertise that dive deep to find "foundations" or on exegetical certainties unmediated by personal, social, and political interests, but by those kinds of expertise that facilitate breadth—a breadth that comes through focusing the role of one's own distinct location in interpretation, and then considering other different locations, thus affirming difference *beyond* the liberal conversationalists' paradigm of tolerance. Such an attending to difference, if in accord with the structure of a cultural-political hermeneutic, moves toward a posture that lives and thinks with and for those outside the conversation, those denied texts, speech, voice—presence and life. In all areas of theological reflection, a cultural-political hermeneutic implies a recasting of authority, truth, and reasoning in terms of a breadth that deliberately gives place to previously ignored voices like those of women, African Americans, gays and lesbians, and other marginalized and oppressed groups. On this view, voices and positions have their relative "authority" or make their "normative" claims in terms of the greater or lesser breadth featured by the communities within which their claims emerge.[44]

A second implication concerns the identity of groups and institutions that are the scenes of theological study. When cultivating a variety of disciplines, methods, and diverse cultural perspectives, *theological study can view its pursuit of difference not as a dilution of the identity of its scene of theological education, but as a way of constituting that identity*. In other words, identity within the interpretive strategy of cultural-political hermeneutics becomes less a matter of being one thing amid or against many other things (say, a theological or religious tradition over against others), and more a matter of being a scene where, in a distinctive way, many things are critically orchestrated, where diverse cultural methods and perspectives are articulated with one another. Just what is meant by "a distinctive way" would depend on a case-by-case analysis. In my own seminary's social location at Princeton Theological Seminary, the constant challenge is to find ways that allow a Presbyterian or Reformed identity to be not just an ecclesial or theological stance over and against other identities, but an identity understood as a distinctive way of orchestrating different identities. There are many ways to distinguish and relate alternative identities, and I cannot enter discussion of those issues here. It is essential to stress, however, that the meaning of the word *identity* is a multifaceted and even a conflictual one, not a homogeneous one.

A third implication focuses on *the need for more focused roles of critical theories in theological education.* In the kind of cultural-political hermeneutic I have proposed, the various critical theories (say, sociology of knowledge, Marxist class analyses, feminist critical theories, and others) are both affirmed more radically than I know them often to be in scenes of theological study, while they also are deprived of the kind of reductionist powers that some may claim for them. If theological study's truth and authority come by highlighting differences to the point of critique, and if this latter critique is taken seriously, then theological study must be exposed to the full force of the critics' claims and counterclaims.

If we really do take seriously, for example, the critique by feminists that theological study is dominated by androcentric structures, then it is part of the labor of theological study to acknowledge, within its structure, the place of gender, literary, and political theories. Without these, theological study's affirmation of feminist projects is either neglected or done naively and paternalistically, and is then often prone to dismissal as "passing fad." A similar place for critical theory must emerge in theological study for the critical insights of Marx, Freud, Nietzsche, and others. At present, systemic study of these thinkers' criticisms are all too often seriously studied only in the divinity schools and religion departments of universities and colleges, or serve only as occasional sparring partners within theological settings.

To make this place in theological education for critical theory need not also mean that theological study is "reduced to" or "explained away by" any one or combination of critical theories. Critical theorists—whether feminist, philosophical, psychological, sociological—also use mediated interpretations, and as such their positions never offer a fulcrum from which all others can be assessed. They, too, must seek their authority within communities seeking a breadth of voices and present lives. Insofar as these critical theories convey the insights of those who are radically marginalized and oppressed, they do have the kind of "privilege" I specified for insights emerging from oppressed groups. This privilege does not entail, however, a power to reduce the complexity of theological study's subject matter to only the categories operative in a given set of critical theories (categories of gender, culture, class, and the like), nor does it mean that insights from critical theorists are immune to criticism from other perspectives and theories.

A final implication may be the most unsettling for theological study. If theological study is marked by a cultural-political hermeneutic that pursues difference to the point of critique emanating from the most radically marginalized ones, from those who are usually absent from scenes of theological study, then this means that *theological study is, strangely, always a turning toward those who are alienated from, and often critical of, that study.* To present this implication is to suggest that the very structure of theological study is not just a matter of identifying and relating interpretive strategies internal to it, but also a challenge to be with, for, alongside, and troubled by those outside our scenes of theological education.

In North American and European scenes of theological study especially, where access to that study often entails not only the expenditure of hard work, but, of more importance, class status, wealth, or access to the right contacts (various old-boys' networks, for example), pursuing the truth and authority of theological study may be especially painful, because the fact that theologians' reasoning is linked to those who are absent from their conversation means crossing not only cultural and national boundaries (something theological educators find it easy to do through jet travel), but also means exposure to and entry into regions of conflict in which gender, racial, economic, and cultural differences are all variously operative. From the viewpoint of a cultural-political hermeneutic, crossing these boundaries is not necessary just to communicate, to express, or to qualify a truth or authority already had in theological study; rather, it is the way theological study's truth and authority *can be had at all.*

Given this last implication, theological study, in all its fields or disciplines, can be viewed as having an interpretive structure that is always carrying it beyond itself and is always unsettled. Not to be thus unsettled is to dwell in untruth. It is to lack authority. The kind of communal authority suggested by a cultural-political hermeneutic will come by moving alongside not only the geographically and linguistically different ones (say, the Maya of the Guatemalan highlands) but also among those who are alienated but "near" (women, African Americans, the North American "underclass"), from whom we North American males are often also alienated.

In summary, this cultural-political hermeneutic provides an interpretive strategy, the structure of which theological study needs to appropriate. It joins the other synchronic strategy of intercultural hermeneutics that I proposed earlier. Together, these two strategies offer important resources for a theological study that intends to struggle, think, and minister within a world that is both multicultural and also experiencing various forms of systemic domination.

My proposal is that these two "synchronic" strategies for navigating the complexities of our present (intercultural hermeneutic and cultural-political hermeneutic) be thoroughly integrated with currently reigning "diachronic" ones. I have *not* proposed that a synchronic hegemony merely replace the diachronic one. That would hardly enable an adequate interpretation of the situations theological educators face today. It would ignore the historical character of situations and the need for historical strategies of interpretation. As I have argued in this essay, however, it is the synchronic strategies of interpretation that are still most ignored by theological educators and in need of disciplined attention in our academies.

NOTES

1. For this essay, I have changed the name of this Guatemalan pastor.

2. For specific documentation of the repression experienced by Guatemalan towns, see Robert M. Carmack, *Harvest of Violence: Mayan Indians and the Guatemalan Crisis* (Tulsa: University of Oklahoma Press, 1988).

3. Edward Farley, *The Fragility of Knowledge: Theological Education in the Church and the University* (Philadelphia: Fortress Press, 1988), 136–37.

4. For examples in theology of the use of both criteria of appropriateness and of intelligibility, see Schubert M. Ogden, *The Point of Christology* (New York: Harper & Row, 1987), 20–21; and David Tracy, *Blessed Rage for Order: The New Pluralism in Theology* (New York: Seabury Press, 1975), 64–73.

5. On notions of diversity and "width" in community as crucial to reasoned judgment, see Francis Schüssler Fiorenza, *Foundational Theology: Jesus and the Church* (New York: Crossroad, 1984), 301–304.

6. Quoted from Richard J. Bernstein, *Beyond Objectivism and Relativism: Science, Hermeneutics, and Praxis* (Philadelphia: University of Pennsylvania Press, 1983), 224.

7. On this method in philosophy, see Israel Scheffler, "On Justification and Commitment," *Journal of Philosophy* 51 (1954): 180–91. For discussion of Scheffler's notions in theology, see Fiorenza, *Foundational Theology,* 302.

8. For feminist hermeneutics, see Mary Ann Tolbert, ed., *The Bible and Feminist Hermeneutics, Semeia,* Society of Biblical Literature (Chico, Calif.: Scholars Press, 1983); and for African American hermeneutics, see as one example, Henry Louis Gates, Jr., *The Signifying Monkey: A Theory of Afro-American Literary Criticism* (New York: Oxford University Press, 1988).

9. Elisabeth Schüssler Fiorenza, *In Memory of Her: A Feminist Theological Reconstruction of Christian Origins* (New York: Crossroad, 1983), 32.

10. Both the predominance of diachronic perspectives and

the suspicion of present revelatory experience are evident in Avery Dulles's study *Models of Revelation* (Garden City, N.Y.: Image Books, 1985).

11. Renita Weems, "The State of Biblical Interpretation: An African American Womanist Critique" (Paper presented at Princeton Theological Seminary, May 17, 1988), 30–31; and Elisabeth Schüssler Fiorenza, "The Ethics of Biblical Interpretation: Decentering Biblical Scholarship," *Journal of Biblical Literature* 107 (1988): 14.

12. On the notion of critical pluralism, see Ihab Hassan, *The Postmodern Turn: Essays in Postmodern Theory and Culture* (Columbus: Ohio State University Press, 1987), 167–82, esp. 182.

13. Ibid., 167.

14. Langdon Gilkey, "Events, Meanings and the Current Tasks of Theology," *Journal of the American Academy of Religion* 53, no. 3 (December 1985): 729–30.

15. See the special issue on "Globalizing Theological Education in North America," *Theological Education* 22, no. 2 (Spring 1986).

16. Anthropology has been described as a "would-be discipline" in Stephen Toulmin, *Human Understanding: The Use and Evolution of Concepts* (Princeton: Princeton University Press, 1972), 380–82.

17. George E. Marcus and Michael M. J. Fischer, *Anthropology as Cultural Critique: An Experimental Moment in the Human Sciences* (Chicago: University of Chicago Press, 1986), 15–16.

18. Just a few examples are Norman Gottwald's use of Marvin Harris's cultural materialism for research in the Hebrew scriptures (Norman K. Gottwald, *Tribes of Yahweh: A Sociology of the Religion of Liberated Israel: 1250–1050 B.C.* [Maryknoll, N.Y.: Orbis Books, 1979]); Bruce Malina's use of Mary Douglas's grid/group theory for New Testament studies (Bruce J. Malina, *Christian Origins and Cultural Anthropology: Practical Models for Biblical Interpretation* [Atlanta: John Knox Press, 1986]); David Tracy's and George Lindbeck's appropriations of Clifford Geertz's theories of culture and religious symbol toward very different theological

ends (Tracy, *Blessed Rage for Order,* 92–93; and George A. Lindbeck, *The Nature of Doctrine: Religion and Theology in a Postliberal Age* [Philadelphia: Westminster Press, 1984], 20–21); and Wolfhart Pannenberg's use of social and cultural anthropological theory in his theological anthropology (Wolfhart Pannenberg, *Anthropology in Theological Perspective,* trans. Matthew J. O'Connell [Philadelphia: Westminister Press, 1985], 315–484). There is also a substantial presence of anthropological perspectives among some of the more sophisticated evangelical scholars interested in missions and intercultural translation of biblical and theological messages; see, for example, Charles H. Kraft, *Christianity in Culture: A Study in Dynamic Biblical Theologizing in Cross-Cultural Perspective* (Maryknoll, N.Y.: Orbis Books, 1979).

19. On the notion of "reflexivity," see Susan J. Hekman, *Hermeneutics and the Sociology of Knowledge* (Notre Dame, University of Notre Dame Press, 1986), 70–71, 80–81.

20. Recent ethnographies illustrating this include the following: Gananath Obeyeskere, *Medusa's Hair: An Essay on Personal Symbols and Religious Experience* (Chicago: University of Chicago Press, 1981); Margorie Shostak, *Nisa: The Life and Words of a !Kung Woman* (Cambridge: Harvard University Press, 1981); and Michelle Rosaldo, *Knowledge and Passion: Ilongot Notions of Self and Social Life* (New York: Cambridge University Press, 1980).

21. Robert Scholte, "Reply," *Current Anthropology* 16 (1975): 256.

22. See, for example, the arguments for capitalist market economy and corporate bureaucracy in Mary Douglas and Aaron Wildavsky, *Risk and Culture: An Essay on the Selection of Technological and Environmental Dangers* (Berkeley: University of California Press, 1982).

23. For summaries of anthropological work as what E. B. Tylor called a "Reformer's science," see Marcus and Fischer, *Anthropology as Cultural Critique,* 128–31.

24. Ibid., 137.

25. Ibid., 157–63.

26. Ibid., 163–65.

27. Paul Rabinow, *Reflections on Fieldwork in Morocco*

(Berkeley: University of California Press, 1977), 39.

28. E. E. Evans-Prichard, "Religion and the Anthropologists," *Blackfriars* 41 (1960): 110–11.

29. Max L. Stackhouse, *Apologia: Contextualization, Globalization, and Mission in Theological Education* (Grand Rapids: Eerdmans, 1988).

30. Ibid., 149, 151.

31. Ibid., 159–61, 165.

32. Bernstein, *Beyond Objectivism and Relativism,* 16–20.

33. Hans-Georg Gadamer, *Truth and Method* (New York: Crossroad, 1975) and *Reason in the Age of Science,* trans. Frederick G. Lawrence (Cambridge, Mass.: MIT Press, 1981). For helpful secondary literature, see Kathleen Wright, ed., *Festivals of Interpretation: Essays on Hans-Georg Gadamer's Work* (Albany, N.Y.: State University of New York Press, 1990) and Joel C. Weinshamer, *Gadamer's Hermeneutics: A Reading of Truth and Method* (New Haven, Conn.: Yale University Press, 1985).

34. Hans-Georg Gadamer, *Truth and Method* (New York: Crossroad, 1975), 324.

35. Ibid., 319.

36. See the summaries in Bernstein, *Beyond Objectivism and Relativism* 79–108.

37. In theology, the most thorough discussion and bibliography of literature supporting this approach to truth and reasoning may be found in Francis Schüssler Fiorenza, *Foundational Theology* 301–21.

38. Whether the North Americans constitute this for the Cakchiquel is another issue that would have to be examined in relation to Cakchiquel cultural experience.

39. Gadamer, *Truth and Method,* 319.

40. Acknowledging this privilege does not entail either romanticizing the oppressed for some noble "intuition" or legitimating their sufferings as some necessary means toward knowledge. The dangers of both romanticization and legitimation require vigilance, but the possibility of these dangers should not prohibit our acknowledging a unique, "privileged" insight available to those who are systematically oppressed.

41. Janice E. Perlman, *The Myth of Marginality: Urban*

Poverty and Politics in Rio de Janeiro (Berkeley: University of California Press, 1976).

42. Edwin Ardener, "Belief and the Problem of Woman," in *Perceiving Women,* ed. Shirley Ardener (London: J. M. Dent and Sons, 1975), 1–17; and Elaine Showalter, ed., *The New Feminist Criticism: Women, Literature, and Theory* (New York: Pantheon Books, 1985), 262–64.

43. Bell Hooks, *Feminist Theory: From Margin to Center* (Boston: South End Press, 1984), v.

44. For a Christian theology responding to this cultural-political hermeneutic, see my formulations in Mark Kline Taylor, *Remembering Esperanza: A Cultural-Political Theology for North American Praxis* (Maryknoll, N.Y.: Orbis Books, 1990).

10

Toward a Fundamental and Strategic Practical Theology

Don S. Browning

Recent philosophical investigations have taught us much about the practical nature of human knowledge. The hermeneutical philosophy of Gadamer and Ricoeur, the critical theory of Habermas, the ordinary language philosophy of Wittgenstein, Peters, and Winch, the pragmatism of Peirce, James, and Dewey, the neo-pragmatism of Bernstein and Rorty, and the philosophy of science of Kuhn all in different ways argue for the priority of practical interests in the formation of our cognitive and moral worlds.[1] Historical reason and practical reason, under the impact of Heidegger and Gadamer, are now seen by many as intimately related, if not identical. If these views are correct, the way we view the past is largely shaped by our present concerns, as indeed the way we deal with the present involves a reconstruction of the past.

These intellectual currents are influencing theological education and the way we envision the structure and movement of theology. This is especially true in the writings on theological education that have come from Edward Farley. The concern with the historicity of knowledge and the importance of the interpretation of situations for the integrity of theological education have been quite prominent in his writings.[2] The heightened prominence of practical knowledge can also be seen in the proposals of Joseph Hough and John Cobb to make "practical theological thinking" and "practical theology" the center of their reform of theological education.[3]

In addition to this appreciation for the practical in these systematic attempts to reformulate theological education, there is additional scattered evidence of the rebirth of the practical in theological education. New efforts to redefine practical theology can be found in Germany, Holland, England, Canada, and Latin America, as well as the United States.[4] These more recent formulations greatly enlarge the province of practical theology. Rather than envision practical theology as primarily theological reflection on the tasks of the ordained minister or the leadership of the church, as was the view of Schleiermacher,[5] these newer trends define practical theology as critical theological reflection on the church's ministry to the world.[6] In the United States, two volumes of essays[7] plus several books dealing explicitly with the reconceptualization of practical theology by Browning, Fowler, Gerkin, Groome, Schreiter, Winquist, Poling and Miller, and McCann and Strain all point to the breadth and vigor of this renewed interest in practical theology.[8]

In spite of this new interest in the practical in recent reconceptualizations of theological education and in practical theology, it is my conviction that the radical implications of the turn to "practical philosophy" have still not been comprehended fully in theological education circles. It seems not to be understood that, if this philosophical turn is taken seriously, all humanistic studies, including theological studies, are practical and historical through and through. In this view, all theology becomes practical theology; historical theology, systematic theology, and what I will call "strategic" practical theology all become moments within a more inclusive fundamental practical theology. Furthermore, because much of the turn to practical philosophy is presently characterized by an emphasis on dialogue and conversation, I will define fundamental practical theology *as critical reflection on the church's dialogue with Christian sources and other communities with the aim of guiding its action toward social and individual transformation.*

I

The Rebirth of Practical Philosophy

I use the phrase "practical philosophy" to refer to a loosely associated group of philosophical positions that emphasize the importance of *phronēsis* (practical wisdom) in contrast to the modern fascination with *theoria* (theoretical knowledge and thinking) or *techne* (technical knowledge and thinking). Since the Enlightenment, the modern experiment increasingly has been dedicated to the improvement of human life through the increase of objective scientific knowledge that is then applied to the technical solution of human problems. The modern university has built itself on the idea of increasing our cognitive grasp of the universe. Issues pertaining to the goals of human action are generally reduced to the technical solution of perceived problems. The goals of action increasingly are held to be self-evident, are thought to be a matter of individual choice, or are taken over uncritically from the surrounding culture. The rebirth of practical philosophy is designed to question the dominance of theoretical and technical reason, to secure in the university a stronger role for practical reason, and to demonstrate that critical reflection about the goals of human action is both possible and necessary, and that, as a matter of fact, practical reason does indeed function in much wider areas of human life than we realize—even, in fact, in the social and natural sciences. Furthermore, the rise of the practical philosophies, especially as influenced by Gadamer, has brought into closer relation historical thinking, hermeneutics, and practical reason or ethics.

These features of the practical philosophies can best

be illustrated by examining certain aspects of the thought of Hans-Georg Gadamer. Many of Gadamer's interpreters have overlooked the strong relation he believes to exist between understanding and what Aristotle called practical wisdom *(phronēsis)*. Gadamer writes: "If we relate Aristotle's description of the ethical phenomenon and especially of the virtue of moral knowledge to our own investigation, we find that Aristotle's analysis is in fact a kind of model of the problems of hermeneutics."[9] Gadamer makes this point in discussing the role of application in both his view of understanding and Aristotle's concept of *phronēsis*. The hermeneutic process aimed at the understanding of a classic text is, for Gadamer, like a moral conversation when moral is understood in the broadest sense. The hermeneutical conversation is like Aristotle's concept of practical wisdom, because neither applies abstract universals to concrete situations. In both hermeneutical conversation and moral judgment, concern with application is there from the beginning.

Hence, understanding or interpretation, whether in law, history, or theology, has for Gadamer from the outset a broadly moral concern with application. As Gadamer writes: "Application is neither a subsequent nor a merely occasional part of the phenomenon of understanding, but co-determines it as a whole from the beginning."[10] Understanding is a kind of moral conversation with a text or historic witness shaped throughout by practical concerns about application that emerge from our current situation.

Therefore, more than we sometimes have acknowledged, hermeneutics is a broadly moral conversation with a tradition's classic religiocultural monuments in which concern with practical application shapes from the beginning the questions we bring to these monuments. When seen from this perspective, understanding and *phronēsis* as practical wisdom interpenetrate and overlap. Richard Bernstein astutely makes this observation when he writes that it is a central thesis of Gadamer's *Truth and Method* that understanding, interpretation, and application are not distinct but intimately related. Bernstein writes:

> They are internally related; every act of understanding involves interpretation, and all interpretation involves application. It is Aristotle's analysis of *phronēsis* that, according to Gadamer, enables us to understand the distinctive way in which application is an essential moment of the hermeneutical experience.[11]

Rather than application to practice being an act that follows understanding, concern with practice, in subtle ways we often overlook, guides the hermeneutic process from the beginning. Gadamer's hermeneutic theory clearly breaks down the theory-to-practice (text-to-application) model of humanistic learning. By analogy, it undercuts this model in theological studies as well. The model it implies is more nearly a radical practice-theory-practice model of understanding that gives the entire theological enterprise a thoroughly practical cast.

The practical nature of the hermeneutical process is even more interesting and complicated when considered from the perspective of Gadamer's theory of "effective history." Gadamer develops the idea that the events of the past shape present historical consciousness. As Gadamer writes, there is a "fusion of the whole of the past with the present."[12] This suggests that when we interpret the classic religious texts of the past, we do not confront them as totally separate and alien entities, even if we consider ourselves unbelievers. Rather, these texts are already part of the believer and unbeliever before they begin their interpretation. Through our cultural heritage, these monuments of culture shape the fore-concepts and prejudices that make up the practical questions that we bring to our efforts to interpret the monuments themselves. Finally, the understanding process is depicted by Gadamer as a fusion of horizons between the practical questions and fore-concepts that we bring to our classic texts and the meaning and horizon of these texts and the questions they put to us.[13]

Gadamerian hermeneutic theory has profound implications for the reconceptualization of the full range of university studies. Not only does it have implications for the reenvisionment of the purposes of philosophy, the social sciences, and theology, but Richard Bernstein and Richard Rorty, with different degrees of debt to Gadamer, have carried hermeneutic theory into the philosophy of the natural sciences.[14] Earlier, Thomas Kuhn's own variety of hermeneutic theory helped first alert us to the tradition-laden and historically situated nature of the natural sciences.[15] These contemporary movements all have undercut foundationalist preoccupations with objectivity and have helped us understand how all the cultural sciences *(Geisteswissenschaften),* and perhaps the natural sciences *(Naturwissenshaften)* as well, can best be understood as dialectical movements from theory-laden practice to theory and back to a new theory-laden practice.

A Preliminary Sketch of the Structure of Theological Studies

So far, I have not argued that Gadamer's hermeneutical theory is a correct model for the humanities. Nor have I argued that his view of hermeneutics is more sound than the subjective and idealistic models of hermeneutics of Schleiermacher and Dilthey. My goal has been to present an interpretation of Gadamer that emphasizes a point that is often lost; that is, that there is an intimate relation in his thought between the hermeneutical process and practical wisdom, or *phronēsis*. Hence my argument is addressed to those already attracted by the conversational model of hermeneutics. Guided by Gadamer's view of the practical nature of understanding and the hermeneutic task, I would like to propose a theory of the structure of theological studies.

I recommend that we conceive of theology as primarily fundamental practical theology that contains within it four submovements: descriptive theology, historical theology, systematic theology, and what I call *strategic* practical theology. This view differs from several well-known proposals for the organization of theology. For instance, it differs somewhat from Schleiermacher's organization of theology into philosophical theology, historical theology, and practical theology.[16] Although Schleiermacher saw practical theology as the teleological goal and "crown" of theology, his view of theology still had a theory-to-practice structure; he understood theology as a movement from philosophical and historical theology to application in practical theology.[17] It is true that this structure is somewhat mitigated by the fact that Schleiermacher understood the whole of theology as a "positive" science in contrast to a "pure" or theoretical science. By positive science, Schleiermacher meant "an assemblage of scientific elements which belong together not because they form a constituent part of the organization of the sciences, as though by some necessity arising out of the notion of science itself, but only insofar as they are requisite for carrying out a practical task."[18] Such a view of theology clearly emphasizes the practical, conditioned, and historically located nature of all theology, and goes far toward making all of theology a basically practical task. Nonetheless, Schleiermacher saw theology as moving from historical knowledge to practical application and, in addition, had little idea about how the practices of the contemporary church play back onto the way we bring our questions to the historical sources.

My proposal also can be distinguished from other current understandings of the structure of theology. Paul Tillich divided theology into historical theology, systematic theology, and practical theology.[19] In the end, this too was a theory-to-practice model, even though Tillich granted that practical theology has a role in formulating the questions that systematic theology answers.[20] Regardless of this minor admission, the weight of his perspective clearly emphasized the theory-practice dichotomy. In his systematic theology, he wrote: "It is the technical point of view that distinguishes practical from theoretical theology. As occurs in every cognitive approach to reality, a bifurcation between pure and applied knowledge takes place in theology."[21] This statement is softened somewhat by the fact that Tillich saw the entire theological task as an existential enterprise, but even here "meaning" rather than the reconstruction of practice was the central thrust of his existential view of theology.

Both Schubert Ogden and David Tracy give heightened visibility to practical theology in their respective proposals for the organization of theology. Ogden indicates in a number of ways that he believes that practical theology is the application to practice of the truth of norms discovered by historical and systematic theology. He proposes a division of theology into historical, systematic, and practical. He gives a strongly cognitive definition of theology proper (systematic theology) as the task of "understanding the meaning of the Christian witness and assessing its truth." And he believes that theology as critical reflection on the truth of the Christian faith should be distinguished from what he calls "witness."[22]

A Revised Correlational Fundamental Practical Theology

My proposal takes its point of departure from the revisionist view of theology found in the work of David Tracy. But whereas Tracy divides theology into fundamental theology, systematic theology, and practical theology, I reverse his pattern by proposing a revised correlational fundamental practical theology that has within it the subspecialties of descriptive theology, historical theology, systematic theology, and strategic practical theology.

The strength of Tracy's proposal is that it is a revised or critical correlational approach to theology. Its weakness is that his vision of fundamental theology is concerned primarily with the conditions for cognitive and metaphysical verification. The principal criteria for the verification of the truth of fundamental theological claims are thought by Tracy to be "transcendental."[23] Although even in his fundamental theology Tracy builds significantly on the hermeneutical theory of Gadamer and

Ricoeur, he seems not to acknowledge that it is a fundamental practical theology that philosophical hermeneutics suggests rather than a fundamental theology concerned primarily with questions of cognitive and transcendental verification.[24]

However, the strength of Tracy's view of theology is easily applicable to a fundamental practical theology. But because of Tracy's revisionist correlational commitments, it would be a critical correlational fundamental practical theology. Fundamental theology, according to Tracy, determines the conditions for the possibility of the theological enterprise. If the conditions are strongly influenced by the close association between hermeneutics and *phronēsis*, as I outlined above, then fundamental theology determines the conditions for the possibility of a theology that would be seen first of all as an enterprise that deals with the normative and critical grounds of our religious praxis. Questions of the truth of Christian belief and conviction would be addressed as issues that are embedded in issues pertaining to practice.

Tracy's revised correlational theology is a *critical* correlational program. The meaning of this can be stated with reference to his understanding of Tillich's correlational approach to theology. Tillich believed that theology is a correlation of existential questions that emerge from cultural experience with answers from the Christian message.[25] Tracy's revised or critical correlational method goes beyond Tillich in envisioning theology as a *mutually* critical dialogue between the Christian message and contemporary cultural experience. Christian theology becomes a critical dialogue between the questions and the answers of the Christian faith and the questions and answers of cultural experience. In fact, according to Tracy, the Christian theologian is obliged to have this critical conversation in principle with "all other 'answers.' "[26]

When Tracy applies the revised correlational model to practical theology, the following definition emerges: "Practical theology is the mutually critical correlation of the interpreted theory and praxis of the Christian faith with the interpreted theory and praxis of the contemporary situation."[27] I propose that this excellent definition of practical theology be extended to become the definition of a fundamental practical theology. Furthermore, this fundamental practical theology should be the most inclusive definition of theology, making descriptive, historical, systematic, and strategic practical theology submovements within the larger framework.

This view insists that the description of situated and theory-laden religious and cultural practices is the first movement of both theology and theological education. That is why I suggest that we call this first movement descriptive theology. Questions of the following kind guide this movement of theological reflection: What, within a particular arena of practice, are we actually doing? What reasons, ideals, and symbols do we use to interpret what we are doing? What do we consider to be the sources of authority and legitimation for what we do? The description of these practices engenders questions about what we *really* should be doing and about the accuracy and consistency of our use of our preferred sources of authority and legitimation. For those who claim to be Christians, this process inevitably leads to a fresh confrontation with the normative texts and monuments of the Christian faith—the source of the norms of practice. Historical theology becomes the heart of the hermeneutical process, but it is now understood as a matter of putting the questions emerging from theory-laden practice to the central texts and monuments of the Christian faith.

This is the second movement within theology and theological education. The question that guides historical theology is, What do the normative texts that are already a part of our effective history *really* imply for our praxis when they are confronted as carefully and honestly as possible?[28] This is the place where the traditional disciplines of biblical studies, church history, and the history of Christian thought are to be located. But in this scheme, these disciplines and all of their technical literary-historical, textual, and social-scientific explanatory interests would be understood as basically practical hermeneutical enterprises. Their technical, explanatory, and distancing maneuvers would be temporary procedures designed to gain clarity within a larger hermeneutic effort to achieve understanding about our praxis and the theory behind it.[29]

The third movement is the turn to systematic theology. Systematic theology, when seen from the perspective of Gadamer's hermeneutics, is the fusion of horizons between the vision implicit in contemporary practices and the vision entailed in the practices of the normative Christian texts. This process of fusion between the present and the past is much different from a simple application of the past to the present. Systematic theology tries to gain as comprehensive a view of the present as possible. It tries to examine large encompassing themes about our present practices and the theory and vision latent in them. The systematic character of this movement of theology comes from the effort to investigate general themes of the gospel that respond to the most generic questions that characterize the situations of the present. This may entail questions that emerge out of the theory-laden practices of such general trends as modernity, liberal democracy, or technical rationality. There is a role for systematic theology within a fundamental practical theology, but it is a submovement or specific movement within a larger practical framework.

Two fundamental questions guide systematic theology. The first is, What new horizon of meaning is fused when the questions coming from our present practice are brought to the central Christian witness? The second is, What reasons can be advanced to support the validity claims of the new horizon of meaning that come from the fusion of present and past? This last question points to the additional obligation of systematic theology to introduce a critical and philosophical component into the theological process. There is, for instance, a role for transcendental judgments in critically testing the metaphysical claims of the Christian faith. But of even more importance, practical claims of the Christian faith need to be tested philosophically. And in the order of things suggested here, transcendental questions are the last rather than the first validity claims to be defended. This is true because many areas of collaboration between Christians and non-Christians are frequently developed without the resolution of transcendental claims. Furthermore, many reflective Christians themselves justify their faith on primarily practical grounds, even though they are quite unclear about the validity of its metaphysical claims. This is not to say that transcendental judgments in defense of metaphysical claims have no place in theology; rather, it is to say that we come to them gradually and even then only develop good reasons for these claims rather than definitive and universally convincing arguments.

My emphasis on the importance to hermeneutics of defending validity claims implicit in these new horizons places me in tension with Gadamer at one significant point. Habermas and Bernstein have severely criticized Gadamer for being a traditionalist and for having no method to test the adequacy of the horizons that emerge out of the hermeneutic conversations between the questions of the present and the witness of the classic texts and monuments.[30] To develop the general criteria for testing the practical validity claims of the Christian faith is the task of theological ethics. Theological ethics should be seen as a dimension of systematic theology.

This, in fact, is the way it generally has been conceived in the history of Protestant attempts to organize the theological disciplines (the so-called Protestant encyclopedia).[31] Without developing a foundationalist view of justifying validity claims that would be incompatible with the hermeneutical and pragmatic view of theology developed here, I will give below some suggestions for how systematic theology can advance what Bernstein calls "the best possible reasons and arguments that are appropriate to our hermeneutical situation in order to validate claims to truth."[32] Such reasons will not satisfy the foundational aspirations for absolute validity and total certainty typical of Cartesianism in science and philosophy or Kantianism in morals. They should, however, constitute reasons that can advance conversations between competing perspectives.

And finally, the fourth movement of theology and of theological education is what I am calling "strategic practical theology." I have chosen the word *strategic* to distinguish this form of practical theology from fundamental practical theology, which is, I am proposing, the most inclusive term for the theological task. There are four basic questions of strategic practical theology. First, how do we understand this concrete situation in which we must act? (The concern with the concrete features of situations in contrast to their general features is what distinguishes strategic practical theology from systematic theology.) Second, what should be our praxis in this concrete situation? Third, what means, strategies, and rhetorics should we use in this situation? And fourth, how do we critically defend the norms of our praxis in this concrete situation? By praxis, I do not just mean ethical practice in any narrow sense of that word, although I certainly mean that in part. Praxis here refers to all the realms of strategic practical theology—ethical, educational, homiletic, liturgic, and poimenic (care). For all these areas, questions of norms, rhetorics, and strategies are relevant. At the same time, the ethical component does have a unique relevance to all of these realms. But in this fourth movement, ethics has to do with the concrete situations rather than the general features of situations typical of the ethical interests of systematic theology. The range of questions that guide strategic practical theology helps us understand the complexity of both this movement of theology and this aspect of theological education.

This is the place in theology where the interpretation of present situations comes together with both the hermeneutical process and our final critical efforts to advance justifications for the relative adequacy of the new horizons of meaning that hermeneutics has brought into existence. It is indeed the crown, as Schleiermacher said, of the theological task. But strategic practical theology is no longer the application to practice of the theoretical yield of Bible, church history, and systematic theology as it was in the old Protestant quadrivium. Concern with questions of practice and application, as Gadamer has argued, has been present from the beginning. Strategic practical theology is more the culmination of an inquiry that has been practical throughout than it is the application of theory to the specifics of praxis.

The traditional fields associated with practical theology will still be present. These might include liturgics, homiletics, education, and care. But in keeping with the move to go beyond yet include the clerical paradigm, strategic practical theology is concerned with areas of praxis that relate to the church's activity in the world as well as its ministries within its own walls. Therefore, a practical theology of care is not just *pastoral* care; it has to do with the church's strategy to create and influence the structures of care in society, most of which are allegedly secular. The same is true with education; it entails not only concern with the religious education of the faithful but with the goals and purposes of all education in modern societies. This view also would include liturgics and homiletics. They would not only be concerned with the church's internal worship and preaching; they also would be concerned with the public liturgies and public rhetoric in both the church and the rest of society. As I indicated above, theological ethics as concerned with the concrete contexts of action would be an abiding concern touching all of these traditional regions of practical theology.

The fourth question of a strategic practical theology—the question of the critical validation of the norms of praxis—I will bring up again toward the end of this essay. Let me conclude this section on strategic practical theology by pointing to how this movement of theology plays back on the entire hermeneutic circle. At the beginning of this discussion, I pointed out how descriptions of present religious and secular practices form the questions that we bring to the hermeneutical process. The practices that emerge from the judgments of strategic practical theology will themselves soon engender new questions that start the hermeneutical circle again. Within the flux and turns of history, our present practices only seem secure for a period before they meet a crisis and pose new questions that take us through the hermeneutical circle once again.

II

Implications for the Movements of Theological Education

The reader will notice that I have spoken simultaneously about the *structure* and *movements* of both *theology* and *theological education*. If one is somewhat convinced by this suggested outline for the structure of theology, what would it imply for theological education? It implies that theological education would be organized around four movements: (1) descriptive theology understood as a "thick description" (to use a phrase of Clifford Geertz) of present religious and cultural practices (and the theories—symbols, myths, ethics—that ground them); (2) historical theology (guided by questions that emerge from movement one); (3) systematic theology (a search for generic features of the Christian message in relation to generic features of the present situation); and (4) strategic practical theology (studies about the norms and strategies of the concrete practices of the church—first for the laity in the world and then for clergy as leaders of both the mission and cultic life of the church). One can imagine these movements being organized serially over a period of three or four years. One can also imagine them being taught simultaneously in a spiral built around successive exercises in the description and normative address of practice-theory-practice situations. But whether they are organized serially or taught simultaneously is less important than that they be recognized as movements of the total fundamental practical theological task. The main point is that both faculty and students would need to understand and agree that something like these four movements constitute the practical habitus of theological education, and approach their studies with some variation of this practical hermeneutical model in mind.[33]

In this view of things, the distinction between university theological education and seminary education for clergy would be modest; all would be the same for both settings except that seminary education for the professional clergy would give additional attention to descriptions of the practices of ordained ministers and would work in its strategic practical theology on the specific leadership practices of ordained ministers. The fact that strategic practical theology serves the church would not mean, in principle, that it would have no place in the university. Just as law, medicine, business, and social work educate the leadership of these institutions in the university, the university can as well, as it does in Europe, Great Britain, and Canada, provide for critical theological studies relevant to the education of the leadership of those religious institutions that have been central to the life of that society. This is a point that Schleiermacher saw well and argued for in his own view of theology as a positive science.

Fundamental Practical Theology and the CPE Model

Possibly the most novel aspect of my proposal is the suggestion to incorporate into the movements of theological education some of the purposes of clinical pastoral education (CPE). Although I have criticized CPE, I also acknowledge important insights to be gained from this model. The clinical pastoral education method goes back to Anton Boisen's suggestion that ministers should learn to study the "human document" as well as the literary text.[34] This developed into a widely popular supplement to ministerial education. Ministry students would spend a ten-to-twelve-week period ministering, under the guidance of an accredited supervisor, to the patients of a general or mental hospital. Although the patient as human document was the main focus of reflection early in the movement, gradually the person of the ministerial student and his or her relation to the patient became the center of attention. The methodology of the CPE movement varies from center to center and frequently degenerates into subjectivism and specialization. Too frequently the interior perceptions and psychological history of the student are central. Also, visions and models of ministry often are restricted to the specialized functions of the modern hospital. This leaves students with narrow understandings of ministry to bring back into the life of the congregation and other nonmedical contexts.

In spite of these criticisms, most students have felt that they received something from the CPE experience that was present in few places in theological education. I suggest that the CPE model actually hit upon a rather unsystematic practical hermeneutical model and gained its power from its rough approximation of the early part of the four movements of theological education outlined above. Its strength lay in the fact that it enacted rather well the first movement—the descriptions of present theory-laden practices. It did this at the same time that the Protestant quadrivium was functioning deductively (from theory to practice) in its movement from Bible, church history, and systematic theology to practical theology. Its main weakness can be found in the unsteady and uncareful progression that the CPE methodology took through the last three steps of the practical hermeneutical process—the movements through historical and systematic theology to strategic practical theology. It also was unable to replicate itself in other than hospital settings. With few exceptions, the CPE model has not been implemented successfully in nonmedical settings like the congregation or other public ministries. Because of this, the CPE model has often produced overly specialized views of ministry that do not serve students well after they leave the hospital.

But in spite of these shortcomings, the CPE model has planted a seed that now needs to be carefully nurtured by a more adequate practical hermeneutical model. In addition, the insights of the CPE model need to be moved out of the medical setting and into theological studies in the university and seminary. This can happen if we understand the full implications of beginning the hermeneutical circle with a careful and multidimensional description of present practices, both religious and secular, and both individual and corporate.

This can be done if one broadens the revised correlational model presented by Tracy. For Tracy, a theology operates on a genuinely revised correlational model if, as he says in his book on fundamental theology, it critically correlates its investigation into the two sources of theology. The two sources are, for him, "Christian Texts and Common Human Experience and Language."[35] As we already have seen, when this formulation is transferred to the arena of praxis, practical theology becomes "the mutually critical correlation of the interpreted theory and praxis of the Christian fact and the interpreted theory and praxis of the contemporary situation."[36] Although one pole of the correlative task actually involves "interpretations" of common experience, Tracy, in effect, elects common *cultural* experience and practices as one of the poles of the correlative process.

In order to make contact between Tracy's revised correlational model and the CPE approach, one needs to refine Tracy's concept of "common human experience" and his more practical reformulation of it into "interpreted theory and praxis of the contemporary situation." Evelyn and James Whitehead, in their *Method in Ministry*, recommend differentiating Tracy's " 'common human experience' . . . into two separable poles of reflection."[37] The Whiteheads divide common experience into "personal" experience and the "corporate" experience of the community. Transferred to the arena of praxis, this division would entail (1) personal interpretations of the practices (religious and secular) of individual agents, (2) interpretations of the practices of their communities and institutions, and (3) interpretations of religiocultural self-interpretations, symbols, and narratives. CPE has its power, I believe, because it takes personal interpretations of individual practices into its systematic reflections. It also permits into reflection interpretations of the practices of the hospital community. And occasionally it relates these two interpretative perspectives to larger interpretations of common cultural experience, for example, the general cultural fear of death and aging, the cultural idolatry of youth, or the cultural reverence for technical reason and medical heroism. However, the power of CPE does not derive from its concern with general or common experience, but from its concern with interpretations of "my experience and practice" and "my community's experience and practice." I propose that something like the full range of the description of experiences and practices (from the personal, to the person's immediate communities, and then to broader religiocultural symbols and stories) be more systematically included in the first movement of theological education in any of its settings.

This first movement, of course, would not be an end in itself; to stop the theological education process with the first step would be subjectivism. But if this first movement is used to refine the questions (the practical prejudices of Gadamer's hermeneutics) that lead back to historical theology, systematic theology, and then finally to the complexities of strategic practical theology, then the spirit and impulse of CPE can have a healthy influence indeed on theological education in all contexts, both the university as well as the seminary that is dedicated to the education of ordained ministers.

Various disciplines can help describe the theory-laden practices of concrete people in their specific communities within the context of larger cultural symbols and narratives. Clearly, psychology and psychoanalysis can uncover aspects of the interpreted practices of individuals. However, these psychological disciplines should not function as natural sciences, exhaustively explaining individual subjective experience. Rather, they should function more as hermeneutic disciplines that permit a unique retrospective glance at the developmental history of the interpretations that the individual brings to his or her social and religious practices.[38] Object relations theory in the writings of Guntrip, Winnicott, Kohut, and others helps us understand ways in which individual experience is actually composed of internalized social experience.[39] A nuanced analysis of individual experience does not necessarily lead to subjectivism and individualism; our inner world leads back to the social world of history, culture, and public issues. When rightly seen, even the interpreted practices of individuals can lead directly to the larger hermeneutical process.

Furthermore, the psychological and psychoanalytic disciplines may help uncover discontinuities between a person's ideals and his or her actual practices. Sociology can function similarly to uncover the unconscious or suppressed interpretations and practices for the communities of the theological student. Also, as Habermas has suggested, psychoanalysis and Marxist social thought can constitute a kind of critical theory uncovering systematic distortions in the communicative practices of individual theological students and their communities.[40] These disciplines, within the context of historical and systematic theology, can also help uncover ideological distortions within the normative religious texts. Furthermore, psychoanalysis and sociology can be used to uncover the depth, or "archeology," to use a phrase of Paul Ricoeur, of broader cultural trends as Freud, Weber, Rieff, and many others have shown.[41]

There is a role for these secular disciplines in the description of individual, communal, and cultural practices. It must be emphasized, however, that the role for the social sciences is partial; they should not be seen as reductively or exhaustively explanatory. These disciplines help us uncover trends that restrict and shape but not necessarily eliminate human freedom.

Yet the description of situated individual, communal, and general cultural practices is never accomplished by the social sciences alone. These practices are also interpreted by the ideals and norms implicit in the theory of these practices. And, insofar as the practices gain their norms from Christian sources, these meanings too play back on them and constitute one perspective on their interpretation. But this raises the following questions: Does the practice in question *really* conform to Christian norms? Is the practice humanly authentic when measured from the perspective of Christian meanings? Such questions move the theological student backward through the practical hermeneutical circle that I described above. Theological education can profit from these depth perspectives on the description of practices, some of which were used with reasonable success in the CPE movement.

I offer a brief illustration of what this approach to theological education might mean, not so much for the details of a theological curriculum, but for a teaching ethos that might permeate the entire process of theological education. For example, what might this point of view mean for teaching an introductory course in practical theology? In addition to assigning students a variety of theoretical readings, I made an assignment for a writing project that necessitated the students' making use of these four movements. I did this by asking them to choose a contemporary issue in religious life in our society that was of vital importance to them. It was to be an issue so vital that it served as a basic motivation behind their interest in theological education. In order to aid them in their thick description of the respective issues they chose (the first movement of a fundamental practical theology), I held a long evening meeting when the nine students of this class told the history of their interest in the issue. One student chose the tension between new age religion and Christianity. Another chose the way psychiatry relates to the religion of its patients. Another was interested in the status and theological understanding of the newly emerging profession of lay ministers in the Roman Catholic Church. Another student chose homosexuality. Another chose the phenomenon of community organizations and the way various churches are using them as extensions of their public ministry. In every case, the students had a significant history of existential concern with their chosen issues. Their initial task was to describe this history at several levels: their personal involvements and motivations, the institutional context of the issue as they saw it, and the religiocultural meanings that surrounded the issue, especially as they experienced them.

This first step of what we are calling descriptive theology was to be carried over into a major paper to be written for the course. But the paper was actually to center on an interview the student was to have with another person who was, in some way, dealing with the student's chosen issue. The students were to begin the paper with a thick description of their own practices and attitudes as they related to the respective issues. More specifically, each student was to record her or his preunderstanding of the issue. For instance, the student who was concerned with homosexuality recorded his own prejudgments about it. The student concerned about the relation of new age religion to Christianity recorded his preunderstanding of that issue. But then the students were to describe, as best they could, the personal, institutional, and religiocultural situation of the interviewee as this related to the selected issue. The student interested in new age religion interviewed a manager of a new age bookstore. The student interested in psychiatry's handling of religion interviewed a psycshiatrist. The student interested in cults interviewed an acquaintance who had converted to the Jehovah's Witnesses. The student interested in homosexuality interviewed a gay graduate student. The papers summarized these interviews and provided thick descriptions of the situations of both the student and the person being interviewed.

Questions about practice (about what good practice would really be) emerged from these thick descriptions of both interviewer and interviewee. This led to the second movement, that is, historical theology. In the midst of this limited project, however, this movement was addressed by asking the student to present the argument of two serious books that could serve as guides to the Christian witness on the issue he or she was investigating. The point, here, was to investigate the historical sources from the angle of vision of the student's description of contemporary practices, the theories implicit within them, and the questions that they pose. The student investigating homosexuality, for instance, used Helmut Thielicke's *The Ethics of Sex* and James Nelson's *Embodiment*.

The next task, which captured some of the features of systematic theology, was not only to lay out the general themes of these guides to the classic Christian sources but to begin a critical dialogue between these guides in an attempt to determine their relative adequacy. In the case of some projects, this task of isolating basic general themes and beginning the process of critically testing their adequacy was enriched by analytic insights from moral philosophy. The task, here, was to give the student an introductory exercise in making critical judgments about the relative adequacy of different interpretive theological perspectives and advancing reasons as to why one view might be better than another. This, of course, is a large task that involves much more than either I can discuss here or the students could adequately address within the context of an introductory course. Nonetheless, they were introduced to the task of critically testing theological arguments.

The fourth movement, however, gave the project its distinctively practical cast and made it a unique assignment in comparison to the students' other theological studies. Here the task was to write the conclusion of their paper for their interviewee rather than for me the professor. They were to attempt to communicate their preferred position on the issue at hand to the person they had interviewed. They were to communicate this position with sensitivity to the views and situation of this person as well as their own situation and preunderstandings of the issue. The students were to look for identities, nonidentities, and analogies between their preferred view and the situated views of their interviewee. The students also were to advance critical reasons for the more adequate position, but to do so in such a way as to make contact with the situation and preunderstandings of the person they had interviewed. In most cases, the students actually went back to their interviewees and shared their paper with them. Hence, the entire project was a dialogue between the students and their subjects around an issue that the classics of the Christian faith also in some fashion address. In virtually all cases, the students reported a change—sometimes quite revolutionary—between their initial preunderstanding and their understanding of the issue at the conclusion of their dialogue. Because they were sensitive to the changes in themselves, they were also more sensitive to the changes that this dialogue invoked in their subjects—changes that were sometimes modest and sometimes profound.

Space does not permit a full commentary on this project. I will add only this: I explained to the students that not all classes in their theological education should be structured in this manner. But I suggested that they might better keep track of the various twists and turns of their theological education if they saw it in its entirety as entailing various deeper investigations of each of these four movements, often considered more discretely and deeply than was the case in this rather large practical synthetic assignment. Theological education should provide an opportunity to both see and practice this process as a whole as well as delve deeply into the various movements and submovements considered both relatively discretely but also, once again, in relation to the entire fundamental practical theological task.

Further Comparisons

There are several recent proposals pertaining to the structure of theology that have either influenced or are similar to the view presented here. If space permitted, I would like to discuss at length the contributions of Juan Luis Segundo, Joseph Hough and John Cobb, and Charles Wood, in addition of those of Johann Baptist Metz, whose views I will discuss more thoroughly. Segundo's view of the hermeneutic circle is very close to mine, but I am somewhat uncomfortable with his rather rigid precommitments.[42] For instance, I agree that "partiality to the poor" is *in some way* part of the central witness of the Christian faith, but there are other surprises in the scriptures that these precommitments may lead us to miss.[43] Furthermore, Segundo's own interpretation of this precommitment may obscure other profound elements of biblical justice.

The proposal to make the capacity for "practical theological thinking" the goal of theology and the central task of theological education in Hough's and Cobb's *Christian Identity and Theological Education* is extremely appealing. I have said so elsewhere in print.[44] Yet in many ways, their excellent proposals are still caught in a theory-to-practice model; their justifiable concern with Christian identity still leads them to move from historical theology to practical theology, almost leaving out systematic theology altogether.[45] And finally, I am deeply impressed with Charles Wood's definition of theology in *Vision and Discernment* as "critical inquiry into the validity of the Christian witness."[46] Wood's view of theology as critical reflection on both Christian belief and activity is clearly congruent with my proposals. But Wood comes dangerously close to a theory-to-practice model in his organization of the structure of theology into the five subdisciplines of historical theology, philosophical theology, practical theology, systematic theology, and moral theology.[47] In beginning with historical theology and moving to practical theology, one detects the older applicational model. Wood tries to correct this by making systematic and moral theology follow and gain from practical theology. Hence, his model becomes something like a theory-practice-theory model. However, I believe it is both theologically and philosophically justifiable to use a more thoroughly practical and hermeneutical model from the beginning—a model more consistent with the full implications of the contemporary turn to practical philosophy.

My concept of "fundamental practical theology" is close to Johann Baptist Metz's concept of "practical fundamental theology."[48] Metz as a fundamental theologian is trying to make fundamental theology practical. In contrast, as a practical theologian, I am trying to expand the idea of practical theology and, at the same time, make it a fundamental and critical discipline. The result is very much the same. Metz and I agree that all theology is practical and that the Christian message is primarily practical in nature.[49] He too emphasizes the "primacy of praxis" over theory and explicitly repudiates the traditional model of practice as the application of theory.[59] He also believes in the importance of beginning theology with a description of contemporary practices, both religious and secular. This leads him to characterize contemporary secular practices as dominated by privatization and the "exchange" principle, and bourgeois religion as primarily in service to these trends.[51]

The differences between Metz's views and mine are few but substantial. I will mention only two. First, Metz is interested in beginning with the description of the contemporary situation, but he does this at the most general level and describes the central dominating global trend, that is, the domination of the exchange principle. In contrast to this, I have suggested beginning theology, and especially theological education, with a more differentiated description of contemporary practices; that is, a description of personal institutional practices and the religiocultural symbols that give them meaning. There is much that Metz's highly molar analysis misses. For instance, even if the exchange principle and privatism dominate much of contemporary social practice, there are still reactions to these trends, some defensible and some less so, that greatly complexify the range of contemporary practices. At this level, Metz's concern with the most generic features of the contemporary situation places his practical fundamental theology closer to what I have called systematic theology. That is, he is searching out, in a significant and creative way, the most general features of the contemporary situation and correlating them with some general themes and categories of the Christian enterprise. Although important, such an approach limits the range of practical issues that could stimulate the theological task.

Second, Metz's model of practical fundamental theology is less dialogical and mutually critical than my vision of a fundamental practical theology. For instance, Metz, in addition to having an extremely molar and generic interpretation of the contemporary situation, has little interest in describing the self-interpretations of contemporary trends, situations, and practices. Hence, Metz shares little of the interest that revised correlational practical theology has in a critical conversation between interpretations (including self-interpretations) of contemporary practices and interpretations of the Christian message. A revised correlational practical theology is interested in the identities, nonidentities, and analogies between interpretations of contemporary practices and interpretations of the praxis implications of the normative Christian events. Metz sees mostly nonidentity and discontinuity between contemporary practices and normative Christian practices. Because nonidentity and discontinuity dominate Metz's methodology, it precludes the possibility, I believe, of hearing and seeing the identities and analogies that may sometimes exist between the Christian message and the self-interpretations of various contemporary secular and religious practices.

There is also little interest, in Metz's view, in allowing a fully critical conversation between the Christian faith and interpretations of contemporary practices. The praxis implications of the *memoria passionis, martis et resurrectionis Jesu Christi* seem to need no test for their validity claims.[52] Indeed, Metz does claim that his practical fundamental theology is apologetic. He works to demonstrate that secular programs of justice require at their metaethical level assumptions entailing a Christian doctrine of a just God suffering with and redeeming both the living and the dead. Yet his apologetic stance stops with showing how other self-interpretations require Christian assumptions. Although this is fair enough, the Christian practical theologian should also go further and enter into a public and critical discourse about the "validity claims" supporting his or her own praxis, especially with regard to more concrete courses of action. Metz has little to say about this issue, and this omission distinguishes his proposals from mine.

Introducing the phrase "validity claims" and the need

for a fundamental practical theology to support the claims it makes introduces for our consideration the critical theory project of Jürgen Habermas. Yet one need not be tied to Habermas's particular version of these validity claims (for instance, his division of them into "comprehensibility, truth, rightness, and truthfulness") to appreciate his insistence that communicative competence entails a willingness to advance reasons for our actions, even to those who do not agree with us and who do not seem to share our faith.[53] It is true that Habermas has been accused by various commentators, especially Bernstein and Rorty, of developing a foundationalist drive for certainty in our social discourse.[54] Of course, such a foundationalism would be in tension with the hermeneutical and historical rationale I have advanced here for the centrality of a fundamental practical theology. But one need not lapse into the relativism of a Richard Rorty to avoid foundationalism. Bernstein's counsel is more appropriate when he writes the following with reference to Gadamer's avoidance of the question of validation.

> I have argued Gadamer is really committed to a communicative understanding of truth, believing that "claims to truth" always implicitly demand argumentation to warrant them, but he has failed to make this view fully explicit. . . . For although all claims to truth are fallible and open to criticism, they still require validation—validation that can be realized only through offering the best reasons and arguments that can be given in support of them—reasons and arguments that are themselves embedded in the practices that have been developed in the course of history. We never escape from the obligation of seeking to validate claims to truth through argumentation and opening ourselves to the criticism of others.[55]

In my own work, I differentiate the validity claims of a fundamental practical theology into five types rather than Habermas's four. I argue that these five validity claims reflect the five dimensions of all forms of practical thinking, whether they be explicitly religious or avowedly secular. I call these dimensions (1) the visional or metaphorical dimension (which inevitably raises metaphysical validity claims), (2) the obligational dimension (which raises normative ethical claims), (3) the tendency-need dimension (which raises claims about the fundamental needs of human nature and the kinds of nonmoral goods that meet them), (4) the contextual dimension (claims about the social-systemic and ecological integrity of situations), and (5) the rule-role dimension (claims about what should be our most concrete behaviors and actions).[56] In fact, I use these five dimensions (I sometimes call them levels) both to describe the theory-laden practices of contemporary situations and to guide the description of the thickness of the Christian witness. Hence, the model is useful to guide description and interpretation at both poles of the revised correlational conversation—the pole of contemporary experience and the pole of the central Christian message.

There is no room here to amplify and justify this division of the validity claims that a fundamental practical theology should address. My goal, rather, is to assert that a critical or revised correlational practical theology must be willing to support its implicit validity claims if it is to take part in the discourse of a free society aimed at shaping the common good. Here I agree with Bernstein. The arguments that a critical practical theology advances cannot be foundational arguments assuring absolute authority. But its arguments can have the status of good reasons that, although not absolutely certain, can advance discourse about the action we should take.

The critical testing of a fundamental practical theology must come at a variety of points in the hermeneutical circle. Sketching out formally the types of validity claims that a critical practical theology might face, however, would be the special province of both systematic theology and strategic practical theology. Furthermore, the actual defense of the validity claims for the purpose of concrete praxis would occur most profoundly at the movement of strategic practical theology.

But it is important to note that when this structure of theology is translated into the rhythms of theological education, one would still begin theology with a thick description of contemporary practices (personal, institutional, and religiocultural) and then only gradually move back to historical theology. One would then move through a systematic consideration of the themes of the faith (considered from the perspective of the questions engendered by present practice), to an ideology critique of these themes and the critical examination of the validity claims of the faith, and finally to the critical and strategic consideration of proposals for the alteration of our present practices. The task of supporting the validity claims of the faith is difficult and challenging but important. Yet it is not the first order of business in theological education. To understand our own present practices in their various situations and the questions these practices evoke is the first task of theological education. How these movements might be organized into a course of study in different situations—the seminary, the graduate department of religion, or even the church—would doubtless vary to some extent. But if the position outlined above has some plausibility, these differences would be more matters of degree and matters of emphasis rather than matters of categorical distinction.

NOTES

1. The list of books pointing toward this turn to practical philosophy is extensive. Representative titles following the order of the names in the text are as follows: Hans-Georg Gadamer, *Truth and Method* (New York: Crossroad, 1982); Paul Ricoeur, *Freud and Philosophy* (New Haven: Yale University Press, 1970); Jürgen Habermas, *Knowledge and Human Interests* (Boston: Beacon Press, 1971); Peter Winch, *The Idea of a Social Science and Its Relation to Philosophy* (London: Routledge & Kegan Paul, 1958); R. S. Peters, *The Concept of Motivation* (London: Routledge & Kegan Paul, 1958); Richard J. Bernstein, *Praxis and Action* (Philadelphia:

University of Pennsylvania Press, 1971), and *Beyond Objectivism and Relativism: Science, Hermeneutics, and Praxis* (Philadelphia: University of Pennsylvania Press, 1983); Richard Rorty, *Philosophy and the Mirror of Nature* (Princeton, N.J.: Princeton University Press, 1979); and Thomas Kuhn, *The Structure of Scientific Revolutions* (Chicago: University of Chicago Press, 1970).

2. Edward Farley, *Theologia: The Fragmentation and Unity of Theological Education* (Philadelphia: Fortress Press, 1983), and *The Fragility of Knowledge: Theological Education in the Church and the University* (Philadelphia: Fortress Press, 1988).

3. Joseph C. Hough, Jr., and John B. Cobb, Jr., *Christian Identity and Theological Education* (Chico, Calif.: Scholars Press, 1985), 81–94.

4. The following are examples from the various countries. Germany: Dietrich Rossler, *Grundriss der Praktischen Theologie* (Berlin: Walter de Gruyter, 1986); N. Mette, *Theories der Praxis* (Dusseldorf, 1978). Holland: J. A. van der Ven, "Practical Theology: From Applied to Empirical Theology," *Journal of Empirical Theology* 1, no. 1 (1988): 7–28; J. Firet, *Dynamics in Pastoring* (Grand Rapids: Eerdmans, 1987). England: Paul Ballard, ed., *Foundations of Pastoral Studies and Practical Theology* (Cardiff: Faculty of Theology, 1986). Canada: M. Viau, *Introduction aux études pastorales* (Montreal: Editions Paulines, 1987). Uruguay: Juan Luis Segundo, *The Liberation of Theology* (New York: Orbis Books, 1976).

5. Friedrich Schleiermacher, *Brief Outline on the Study of Theology* (Richmond: John Knox Press, 1970), 92.

6. An excellent statement of this approach can be found in the early article by Alasdair Campbell, "Is Practical Theology Possible?" *Scottish Journal of Theology* 5, no. 25 (1972): 217–27.

7. The two volumes of essays are Don S. Browning, ed., *Practical Theology: The Emerging Field in Theology, Church and World* (San Francisco: Harper & Row, 1983); and Lewis S. Mudge and James N. Poling, eds., *Formation and Reflection: The Promise of Practical Theology* (Philadelphia: Fortress Press, 1987).

8. The book-length studies are Don S. Browning, *Religious*

Ethics and Pastoral Care (Philadelphia: Fortress Press, 1983); James Fowler, *Faith Development and Pastoral Care* (Philadelphia: Fortress Press, 1987); Charles Gerkin, *Widening the Horizons* (Philadelphia: Westminster Press, 1986); Thomas Groome, *Christian Religious Education* (San Francisco: Harper & Row, 1980); Robert Schreiter, *Constructing Local Theologies* (Maryknoll, N.Y.: Orbis Books, 1985); Charles Winquist, *Practical Hermeneutics* (Chico, Calif.: Scholars Press, 1980); James Poling and Donald Miller, *Foundations for a Practical Theology of Ministry* (Nashville: Abingdon Press, 1985); and Dennis McCann and Charles Strain, *Polity and Praxis* (New York: Winston, 1986).

9. Gadamer, *Truth and Method*, 289.

10. Ibid.

11. Bernstein, *Beyond Objectivism and Relativism*, 38.

12. Gadamer, *Truth and Method*, 273.

13. Ibid., 273–74, 337–41.

14. Bernstein, *Beyond Objectivism and Relativism*, 173–74; Rorty, *Philosophy and the Mirror of Nature*, 192–209.

15. Kuhn, *The Structure of Scientific Revolutions*, 41, 53.

16. Schleiermacher, *Brief Outline*, 25–27; John Burkhart, "Schleiermacher's Vision for Theology," in *Practical Theology*, ed. Browning, 42–60.

17. Schleiermacher, *Brief Outline*, 91–126.

18. Ibid., 19.

19. Paul Tillich, *Systematic Theology*, vol. 1 (Chicago: University of Chicago Press, 1951), 29.

20. Ibid., 33.

21. Ibid.

22. For discussions of Ogden's view of the organization of theology, see his *On Theology* (San Francisco: Harper & Row, 1986), 7–16, and "The Concept of a Theology of Liberation: Must a Christian Theology Today Be So Conceived?" *The Challenge of Liberation Theology: A First World Response*, eds. Brian Mahan and Dale Richesin (Maryknoll, N.Y.: Orbis Books, 1981). To be fair to Ogden, he does say that theology as a whole should be conceived as practical "in a broad sense." But if this is so, Ogden should come up with a different flow to the structure of theology and also come to

understand the importance of questions coming from practice as animating the theological task.

23. David Tracy, *Blessed Rage for Order: The New Pluralism for Theology* (New York: Seabury Press, 1975), 52–56.

24. Ibid. 49–52.

25. Tillich, *Systematic Theology*, 36.

26. Tracy, *Blessed Rage for Order*, 46.

27. David Tracy, "The Foundations of Practical Theology," in *Practical Theology*, ed. Browning, 76.

28. Gadamer, *Truth and Method*, 273.

29. Tracy, *Blessed Rage for Order*, 75–76; Paul Ricoeur, *Critical Hermeneutics and the Human Sciences: Essays of Language, Action, and Interpretation* (Cambridge: Cambridge University Press, 1981), 149–64.

30. Bernstein, *Beyond Objectivism and Relativism*, 42–44; Habermas, *Knowledge and Human Interests*, 301–17, and *Communication and the Evolution of Society* (Boston: Beacon Press, 1979), 201–203.

31. Wolfhart Pannenberg, *Theology and the Philosophy of Science* (Philadelphia: Westminster Press, 1976), 410.

32. Bernstein, *Beyond Objectivism and Relativism*, 153.

33. Farley, *Theologia*, 35.

34. Allison Stokes, *Ministry After Freud* (New York: Pilgrim Press, 1985), 51–62.

35. Tracy, *Blessed Rage for Order*, 43.

36. Tracy, "The Foundations of Practical Theology," in *Practical Theology*, ed. Browning, 76. For an adaptation of Tracy's model to a practical theology of care, see my "Mapping the Terrain of Pastoral Theology: Toward a Practical Theology of Care," *Pastoral Psychology*, 36, no. 1 (Fall 1987): 20.

37. James Whitehead and Evelyn Whitehead, *Method in Ministry* (New York: Seabury Press, 1980), 12.

38. This is the basic meaning of Paul Ricoeur's view that psychoanalysis helps us uncover the "archeology of the subject." See his *Freud and Philosophy* (New Haven: Yale University Press, 1970), 419–58.

39. For a review of the object relations school of psychoanalysis, see Jay Greenberg and Stephen Mitchell, *Object Relations in Psychoanalytic Theory* (Cambridge: Harvard University Press, 1983).

40. Habermas, *Knowledge and Human Interests*, 274–300.

41. For the best review of how both psycholanalysis and Weberian sociology can be used to uncover cultural trends, see Philip Rieff, *Freud: The Mind of the Moralist* (New York: Doubleday, 1961), and *Triumph of the Therapeutic* (New York: Harper & Row, 1966).

42. Segundo, *The Liberation of Theology*, 9.

43. Ibid., 33.

44. Hough and Cobb, *Christian Identity and Theological Education*, 104. For my positive response to their proposals, see Don S. Browning, "Globalization and the Task of Theological Education," *Theological Education*, 23, no. 1 (Autumn 1986): 43–59.

45. Hough and Cobb, *Christian Identity and Theological Education*, 29–30.

46. Charles M. Wood, *Vision and Discernment: An Orientation in Theological Study* (Atlanta: Scholars Press, 1985), 20.

47. Ibid., 39–55.

48. Johann Baptist Metz, *Faith in History and Society* (New York: Seabury Press, 1980), 5–8.

49. Ibid., 50–70.

50. Ibid., 50.

51. Ibid., 34–36.

52. Ibid., 111.

53. Habermas, *Communication and the Evolution of Society*, 58, and *Theory of Communicative Action*, vol. 1 (Boston: Beacon Press, 1981), 325–29.

54. Richard Rorty, *Consequences of Pragmatism* (Minneapolis: University of Minnesota Press, 1982), 173–74; Bernstein, *Beyond Objectivism and Relativism*, 197–207.

55. Bernstein, *Beyond Objectivism and Relativism*, 168.

56. Browning, *Religious Ethics and Pastoral Care*, 53–71, and "Practical Theology and Political Theology," *Theology Today* 42 (April 1985): 207–12. For a fuller discussion of these issues, see my *A Fundamental Practical Theology: With Descriptive and Strategic Proposals* (Minneapolis: Fortress Press, 1991).